D0984757

MODUS VIVENDI LIBERALISM

A central task in contemporary political philosophy is to identify principles governing political life where citizens disagree deeply on important questions of value and, more generally, about the proper ends of life. The distinctively liberal response to this challenge insists that the state should as far as possible avoid relying on such contested issues in its basic structure and deliberations. David McCabe critically surveys influential defenses of the liberal solution and advocates modus vivendi liberalism as an alternative defense of the liberal state. Acknowledging that the modus vivendi approach does not provide the deep moral consensus that many liberals demand, he defends the liberal state as an acceptable compromise among citizens who will continue to see it as less than ideal. His book will interest a wide range of readers in political philosophy and political theory.

DAVID MCCABE is Associate Professor in Philosophy at Colgate University. His previous publications include a number of articles within books and journals on social and political philosophy.

MODUS VIVENDI LIBERALISM

LIBERALISM

Theory and Practice

DAVID McCABE

Colgate University

CAMBRIDGE
UNIVERSITY PRESS

CAMBRIDGE UNIVERSITY PRESS
Cambridge, New York, Melbourne, Madrid, Cape Town, Singapore,
São Paulo, Delhi, Dubai, Tokyo

Cambridge University Press
The Edinburgh Building, Cambridge CB2 8RU, UK

Published in the United States of America by Cambridge University Press, New York

www.cambridge.org
Information on this title: www.cambridge.org/9780521119788

First published 2010

Printed in the United Kingdom at the University Press, Cambridge

A catalogue record for this publication is available from the British Library

Library of Congress Cataloguing in Publication data
McCabe, David, 1963–
Modus vivendi liberalism : theory and practice / David McCabe.
p.   cm.
ISBN 978-0-521-11978-8 (Hardback)
1. Liberalism.   2. Political science–Philosophy.   I. Title.
JC574.M42 2010
320.51–dc22   2009042807

ISBN 978-0-521-11978-8 Hardback

Contents

Acknowledgments

Most of what I understand about making philosophical arguments I owe to my advisor at graduate school, John Deigh. In his staunch commitments to rigor, clarity, and intellectual probity, John offered an exemplary model of how philosophical work should be done. This book no doubt falls short of those standards in various respects, but it is a pleasure to acknowledge my extensive debt to him.

The bulk of this book was written after I joined the faculty at Colgate University. Its appearance has been accelerated by the University's generous support of faculty research and by its fine library staff. My students at Colgate have offered a consistently high level of philosophical engagement that has been an important stimulus to my thinking. Most importantly, my colleagues in Colgate's departments of Philosophy and Religion have provided an environment for careful reflection as rewarding as it is enjoyable.

I also worked on this book, and presented some of its ideas, while a Fellow at the Centre for Ethics, Philosophy, and Public Affairs at the University of St. Andrews, under the direction of John Haldane. I thank the St. Andrews Philosophy departments in general, and John in particular, for their hospitality and for the opportunity to exchange ideas. I made final revisions while holding the McCullough Chair in the Philosophy Department at Hamilton College, and I am grateful to Hamilton and to my colleagues there for their warm and stimulating support.

Chapter 4 is a revised version of an essay that originally appeared in *Ethics* III (April 2001), and Chapter 5 reworks some material from an essay that appeared in *Ethics* 110 (January 2000). I am grateful to *Ethics* and the University of Chicago Press for permission to use that material here.

This book has benefited from the criticisms and input, direct and indirect, of many people. I wish to acknowledge in particular Robert Audi, Jerome Balmuth, Stanley Brubaker, Kai Draper, James Harris,

Jonathan Jacobs, the late Susan Moller Okin, Barry Shain, and John Skorupski. Paul Baumann, model editor of *Commonweal*, has been a consistent supporter of my work in ways I appreciate very much. George Sher early in my career offered friendly but devastating criticism of a view I had advanced, and his critique has been influential in my subsequent approach to political theory. Finally, David Dudrick, my colleague at Colgate, deserves special mention for being such a generous and constructive interlocutor as I struggled to figure out precisely what I wanted to say here.

At Cambridge, Hilary Gaskin has been an ideal editor from start to finish – unfailingly gracious, professional, and supportive; without her ministrations this book would not exist. I am also thankful for the exceptionally thorough reports from outside readers on an earlier version of this book. Though I am sure I have not addressed all their worries, this book has been immeasurably improved as a result of their comments.

My wife, Kate Lucey, has offered steadfast and loving support of this project, often when I feared it had got the best of me; I hope I have repaid her confidence. My father, Frank McCabe, provided a life-long model of responsible engagement in the world that I have tried to honor on every page here. Though he did not live to see its publication, I take some pleasure in dedicating this book to his memory, as I know of no one who has demonstrated more conclusively the importance of philosophical reflection to a life well lived.

PART I

Starting assumptions

CHAPTER I

The liberal project

THE LIBERAL PROJECT

From theorists concerned with the course of ideas and institutions over time, one often hears claims about the various "projects" that characterize historical periods. Such talk is often not salutary: speaking of "the Enlightenment project," for example, or "the project of modernity" tends more often to hide tendentious assumptions than to denote a clear subject of inquiry. What Enlightenment project?, we want to ask. What do you mean by modernity? To philosophers such broad reductionism is especially unwelcome, as it leaves little room for the careful consideration of nuance and distinction that is their stock-in-trade.

Mindful of these concerns, I nonetheless intend the following book as an assessment of what I shall call the liberal project, as understood and advanced by its most forceful contemporary advocates. In referring to this project I mean to deny neither that contemporary liberal theory (or the liberal tradition as a whole) exhibits great diversity, nor that failure to attend to that diversity can result in a narrow reconstruction of a complex body of thought. But such considerations should not condemn from the outset any attempt to discern and assess what is central and distinct in liberal thought, to identify key elements that characterize the liberal account of political association.

The liberal project I understand as the attempt to mount an argument that achieves two distinct goals: one concerning the argument's conclusion for political practice, the other having to do with the nature of the argument itself. First, the theory should provide a compelling defense of the general model of political association, including the chief distinguishing structural features, that characterizes liberal states. I do not pretend that the phrase "liberal state" is entirely uncontroversial, and liberals continue to disagree over how such a state should conduct itself (what its policies should be with respect to economic justice, affirmative action, international affairs, and so on). Without denying the urgency of such debates, my concern here is with the consensus that holds at a level above such disputes, the broad vision of political association shared by adversaries within those debates that nonetheless makes it sensible to group all of them, despite their differences, as liberals.

The essentials of that vision have been well conveyed by Isaiah Berlin. Liberal regimes, he says, aim to create conditions

> in which as many individuals as possible can realize as many of their ends as possible, without assessment of the value of these ends as such, save in so far as they may frustrate the purposes of others. They wish the frontiers between individuals or groups of men to be drawn solely with a view to preventing collisions between human purposes, all of which must be considered to be equally ultimate, uncriticizable ends in themselves.[1]

To create a social world responsive to this ideal, liberal states embrace two commitments that I shall concentrate on throughout my argument. First, all citizens are to have the broadest possible sphere of liberty within which to pursue whatever ends they choose so long as they do not harm others. This commitment finds most famous expression in Mill's harm principle, and I shall sometimes refer to it as such. Second, the state should take no steps to direct individuals towards particular goals or activities it regards as more valuable than any others. This constitutes the familiar prohibition against state paternalism.[2] Both commitments denote ideal types, and it may be that no existing liberal regime consistently lives up to both – that all extant liberal regimes both restrict personal liberty in ways that cannot be justified solely by the harm principle (consider public decency rules, for example) and promote certain goals (fine art, scholarship) deemed especially worthy. It is also true that some self-described liberals have of late argued that liberal states may advance especially worthwhile goals despite the opposition of some citizens. Notwithstanding such qualifications, these two commitments figure especially prominently in public debate within liberal regimes and in the conception of such regimes invoked by champions and critics alike. Both also connect directly to the principle of state neutrality that many see as epitomizing the liberal model of politics. Keeping the two commitments at the forefront of the discussion thus

---

[1] Isaiah Berlin, "Two Concepts of Liberty," in *Four Essays on Liberty* (New York: Oxford University Press, 1969), 153, n. 1.

[2] Note that these are discrete commitments: the harm principle alone does not prohibit the state from promoting certain activities and goals, and anti-paternalism alone does not guarantee freedom to engage in activities that offend but do not harm others.

helps sharpen the contrast between the liberal model of politics and other accounts.

If the first defining goal of the liberal project is to defend a familiar political structure, the second concerns the process of reasoning by which that structure is defended. The main idea here is that liberal theorists are committed to an account of political legitimacy which states that the fundamental principles structuring the political realm must be such as can be rationally vindicated to citizens subject to it. In his prize-winning essay, "The Theoretical Foundations of Liberalism," Jeremy Waldron captures the idea thus:

> If life in society is practicable and desirable, then its principles must be amenable to explanation and understanding, and the rules and restraints that are necessary must be capable of being justified to the people who are to live under them. … The view that I want to identify as a foundation of liberal thought is based on this demand for a justification of the social world.[3]

Delivering on this demand for justification is not, for liberals, chiefly a pragmatic issue having to do with motivating citizens to subscribe to the rules and practices of liberal regimes, though it is partly that. It is fundamentally a normative requirement for any adequate account of legitimate political association. So while there is variation in the considerations offered to defend the liberal state (there are liberalisms grounded in personal autonomy, value pluralism, and so on), any liberal advancing such an account must believe it is persuasive enough to merit the assent of reasonable citizens who consider it. This second aspect of the liberal project I shall call the justificatory requirement (JR).

Straight away we can note important ambiguities in JR. To begin with, who is bound by it? Does it apply only to theorists defending the basic constitutional structure of the political community, or does it extend to anyone acting in a political capacity within that structure, or, indeed, to any engaged citizen at all? A body of important work has arisen over the last few decades exploring these matters, with particular attention to the appropriateness of relying on religious beliefs in political argument, and those discussions suggest the rich and nuanced issues at stake.[4] A second, related question concerns the topics to which JR

---

[3] Jeremy Waldron, "Theoretical Foundations of Liberalism," *Philosophical Quarterly* 37 (April 1987), 134–5.

[4] Especially influential contributions to this debate include Robert Audi, *Religious Commitment and Secular Reason* (Cambridge: Cambridge University Press, 2000), Kent Greenawalt, *Private Consciences and Public Reasons* (New York: Oxford University Press, 1995), and Michael Perry,

applies. Does it apply only to large-scale, defining issues within a political community (the relation between church and state, status and protection of basic liberties, etc.), or must all decisions made by political
bodies satisfy JR (e.g. whether to preserve open areas, which works of art
to subsidize, etc.)?

To resolve these matters adequately would take me far afield of my
central concern here. Instead, I shall follow the general intuition that
I believe John Rawls had in mind when he suggested that JR applies
chiefly to "'constitutional essentials' and questions of basic justice."[5]
Though Rawls's approach invites the objections of being both arbitrary
(because it exempts some ultimately coercive exercises of state power
from JR) and incomplete (because what qualifies as a matter of basic
justice may itself depend on arguments that cannot themselves meet JR),
it is nonetheless grounded on an unassailable intuition – namely, that
the importance of satisfying JR stands in direct proportion to the importance of the state action in question. It is, for example, far more urgent
that JR be satisfied when we are imagining the basic constitution for the
polity, or citizens' religious liberties, than when we are considering how
the state shall dispose of some infinitesimal portion of its national tax
revenues. And we can grant that there is no firm and fixed border separating the important from the unimportant within the context of state
policy while still distinguishing matters that have great importance from
those that do not. I shall assume that the liberal arguments I explore,
and the two liberal commitments I am focusing on, involve matters of
great importance within a political community, so that if JR applies at
all, it applies to them.

The final ambiguity in JR points to an especially deep worry that will
recur at various points in my argument. What precisely does it mean to
say that political principles must, as Waldron puts it, be "capable of being
justified" to those who live under them, or that they should be, in Kent
Greenawalt's phrase, "generally accessible" to citizens?[6] If we take this to
mean that the argument for those principles will inevitably be endorsed
by any intelligent citizen who considers it (like modus ponens, perhaps),
this presents an exceptionally strong requirement, one that no political
principles may meet. But just as surely JR requires that some significant number of citizens will be persuaded by the argument in question.

Love and Power: The Role of Religion and Morality in American Politics (New York: Oxford
University Press, 1991).
[5] John Rawls, *Political Liberalism* (New York: Columbia University Press, 1993), 214ff.
[6] Greenawalt, *Private Consciences and Public Reasons,* 26ff.

Finding the right position between these two extremes is no easy task, and I shall explore it at some length in both Chapter 5 (when discussing Rawls's account of justification) and Chapter 7 (when considering how modus vivendi liberalism stands *vis à vis* the ideal of justification). Here it must suffice to see JR as requiring that the argument for the liberal state be one that merits and for that reason strongly tends to elicit assent in citizens who consider it in the appropriate way (i.e. they accept a basic commitment to moral equality, follow canons of logical inference, endorse clearly grounded empirical claims, and so on).[7]

The importance of JR to the liberal project figures centrally in the argument of this book. No doubt many citizens, for a range of reasons, believe the liberal state constitutes an ideal form of political life and see it as a harmonious extension of ideals authoritative in their private lives. But such citizens are not, I want to stress, those whom contemporary liberal theorists most need to address. The really important audience here consists of persons who, prior to being presented with the liberal's argument, either endorse some illiberal vision of political association or are unsure of the appeal of the liberal account. It is this person, whom I shall refer to as the critic and whose doubt about liberal principles is usually rooted in a quite different set of authoritative ideals, who gives genuine urgency to the task of articulating an adequate liberal theory, his concerns that must be addressed if liberal states can reasonably claim authority over him. As Waldron notes, "If there is some individual to whom a justification cannot be given, then so far as *he* is concerned the social order had better be replaced by other arrangements, for the *status quo* has made out no claim to *his* allegiance."[8] Adopting T. M. Scanlon's terminology, we might say the argument for liberalism must be one the critic cannot reasonably reject. This is the acid test for an adequate liberal theory.

A key assumption driving this book is the belief that liberals have not adequately engaged with the critics' concerns. Consider in this context Michael Ignatieff's praise for Isaiah Berlin as "the only liberal thinker of real consequence to take the trouble to enter the mental worlds of liberalism's sworn enemies."[9] Given the importance of the ideal of justification,

---

[7] This way of putting the idea was suggested by an anonymous reader. The idea is similar to Rawls's cashing out liberal legitimacy in terms of principles that all citizens "may reasonably be expected to endorse," given features of "their common human reason" (*Political Liberalism*, 137).

[8] Waldron, "Theoretical Foundations of Liberalism," 135.

[9] Michael Ignatieff, *Isaiah Berlin: A Life* (London: Chatto & Windus, 1998), 249, quoted in Steven Lukes, *Liberals and Cannibals: The Implications of Diversity* (New York: Verso, 2003), 111.

Ignatieff's accusation points to a potentially serious indictment of liberal theory generally (assuming, as I shall, that some of those enemies are neither unreasoning nor deeply immoral). The worry is exacerbated by the fact that the worldviews, values, ideals, and so forth held by liberalism's defenders quite often are not shared by the critics to whom justification must be given. Indeed, it is likely that the very dispositions that qualify one for success as a political theorist (an unusually high degree of comfort with uncertainty, special interest in rational deliberation and self-scrutiny, enjoyment in challenging accepted views, and so on) also dispose one favorably to the general character of liberal regimes – a fact that would explain the phenomenon Ignatieff laments. Any argument sufficiently powerful to overcome the critics' objections will have to begin by understanding the depth of those objections.

Accordingly, this book tries to give serious and careful consideration to those objections. It assumes that there exist thoughtful critics of liberal regimes who have identified serious drawbacks to that model of politics, and it proceeds by asking whether the accounts offered by contemporary liberals are sufficient to allay those worries. I shall argue that the dominant strains of liberal theory fail by this criterion: existing arguments for the liberal state are not decisive against the critics' objections, and the steps liberals might take to bolster those arguments are either inconclusive or ruled out by JR.[10] But this does not mean, I shall argue, that liberal states cannot be given an adequate defense consistent with the guiding ideals of the liberal project. In the second half of the book I pursue an alternative defense of liberalism, one largely neglected in the tradition, that I believe offers a better chance of generating agreement on the general structure of liberal regimes.

OUTLINE OF THE ARGUMENT

At various points in my argument I imagine the critic objecting to the liberal model on the grounds that it has unacceptable costs on human well-being. The force of that objection obviously hinges on the idea that how a particular model of political organization affects human well-being

---

[10] Andrew Mason has gestured to a similar possibility: "I have considerable doubts about the possibility of showing that any particular conception of justice, or even any set of liberal principles more abstractly conceived, can meet [the liberal] standard of justification, but I shall not pursue the point here, for it threatens the dominant liberal conception of political community itself" (*Community, Solidarity, and Belonging* [New York: Cambridge University Press, 2000], 73).

constitutes an important axis in assessing that model. Accordingly, Chapter 2 begins by discussing briefly the status of that assumption within political philosophy generally and the liberal project in particular. It then moves on to sketch an account of well-being that centers on the importance of engaging with objectively valuable goals and activities. Some readers might object to the absence of a rigorously worked out philosophical defense of that account, but such criticism is beside the point. The important question is not whether some such account is ultimately defensible through philosophical argument (I think it is), but whether endorsing it is a reasonable belief of the sort of critic whom liberal theory needs to persuade and so one with which any case for liberalism must be compatible. In the rest of Chapter 2 I defend a pluralist account of the goods that contribute to well-being and argue that no particular constellation of these is superior to all others.

I then turn to assess the most influential recent attempts to deliver the liberal project. I begin in Chapter 3 with the argument that the ideal of personal autonomy is supremely important and suitably protected only by liberal regimes. Chapter 4 takes up the more modest claim that autonomy, even if not essential to a good life, so powerfully infiltrates liberal society that liberal states have good reason to privilege that ideal. Chapter 5 considers an argument that seeks to bypass claims about well-being and appeals instead to an implicit consensus among liberal citizens on basic political norms and canons of reasonableness appropriate to political deliberation. In each case I conclude that the arguments for liberalism are not compelling enough to persuade the thoughtful critic: liberal states generate real costs, and the truth of value pluralism makes it impossible to conclude confidently that those costs are outweighed by the benefits liberal states provide. This fact raises the possibility that liberalism might best be defended by appeal to value pluralism itself. In Chapter 6 I survey various attempts to make this argument and suggest that they too ultimately fail.

Part III then pursues an alternative way of defending liberalism, one that abandons the strong normative ambitions of the previously canvassed arguments and endorses liberalism as a modus vivendi among citizens who remain deeply divided on the basic norms that would ideally govern political life. Modus vivendi liberalism (MVL) has been something of a black sheep in the extended family of liberal thought, and Chapter 7 seeks to rehabilitate it against its detractors. In the course of that argument I defend a construal of JR that, while less robust than that endorsed by other liberals, remains faithful to the central ideal JR captures.

Chapters 8 and 9 consider the practical implications of the modus vivendi approach, concentrating on two important areas where the liberal
state's authority has been challenged: gender equality, and compulsory
education. The concluding chapter acknowledges the shortcomings of
MVL and tries to show that they do not constitute strong objections to
the MVL approach.

CHAPTER 2

Well-being and value pluralism

POLITICAL PHILOSOPHY AND THE CLAIMS OF WELL-BEING

In considering the prospects for a successful defense of liberalism I shall frequently invoke the critic's objection that the liberal state does not advance human well-being as well as some illiberal models would. This objection assumes that any model of political organization should be evaluated, in significant measure, by how well it advances human well-being. In contrast to the justificatory requirement mentioned in the previous chapter, this is not a distinctively liberal constraint on acceptable political argument. It is possible either (1) to invoke claims about well-being in advancing a political argument that rejects JR entirely or (2) to advance an argument that satisfies JR but excludes considerations of well-being (or gives them very little weight). But I believe either form of argument would be significantly problematic.

Since my aim in this book is to assess the liberal project, arguments along the lines of (1) are, strictly speaking, not germane to my overall task. Still, it's worth noting that any such argument violates a basic normative commitment of mainstream political theory, publicly endorsed by virtually all extant governments, according to which political power, since it properly serves the interests of those subject to it and so owes its authority ultimately to them, must be organized and exercised on grounds broadly justifiable to citizens. One might deny this if one believed that human beings differed enough in their inherent abilities – their rationality, moral character, self-restraint, and the like – such that some had jurisdictional authority over others by their very nature, as it were. On that alternative, as Rousseau dryly noted in the *Contrat Social*, we must conclude that either rulers are men and the ruled beasts, or the ruled men and rulers gods. Such an approach may not be incoherent, but it is today simply a nonstarter, both in political theory and public political discourse generally.

What of option (2), i.e. the possibility of a persuasive political argument that satisfies JR but excludes the relevance of judgments about well-being? This option is widely regarded as far more plausible than (1), and several theorists have recently argued not only that one can defend the liberal state through an argument excluding such considerations, but that only such an argument can succeed. In the chapters below I consider various ways of advancing such exclusionary arguments. Still, it will be helpful now to indicate the serious obstacles that face this approach and so bolster the view that considerations of well-being are ineluctably relevant in political argument.

A first problem for the exclusionary approach arises from the internal logic of JR. The view that any form of political association should be assessed in some significant degree by its impact on well-being is surely a reasonable one for citizens to hold (and one that, not coincidentally, has been endorsed by most canonical political theorists). So if we accept JR, it follows that any argument justifying the liberal state to such citizens cannot require the rejection of that view and must instead be consistent with it. But if so, including as relevant the question of how human well-being fares under that model should not undermine that argument. Seen this way, JR itself recommends against the exclusionary view.

Here the exclusionist might reply that even if we grant the reasonableness of the inclusionist approach, it is equally reasonable to deny concerns over well-being a critical place in assessing political argument, and so for this reason JR requires that in political argument we simply set such concerns aside.[1] Bracketing those views, she may add, is quite different from requiring their rejection. But it is not at all clear that denying the relevance of well-being in political argument is reasonable. Imagine that you object to the model of political organization I have just defended on the grounds that people living within it are likely to be very badly off, judged by the major indicators of well-being. It would be utterly fatuous of me to declare your objection irrelevant to my argument: the well-being of those inhabiting any political arrangement surely constitutes a direct and extremely plausible independent criterion. My response would more likely be to contest your judgments, or, less likely, to argue that such losses are somehow offset by other extraordinarily important values. Exclusionists may believe that political arrangements arrived at through an argument that both excludes questions of well-being and satisfies JR are bound to do quite well in terms of promoting the well-being of those under them.

---

[1] This worry was forcefully raised by an anonymous reader.

That may be: my point is that such a claim does not occur after the argument for the liberal state is concluded, but instead does important work within that argument.

A further reason against the exclusionary approach involves the way it implicitly construes political theorizing, and moral philosophy generally. Consider perhaps the most influential version of that approach, according to which excluding considerations of well-being from political justification is required by the principle of respecting other persons. Note that this approach cannot defend itself on the grounds that it ultimately advances others' well-being, nor can it understand the idea of respecting others in terms of taking account of their interests or well-being. Instead, the approach usually appeals to the extraordinary value of human agency, grounded in our capacity for rational self-direction. But we can, I think, acknowledge that value without believing that it necessarily trumps competing considerations of well-being in assessing political arrangements. Indeed, the account of value pluralism defended in the next section cautions against resolutely enthroning any one value over all others and suggests that political theory should be responsive to a range of values. The advancement of human well-being is surely among these.[2]

Even if some version of the exclusionist approach could be made philosophically defensible, it would itself be just as controversial as the non-exclusionist approach it would seek to block. This constitutes a final problem for liberals who advocate exclusion. For if judgments reasonably differ on whether questions of well-being belong in political argument, it hardly seems a fair solution to simply bracket such questions: that sides with only one of the reasonable positions. (This is like the state's resolving the abortion question by deciding it shall not take a stand on whether the fetus is a person.) Indeed, it is either arbitrary or self-refuting to defend the exclusionist position as a constraint on how political argument may be conducted, since that constraint cannot itself be defended (given the reasonableness of non-exclusionist approaches) in ways that satisfy it. In the end, all we can do is compare the different sorts of arguments on their own merits and see which on balance is most compelling (though I have tried to suggest why the burden of proof falls on the exclusionist).

---

[2] I recognize that some theorists do argue that human well-being is best advanced by a liberal state that excludes judgments about well-being from its deliberations. This position is not incoherent, and I shall consider variants of it in the chapters below. But note that it does not recommend excluding questions of well-being in assessing political models; it relies on them in defending a particular political model.

For these reasons, then, I shall assume that a successful argument for the liberal state will both satisfy JR and address the critic's concerns over the prospects for well-being under that model of political life. Nowhere in this book do I defend with any specificity the elements that comprise human well-being. I need not: the challenge for liberal theory I take up here concerns its success not against a philosophically resourceful defense of such an account, but against the critic who endorses a version of such an account in terms that represent a reasonable exercise of human reason. The objections of such a critic will appear in their strongest light, however, to the degree that his conception of well-being is independently appealing. It will strengthen his case, then, if I say something about both the structure and the substantive content of the conception of well-being advanced by the sort of critic I have in mind.

The central structural feature of that conception is its rejection of relativism, subjectivism, and skepticism. Here I assume that a good life is in large part characterized by engagement in worthwhile activities, relationships, and experiences, the value of which is a function of features intrinsic to the sorts of goods they are and does not derive simply from the fact that they are desired, pursued, or otherwise endorsed by agents. Exactly how this value is to be explained, and the nature of its ontology, are deep questions I shall not sort through here. I simply take for granted that any strongly subjectivist account of the good is too deeply at odds with our basic experience of human agency to have much appeal as a general theory of human well-being.[3] I also assume that the activities, relationships, and experiences that are of value in the world are to some considerable extent discernible to human reason, and that by reflecting on such things as human history, great works of art, personal experience, and enduring consensus across cultures we can identify at least some of these goods and make plans for achieving them. Admittedly, the rejection of skepticism does not strictly follow from the rejection of subjectivism (though some might think it a terribly cruel world that would offer

---

[3] Powerful objections to subjectivism abound. See, for example, George Sher, *Beyond Neutrality: Perfectionism and Politics* (New York: Cambridge University Press, 1997), ch. 8, and Warren Quinn, "Putting Rationality in its Place," in *Virtues and Reasons: Philippa Foot and Moral Theory*, ed. Rosalind Hursthouse *et al.* (Oxford: Clarendon, 1995), 181–208. Donald Regan has recently offered what he calls "an embarrassingly brief and far from original" argument that conveys the main idea: "We think that as agents we choose our projects. But choice requires standards, which must guide the choice and which therefore cannot be created in the act of choosing. Our self-conception as agents therefore requires that there be independent standards by which potential projects can be judged" ("The Value of Rational Nature," *Ethics* 112 [January 2002], 273–4).

objective goods but deny us knowledge of what they are). Nonetheless, if political philosophy must give central importance to human well-being, and if there are good reasons to reject both subjectivism and skepticism about the good, then the viability of political philosophy as an enterprise implies some ability to identify elements that comprise the human good, however thin those may be.

The realization that many of us already make such judgments with great confidence, that in fact they are inescapable, reveals some of the substantive features of well-being that characterize the critic's account of well-being. The argument here appeals in part to strong consensus within and across cultures. Even the most ardent relativist cannot deny that there exists widespread agreement on various important goods – friendship, reciprocated love, close family affection, intellectual achievement, aesthetic engagement, sociability, recreation, and feelings of communal belonging, to name a few – and that in virtually all communities a good life is seen as involving such goods. Here again I offer no philosophical defense of the value of such goods, but here again none is needed. Since I am concerned throughout with the possibility of articulating a defense of liberalism that might convince a serious and reasonable critic who endorses an ideal of the good consistent with such values, all my argument requires is the more modest claim that someone who sees a good life as involving such goods is not unreasonable. With this I assume no reader will disagree.

VALUE PLURALISM: FOUR THESES

The conception of well-being I rely on, and the arguments I offer throughout this book, are deeply informed by a commitment to value pluralism. The list of contemporary theorists who endorse pluralism constitutes a formidable group, whose numbers seem only to be growing.[4] And though the accounts offered by these theorists differ in various respects, it will nonetheless be helpful to say something about the overall structure of that view.

---

[4] Contemporary pluralists include Isaiah Berlin, Bernard Williams, Susan Wolf, Thomas Nagel, Stuart Hampshire, and Joseph Raz. John Rawls is sometimes classified as a pluralist, though his position is ambiguous. His pluralism concerns chiefly not the various values worth pursuing in a life, but the diverse ways in which those values are derived and defended, and even there he does not so much endorse the truth of pluralism as argue that pluralism is a reasonable position to endorse. Indeed, Berys Gaut cites Rawls as one of the few philosophers who have argued against value pluralism as a coherent approach to morality (Gaut, "Moral Pluralism," *Philosophical Papers* 22, no. 1 [1993], 17–40).

The obvious place to begin is by noting that pluralism hinges on, and is born from, a rejection of monism in value theory. This contrast is more often asserted than explained,[5] however, and it is difficult to specify the essence of monism in a way that all will agree with. The general spirit of monist theories of value is perhaps best captured by a cluster of claims which, though they may not logically imply one another, hang together in a mutually reinforcing way. To begin with, monists believe that whatever has value does so by virtue of its possessing some single common quality (e.g. its having been willed by God, its correspondence to our nature as living organisms, its productivity of happiness). Because all value is a function of this one common property, monists also believe that when faced with two valuable options, it will always be the case either that one is more valuable than the other or that they are equally valuable. This extends as well to a person's overall quality of life, such that if a person is deciding which activities and ideals to pursue, it must be the case that one set is better than the others or that they are of equal value. For this reason monists also embrace a model of decision-making in which either there is always a single best option, or if there is more than one acceptable option that is because the choices compare equally in terms of the single decisive moral criterion (for example, two options may reasonably be expected to produce the same amount of overall happiness). Critics often make the further charge that the monist must see deliberation as involving the application of quasi-mathematical formulae and criteria, but this seems unwarranted, and there is no reason monism cannot be combined with the recognition of a more supple capacity for evaluative judgment.

To this general monist account of value, deliberation, and determinacy, value pluralism stands in sharp contrast. I suggest that its essential features are captured in four theses. The first, which I will call the uncombinability thesis, asserts that no single life can combine maximal amounts of the various goods and virtues worth pursuing, and so to achieve some important values we must often sacrifice others. Consider, for example, the difficult choice among scholarly excellence, friendship, and the good of family life: the commitment needed for engaged and successful involvement in any of these pursuits invariably cuts into the time and energy one can devote to the others. Many choose to concentrate predominantly, perhaps even exclusively, on one, while others seek some balance

---

[5] As is the alleged dominance of monism in the history of moral philosophy. Michael Stocker goes so far as to suggest that among important moral philosophers "there have been very few evaluative monists," at least in the sense of monism frequently invoked in discussions of pluralism (*Plural and Conflicting Values* [Oxford: Clarendon Press, 1990], 166).

among them. The uncombinability thesis stresses that success in some of the goods often entails less achievement in others, contrasting with the view that one might combine all important goods without loss in any.[6] Nor does the uncombinability problem arise, as the previous example may suggest, merely because of limitations on our time: many goods and virtues are constitutively uncombinable as well. For example, the kind of good associated with Faustian ideals of self-creation cannot be combined with a life of dutiful service to a divine being or moral cause, any more than one person can possess the skills and disposition that make one both a successful mediator and a passionate and unyielding advocate of a single cause. Uncombinability does not reflect our own shortcomings, but is an intrinsic feature of the values we recognize.

The uncombinability thesis does not by itself, however, lead to value pluralism, for it might still be possible to assess the relative value of competing virtues and goods and to choose on the basis of such assessments. What value pluralism stresses in addition is that reason does not validate as objectively superior many of those uncombinable goods. For example, professional excellence as a philosopher constitutes one worthwhile end, but so does close involvement in the raising of one's children and in sustained friendships. This claim – that with respect to many goods and virtues reason does not reveal any one as intrinsically superior to any other – I shall call the noncomparability thesis, and it is the critical move by the pluralist. The plausibility of the uncombinability thesis will strike many both as undeniable, confirmed by both conceptual argument and personal experience, and as posing little threat to a familiar view of the world as cohesively ordered and unified from the moral point of view. The noncomparability thesis, in asserting that many of those uncombinable goods cannot be judged more or less valuable than others, has deeper and more disturbing ramifications.

The noncomparability thesis should not be confused with the closely related claim of incommensurability, frequently stressed in pluralist accounts, which asserts that the value of different options often cannot be charted on a common metric. Incommensurability is often thought to raise serious problems for any attempt to judge between options, via a line of argument nicely summarized by Michael Stocker. "It makes no sense to talk about a given amount of pleasure being greater than a given amount of understanding: 'This act leads to more pleasure than that act leads to

---

[6] For an exemplary critique of an account that appears to deny the uncombinability thesis, see Stuart Hampshire's discussion of Aristotle in *Innocence and Experience* (Cambridge, MA: Harvard University Press, 1989), 27ff.

understanding' and 'The gain in pleasurableness of this act over that act is greater than the gain in understanding of that one over this' are nonsense. Thus, plural values do not allow for sound judgment and action."[7] Though tempting, this is not, as Stocker notes, exactly the argument pluralists want: the problem to which incommensurability gives rise (i.e. that we often cannot assess the value of one option relative to another) needs to be kept distinct from the fact of incommensurability itself (i.e. that there is no single axis on which to plot the relevant values). For while it may be true that noncomparability arises only when incommensurability is present, incommensurability does not guarantee noncomparability. Even when the value of two options cannot be charted on any common metric of value, it is often clear that one is better than the other. Consider my choice between an excellent massage or a unique opportunity to discuss with my favorite novelist her life's work. Here there is no doubt which option is more valuable, but we cannot defend this judgment in terms of a single value offered in both options: the goods involved are simply too diverse.[8]

Since incommensurability alone does not entail that no one option can rightly be judged superior, I have stressed the noncomparability thesis as central to value pluralism. But I am not denying that incommensurability offers the best explanation of noncomparability. For if values could always be measured against one another, then when faced with options connected to different values we could always determine whether one was better or whether they were roughly equal; since we often cannot do

---

[7] Stocker, *Plural and Conflicting Values*, 167. Stocker himself believes the quoted argument overstates significantly the problem incommensurability poses in making decisions, and my distinction between incommensurability and noncomparability is inspired by his account.

[8] That we are able to judge certain options as obviously better than others even when the values at stake cannot be charted on a single metric is a puzzling phenomenon to which value pluralists need to give more attention. One line of explanation would be to say that there is just more value *per se* in meeting with the novelist than in receiving a massage, but unless we are told on what basis the judgment of greater value is being made, this explanation is not helpful. After all, we tend to think that when options are valuable it is because they make available *some particular* value, not because they make available *value itself*. Even if the value of different options could be ultimately explained by their falling under what Stocker calls "an all-encompassing highest category of value as such," the fact remains, as Stocker points out, that "their plurality has to do with differences in the nature of what differs, and not simply in different amounts of a common nature. They differ *qua* value, not simply in amount of value" (Stocker, *Plural and Conflicting Values*, 177); Raz makes a similar point, arguing against the idea that there is something behind our rankings of value that we refer to in arriving at such rankings (Joseph Raz, *The Morality of Freedom* [Oxford: Clarendon Press, 1986], 327). Alternatively, then, we might be tempted to say that the basis of the judgment of greater value is the extent to which pursuing that option leads to a good life, and that satisfying one's serious intellectual interests is more important for such a life than transient and low-level physical pleasure. But this just argues in a circle: since a good life involves the successful pursuit of valuable ends, we cannot explain the value of those ends by the fact that pursuing them contributes to a good life.

this, the values must not be commensurable.[9] This explanation is valuable because it helps us resist the temptation to think that noncomparability arises only when we have imperfect or incomplete knowledge. As Raz asserts, "Where there is incommensurability, it is the ultimate truth. There is nothing further behind it, nor is it a sign of imperfection."[10]

With this in mind consider again the previous example. A life of scholarship may offer travel, fame, and sustained intellectual growth; friendship offers enjoyment, emotional support from one's peers, and sociability; family life offers stability, deep openness, and unconditional attachment. If, as incommensurability asserts, the values connected to each of these domains differ so significantly from one another, then it will be the case that, from the standpoint of general axiology, we have no grounds on which to judge any one of them, *qua* the distinct good it offers, superior to the others. The diversity of goods involved prevents any such general ranking, even if in particular cases there may be reasons, drawn from the specifics of the case, recommending one option over another. Advocates of incommensurability further assert that any attempt to deny this diversity by introducing some single measurement (such as the production of happiness, or desire-satisfaction) from which any other good derives its value will necessarily misrepresent the nature of the goods in question.[11] We value each not because of its connection to or production of something else, but because of its intrinsic nature.

Confronting the noncomparability that such incommensurability entails, experiencing what Thomas Nagel has called the fragmentation of value, can be both frustrating and disturbing. For, when coupled with the fact of uncombinability, it means not only that we cannot achieve all the

---

My own suspicion is that we often make sound choices between incommensurables by drawing on a ranking system that ranges from the trivial to the very important. When choices lacking any common criterion of value appear close to one another on that scale, we are likely to face noncomparable options. But when the choices are far apart, with one value being offered in significant measure and the other offered in only a trivial degree (as in the example involving the massage and the novelist), we can clearly see one as better even though the options are incommensurable. I doubt that such a scale charting significance is open to the objection of a competing scale charting something of incommensurable value, because no competitor to the idea of significance appears plausible: judgments of value are inherently judgments of significance.

[9] That incommensurability is not rough equality is argued in Raz, *The Morality of Freedom*, 330ff. The argument holds for noncomparability as well.

[10] Raz, *The Morality of Freedom*, 327.

[11] For a nice example of an attempt to vanquish the problem of incommensurability via a desire satisfaction account of the good, see James Griffin, "Are There Incommensurable Values?," *Philosophy and Public Affairs* 7 (1977), 39–59. From the pluralist point of view, Griffin's solution merely proves the unsolvability of the problem, for his solution depends on what is, to the pluralist, a too narrow conception of what has value (i.e. desire satisfaction alone).

values worth pursuing but also that we cannot arrive at a single ranking of those values that accords each its uniquely appropriate place. It follows as well that our lives will lack certain important goods whose absence is not outweighed by those we do achieve. For this reason, Berlin concludes, "the notion of total human fulfillment is a formal contradiction."[12]

We are thus led to the third thesis of value pluralism, involving the underdeterminacy of reasons for actions. For if important goals, virtues, and ideals are fundamentally uncombinable and noncomparable, and if our reasons for action derive from the values at stake, our choices will often be underdetermined by reasons. Reflection on the values worth pursuing in a life reveals no one option as intrinsically superior to all others. There will often, then, be no single answer as to how resolve difficult choice situations, just as there is no one best way to lead a life.

The underdeterminacy thesis is especially critical to assessing the liberal project, but we need to avoid two misunderstandings of it. The first is to think that it implies that our choices on questions of value are always unconstrained by rational considerations. The difference between that extreme position and underdeterminacy can be brought out by considering Sartre's well-known example of the young man in Nazi-occupied France who must choose between joining the Free French forces in England or staying in France with his mother, for whom he is, as Sartre puts it tenderly, "her only consolation." After discussing both options, Sartre concludes that in such dilemmas we cannot rely on general principles and that "the only thing left for us is to trust our instincts."[13]

Many readers (not all of them first-year philosophy students) have interpreted Sartre's example as showing that moral choices are ultimately beyond the sway of reasons. But, as Charles Taylor has argued, this is quite the wrong lesson to draw from the example. For had the young man been torn between caring for his mother and going to the wine country to enjoy that year's harvest of Beaujolais, we would not say he was faced with a genuine ethical dilemma: seriously deliberating over that choice would reveal not a lack of determinacy in the structure of moral reasoning, but simply the moral callousness of the young Frenchman. What Sartre's example instead shows is that we may face situations where the relevant reasons for one option do not outweigh reasons for another.[14]

[12] Berlin, "Two Concepts of Liberty," 168.
[13] Jean-Paul Sartre, *Existentialism and Human Emotions*, trans. Bernard Frechtman (New York: Philosophical Library, 1957), 24.
[14] Charles Taylor, "What is Human Agency?," in *Human Agency and Language: Philosophical Papers*, vol. I (New York: Cambridge University Press, 1985), 29ff.

It is critical to see here that it does not follow from the fact that one's reasons for one option do not conclusively defeat reasons for another either that one's choice is irrational or that one is beyond the reach of objective reasons. That would follow if one held that a choice is rational only if made on the basis of reasons that defeat all others, but to insist on this all-defeating requirement would be to assume a conception of rationality that rules out underdeterminacy from the start. It would also, given the frequency with which we encounter noncomparable options, unacceptably consign large areas of human agency to a realm beyond the scope of objective reasons.[15] Our world has an objective structure of value to which choice-making should be responsive even if there are times when no one such value conclusively defeats all others. This rejection of both relativism and subjectivism constitutes the fourth central thesis of pluralism.

If the first misunderstanding of the underdeterminacy thesis arises from overlooking constraints on the values to which one can reasonably appeal, the second involves failing to see that an agent can often have decisive reasons, particular to his circumstances, to choose one option over another even when it is not intrinsically superior. We must keep in mind, that is, that the noncomparability thesis states that reflection on the values in the world does not reveal any particular goals, virtues, ways of life, and so on as superior to all others. This thesis is asserted from, as it were, the general standpoint of value theory. That general claim does not entail that underdeterminacy obtains whenever any agent chooses between intrinsically noncomparable options. What a particular person has reason to do is often shaped by the ongoing relationships, histories, aptitudes, and the like that characterize a particular human life. Such agent-relative constraints on what one has reason to do arise in numerous ways and may reflect either moral or non-moral considerations. For example, previous promises or indebtedness may provide conclusive reasons to choose one course of action over another. (Has the young man promised the other Free French fighters that he would join them? Did his own mother make extraordinary sacrifices to raise him?) Or again, one's distinct talents and personality may dispose one to greater success in some pursuit than others and so provide strong reason to pursue it over

---

[15] "Rational action is action for (what the agent takes to be) an undefeated reason. It is not necessarily action for a reason which defeats all others" (Raz, *The Morality of Freedom*, 339). Cf. Stocker's claim, in *Plural and Conflicting Values*, that anyone who recognizes the extent of value incommensurability while still believing that human agency is not largely a matter of choosing irrationally among options must also believe that we can make rational choices even when faced with plural and incommensurable values. A main goal of Stocker's book is to show how we do just this.

alternatives. (Is our Frenchmen so cowardly that he would be useless to the Free French? Will he be so miserable caring for his mother that he will be no comfort to her?)

The most significant kinds of agent-relative constraints arise from the fact that one may have already undertaken, perhaps well before one recognized the plurality of values, a defining commitment to lead one's life in a particular way. In such cases it may again be true that while no single response is intrinsically better, one still has conclusive reasons to choose in one way over another because of the values of commitment and integrity. Susan Wolf invokes a scene from Peter Weir's film *Witness* to elucidate this point.[16] In the film, the street-tough cop John Book masquerades as a member of a pacifist Amish community. One day Book and a group of Amish are confronted by an obnoxious brute who insults and manhandles them. When Book gestures towards a physical response, one of the Amish men replies, "That is not our way." Unable to contain himself (for reasons which any non-Amish audience quickly understands), Book punches the lout in the face.

One of the points Wolf makes through this story is that even if pluralists can recognize Book's code of conduct and that of the Amish as noncomparably valuable, they can also recognize that while it was acceptable for Book to lash out, it would have been troubling for one of the Amish to do the same. The reason is that each member of the Amish community has undertaken to lead a life in accordance with certain ideals. To respond as Book does would constitute a falling off from the sort of commitment and integrity which, Wolf suggests, characterize any good life. Note also, though Wolf does not press this point, that it would be wrong to regard these ideals of commitment and integrity as constraints on our capacity for self-expression (though they are constraints on the reasons to which we may properly appeal); rather, maintaining commitments and demonstrating integrity are central both to having a self which one can express in one's actions and to navigating manageably the encounters with plural values one is bound to experience.

These ideas of commitment and integrity further distinguish pluralism from both relativism and subjectivism. For some might think that if what is right for Book is wrong for the Amish, then morality is in some sense relative. Yes, in some sense. But the nature of the relativism thereby validated is sharply limited, and defanged, by two considerations. The first I have just discussed: one cannot justify one's action by

---

[16] Susan Wolf, "Two Levels of Pluralism," *Ethics* 102 (July 1992), 785–98.

just any worthwhile ideals. One must be able plausibly to claim that one regards those ideals as authoritative, and one main way such claims are made good is by a history of commitment. Someone who was Amish, for example, could not act as Book does without both casting doubt on the commitments that have heretofore characterized his life and revealing himself to be a person whose guiding ideals in life are subject to change depending on the circumstances he finds himself in (which is to say, a person with no guiding ideals).[17] The other consideration constraining the threat of relativism is the fact that the range of acceptable ideals that can legitimately govern one's behavior is finite, as the Sartre case shows. Book's preparedness to use modest physical force to combat humiliation is one such ideal, the Amish commitment to non-violent stoicism another. But pleasure in hurling abuse on those innocently going about their business, displayed by the bully in the film, is never acceptable.

Nor has pluralism collapsed into subjectivism. The pluralist is not suggesting that the mere desire to follow the Amish way of life is what makes it valuable. What make it valuable are the actual goods it promotes (self-sacrifice, close connection to the land, communal affiliation, and so on). Similarly, the value of integrity and commitment does not derive from the fact that persons want them: if that were the case, there would be nothing wrong with someone who had no consistent ideals in life and saw no value in them. But integrity and commitment are traits all human beings have reason to develop, and their value does not depend on their being desired.

Keeping this last point in mind strengthens pluralism against the worry that it sanctions a too permissive approach to deliberation and practical agency. The defense draws on normative and psychological factors that are somewhat hard to disentangle. From the normative perspective, a life characterized by strong commitment to certain ends has greater depth and offers more opportunity for accomplishments of genuine weight than one spent flitting from one set of goals to another. Persons engaged in the latter are always at risk of being swamped by what the novelist Milan Kundera has called the unbearable lightness of being – a lack of felt solidity both to one's self and one's projects – which often expresses itself in obsessive and ultimately meaningless rituals, and which is itself frequently the

---

[17] I am not denying either the possibility or importance of radical conversion. But when such cases arise, the authenticity of conversion is demonstrated only by steadfast commitment to the new ideals for a substantial time after the moment of conversion. Even in these cases, then, there is no escaping the importance of integrity and commitment.

symptom of a pathology brought about by living in inhumane conditions (as in Kundera's novel).

The psychological point concerns the fact that pursuing worthy ideals and goals tends both to strengthen one's belief in their value and to diminish the appeal of forsaken alternatives, a dynamic that Joseph Raz calls competitive pluralism.[18] Though the dynamic results in a narrowed conception of values in the world, it is not wholly regrettable. Sustained confidence in the value of one's goals helps one both to navigate what might otherwise be a series of difficult encounters with competing values and to carve out a way of life with clarity, purpose, and definition. In addition, a life marked by commitment and integrity offers greater opportunities to synthesize disparate events into a coherent and unified narrative, one that can make sense of and perhaps even redeem what had earlier figured as disconnected or senseless failures. This validation of one's past, which Alexander Nehamas discerns in Nietzsche's idea of justifying one's life aesthetically, is achieved by conferring on one's life a certain unity and direction, an outcome more likely the more one displays commitment and integrity.[19]

Summing up, then, the value pluralism I shall rely on is marked by four theses:

1. *Uncombinability* It is not possible to combine in a single life, to any substantial degree, all of the goals, virtues, ideals, and so forth that add value to a life and enhance our well-being: any life must inevitably lack certain important goods, because of either our own limitations or the incompatible nature of the goods in question.

2. *Incommensurability* Among such uncombinable goals, ideals, and so forth are some whose value differs in kind so much from one another that we cannot compare their relative value, and so cannot determine whether sacrifices in one are outweighed by achievements in the other – indeed, the very idea of such a balancing is in many contexts nonsensical.

3. *Noncomparability* The conjunction of the first two theses means that reason does not reveal any one particular set of goals, combination of virtues, or way of life as intrinsically best for human beings. Though powerful reasons relating to a person's particular circumstances may

---

[18] Raz, *The Morality of Freedom*, 404–7.
[19] Alexander Nehamas, *Nietzsche: Life as Literature* (Cambridge, MA: Harvard University Press, 1985).

recommend one set over another, there is no single group of goods, virtues, ideals, and so forth that all ought to pursue.

4. *Objectivism about values and reasons* In contrast to both relativism and subjectivism, pluralism allows that the appropriateness of our choices is constrained by objective reasons. These constraints reflect chiefly the objective value of various goals, virtues, and so on, but also the importance of commitment and integrity in any person's life.

PART II

The failure of the main arguments

CHAPTER 3

Liberal autonomy: the universalist case

THE LIBERAL IDEAL OF AUTONOMY

In this chapter I assess the case for liberalism grounded in the universal value of the ideal of personal autonomy. By a universal value I mean one whose worth is not a function of circumstantial facts about any particular society but is instead of such weight that a person either cannot lead a good life without it or is overwhelmingly less likely to do so. The argument considered in this chapter claims both that personal autonomy is such a universal value and that only robust liberal regimes adequately protect it.

The notion of autonomy relevant here concerns neither the will's capacity to be *causa sui,* in the sense relevant to metaphysical debates over free will and determinism, nor the (related) idea of moral autonomy central to Kant's ethics. Both issues would be addressed in any comprehensive account of autonomy, but their complexities raise deep questions that can be ignored in the debate over autonomy-based liberalism. In that debate the ideal of personal autonomy contrasts neither with causally determined behavior nor with acts that fail to conform to a principle of universalizable self-legislation, but with actions and choices that run afoul of the ideal of individuals' determining their own course in life, with persons whose goals and choices do not reflect judgments they have made for themselves and so fail in important ways to author their own lives.

As stated, the idea is lamentably vague. We can make it somewhat clearer by drawing on the spate of recent work on autonomy in the philosophical literature. That work suggests that autonomy's elements can be plotted on two axes. The first involves an individual's own capacities. An autonomous person possesses adequate rationality both to engage in means-ends reasoning and to identify and respond to values in some appropriate way.[1] Given the occurrence in human beings of desires that

---

[1] On the importance of means-ends reasoning, see e.g. Raz, *The Morality of Freedom,* 372–3; on the need to be responsive to values, see Sher, *Beyond Neutrality,* 48–51, 57.

run contrary to important goals, the autonomous person is also able, to some extent, to govern her actions by her important goals and to control desires that run against those goals.[2] Related to these ideas is the notion that autonomous persons pursue goals whose value they have endorsed for themselves. This does not mean that in explaining why an autonomous person is committed to certain goals no mention may be made of the efforts and influences of others; such independence is both conceptually and empirically impossible. But autonomy does require that formative processes of education and socialization proceed by appealing to a person's capacity for rationality, so that her choices and actions reflect reasons whose force she recognizes: following Gerald Dworkin, we can dub this the criterion of "procedural independence." It is violated most plainly by those seeking to engender commitments through processes like brainwashing or hypnosis which bypass a person's capacity for rational assessment.[3]

Rounding out the requirements for autonomy on the individual axis, autonomy also essentially involves some degree of critical examination, self-reflection, and a willingness to revise commitments when presented with sufficient reasons. In contrast to the general consensus on the elements in the previous paragraph, appeal to these last ideas often generates controversy, with some objecting to putting too much weight on them when discussing autonomy in the context of political argument.[4] These

---

[2] The importance in autonomy of such self-control has been powerfully advanced in the work of Harry Frankfurt (see especially his "Freedom of the Will and the Concept of a Person," in *Free Will*, ed. Gary Watson [New York: Oxford University Press, 1982], 81–95), and Gerald Dworkin (*The Theory and Practice of Autonomy* [New York: Cambridge University Press, 1988]). Susan Wolf dubs this general account "the deep self view" and includes among its advocates Charles Taylor and Gary Watson. See Wolf, "Sanity and the Metaphysics of Responsibility," in *Responsibility, Character, and the Emotions*, ed. F. Schoeman (New York: Cambridge University Press, 1988), 46–62.

[3] Gerald Dworkin, "Autonomy and Behavior Control," *Hastings Center Report* 6 (February 1976), 23–8.

[4] For expressions of such doubts see Robert Noggle, "The Public Conception of Autonomy and Critical Self-Reflection," in *Southern Journal of Philosophy* 35 (1997), 495–515, and Richard Double, "Two Types of Autonomy Accounts," *Canadian Journal of Philosophy* 22, no. 1 (March 1992), 65–80. Stephen Wall also seeks to downplay the connection between autonomy and self-reflection, though Wall somewhat undermines his position in suggesting that part of autonomy's value derives from its enabling persons to choose goals that match their talents and interests well. As Wall himself recognizes, gaining such insight is likely to involve a fair amount of self-scrutiny (*Liberalism, Perfectionism, and Restraint* [Cambridge: Cambridge University Press, 1998], 153, n. 34). A decisive argument for the importance to autonomy of critical examination and openness to revision is offered in Wolf's "Sanity and the Metaphysics of Responsibility." Wolf's discussion of the fictional tyrant JoJo vividly demonstrates how one who is denied these may actively shape his life in accordance with goals he values highly while still failing to be autonomous. Even if we agree that JoJo has a self that determines his actions (which Noggle suggests is all that is required for autonomy), we can still ask whether JoJo has played any active role in shaping the

concerns raise genuine worries, as I shall suggest below, but for now they can be addressed if we see autonomy not as requiring the continuous deployment of skills of critical examination, self-reflection, and revision, but instead as having the skills and willingness to do so when reason recommends. After all, some amount of critical examination is needed if one is to choose goals on the basis of reasons; self-reflection helps one to assess how well goals correspond to one's talents and temperament and to recognize when one is motivated by desires at odds with values one holds dear; and willingness to revise one's commitments when faced with sufficient reasons is logically entailed by the idea of choosing goals on the basis of reasons whose power one appreciates.[5]

The other axis relevant to autonomy concerns a person's social context. Here two ideas stand out. First, to be autonomous in any area one must be free from the coercion of others.[6] Since autonomy involves pursuing goals one endorses through one's capacity for reasoning about values, it provides a strong *prima facie* reason for allowing persons to act on ends they see as worthwhile. The other social element of autonomy involves having an adequate range of valuable options.[7] This reflects not only the idea that a self-authored life involves choosing a goal from a plural set, but also the importance of critical examination: insofar as the values individuals reflect on are presented largely through ongoing activities that precede them, they can compare values in the way autonomy requires only if they have a range of acceptable options.

While these considerations capture the broad vision of self-direction at the heart of autonomy, they do not appear to constitute a distinctively liberal ideal that the critic might oppose. After all, who could reasonably

---

self he has become. When the answer is no (as in the JoJo case), the importance of respecting his decisions (said to follow from the ideal of respecting JoJo himself) becomes much less clear. Lawrence Haworth has argued powerfully that respect for another's choices is appropriate only when those choices have been shaped autonomously. See his "Autonomy and Utility," in *The Inner Citadel: Essays on Individual Autonomy*, ed. John Christman (New York: Oxford University Press, 1989), 155–69.

[5] Two clarifications are in order here. First, learning that one erred in one's original assessment of the value of a goal does not entail that one no longer has reason to continue in it: that one has already invested effort in that pursuit, and that others may now be depending on one's continuing in it, are just two reasons against abandoning it. Second, the preparedness to revise when presented with sufficient reasons does not mean that one must be constantly revising.

[6] This point is somewhat controversial. The familiar example of the man who hands over his money at gunpoint generates conflicting judgments: some see him as autonomous but not free, others as not autonomous because not free. But all agree that if autonomy is valuable, then so is freedom. We value not merely having the capacity for autonomy, but exercising it as well.

[7] This idea is captured most famously by Mill in ch. 3 of *On Liberty*, and has been endorsed more recently by Thomas Hurka ("Why Value Autonomy?," *Social Theory and Practice* 13, no. 3 [Fall 1987], 361–82) and by Raz, *The Morality of Freedom*, 373ff.

object to the notion that there is value in rationality, in choosing on the basis of reasons, in having some amount of personal liberty, and so on? Autonomy becomes controversial, and an *ideal* of autonomy emerges that is distinctively liberal, I believe, when the value of autonomy is seen as providing a reason for amplifying as far as possible the elements of autonomy on both the personal and social axes: if critical reflection is part of autonomy, then the ideal of autonomy sees more critical reflection as better than less; if liberty is as well, then the ideal argues for the maximal realm of liberty possible; if having options available is good, then having more options is better; and so on. This account of the liberal ideal of autonomy, which sees liberal states as celebrating a more robust exercise of capacities whose value critics to some degree recognize, is admittedly imprecise, and it allows that judgments of relative autonomy are complex and likely to be controversial. But this I see as a strength of the account. For autonomy is better understood in terms of a spectrum rather than as something one either has or lacks *simpliciter*, and this, I shall argue, leads to serious problems for autonomy-based liberalism.

AUTONOMY AS A PRECONDITION OF THE GOOD LIFE

There are three main strategies for defending the universal value of the liberal ideal of autonomy. The first sees autonomy as a necessary precondition for any good life. The second emphasizes autonomy's instrumental value in helping individuals achieve goods whose value is not itself a function of the value of autonomy. The third defends autonomy as having such enormous intrinsic value that it must figure in any genuinely good life. These claims are not mutually exclusive, but our discussion will be clearer if we consider them separately. In the following two sections I consider the latter two arguments. Here I take up the argument for autonomy as precondition, built around the idea that only liberal regimes adequately register the relation between one's pursuits and one's conception of value that must obtain if one is to lead a good life.

The general idea behind this argument, dubbed by Richard Arneson the endorsement constraint, is that one's life goes better only if one pursues or achieves goals, relationships, character traits, and the like whose value one endorses.[8] If so, and if political arrangements are to be assessed in terms of how well they advance the well-being of those under them,

---

[8] Will Kymlicka succinctly captures the core idea: "No life goes better by being led from the outside, according to values the person doesn't endorse. My life only goes better if I'm leading it from the inside, according to my beliefs about value" (*Liberalism, Community and Culture*

we have strong grounds for ensuring that citizens are most free to pursue whatever goals they endorse as valuable: their lives can go better in no other way. We also, on similar grounds, appear to have good reasons against both coercing citizens and directing them towards goals they don't endorse. And since the endorsement constraint does not rely on skepticism or subjectivism about the good, it allows liberals to defend their distinctive commitments without endorsing those controversial positions.

The route from the endorsement constraint to liberal states faces three serious problems, however. First, the very idea of leading a life from the inside is unclear, largely because of the obscurity of the contrast case. What would it be like to lead a life from the outside?[9] Paradigm cases here would perhaps include someone who goes to medical school just to remain in the parents' will, or who dates someone of the other sex only to avoid being thought gay. Should we say, then, that leading a life from the outside consists in pursuing goals and engaging in activities not because one finds them valuable in themselves but because doing so will get one something else that one values? That answer is too strong. According to it, we fail to lead our lives from the inside when we earn money by working in a job we don't see as intrinsically valuable, for example, or clean our houses, or visit doctors. This answer does not explain why falling short of the endorsement constraint is so bad.

Alternatively, we might say that one leads a life from the outside when one engages in activities that one does not believe one has strongest reason to engage in, as specified by one's deepest values. The problem with this approach, though, is that the paradigm cases mentioned above would satisfy the endorsement constraint. What each person most values in those cases is either to achieve some good or to avoid some harm, each wants that more than he or she wants to avoid the activity in question, and so each is motivated by his own values.

Perhaps, then, one leads a life from the outside whenever one is not doing what one most wants to do. This seems to explain both paradigm cases, for in each the person ideally prefers either to achieve the good or to avoid the harm by engaging in some other activity. But this third answer can't be right either. Many of us frequently find that we cannot do what

[New York: Oxford University Press, 1989], 12; see also 13, 18, and 19). Amy Gutmann talks about living according to one's own best lights in *Democratic Education*, rev. edn. (Princeton: Princeton University Press, 1999). Arneson, who criticizes the endorsement constraint, focuses his critique on Ronald Dworkin's argument in Dworkin, *Sovereign Virtue: The Theory and Practice of Equality* (Cambridge, MA: Harvard University Press, 2000). See Arneson, "Human Flourishing versus Desire Satisfaction," *Social Philosophy and Policy* 16 (Winter 1999), 113–42.

9 I am grateful to John Deigh for raising this question in discussion with me.

we ideally want to do (teach at Cambridge, say, or perform at Carnegie Hall). If pursuing those options means we're not leading a life from the inside, the endorsement constraint is ridiculously demanding.[10]

At this point, advocates of the ideal of leading a life from the inside will reply that I have ignored a crucial distinction. It is one thing, they will say, if one cannot engage in activities one endorses because of one's own limitations or the permissible decisions of others, and quite another if one is prevented by restrictions unreasonably imposed by others. This brings us, I think, to the heart of what disturbs liberals in the paradigmatic cases: namely, that someone or some group has structured the available options in an objectionable way. In both cases others have attached penalties and rewards to activities in a way that strongly influences what one has most reason to do. It seems, then, that leading a life from the inside is determined neither by the degree to which one endorses the intrinsic value of one's activity nor by the strength of reasons for doing it, but by reference to the conditions within which one chooses. But precisely here lies the problem for the endorsement constraint: those who stress it believe the conditions under which persons choose should be marked by the greatest liberty possible and a strong prohibition against state paternalism. Whether they are right is the subject of this book. But if the concept of leading a life from the inside is to figure as a *reason for* securing those conditions, it must be more than just a description of choices made under them.[11]

Even if the idea of leading a life from the inside could be made intelligible, is it really true that no one's life goes better by engaging in activities they don't endorse? Many critics believe that certain activities, relationships, experiences, and so on are intrinsically valuable, and that a good life is in large measure marked by engagement with these. This view contrasts with subjectivist accounts, which understand the good for persons in terms of their desires, life-plans, or other features distinct to their mental states. Now while the endorsement constraint follows naturally from

---

[10] The root of the problem is evident in Kymlicka's argument. Though his defense of liberal regimes hinges on his worry over the loss of value that results when persons do not lead lives from the inside (thereby suggesting that this is at least a possibility), he also offers an argument which has as its premise the idea that no one can avoid living a life from the inside (cf. the passage on p. 34 of *Liberalism, Community and Culture* that begins: "Since lives have to be led from the inside ..."). Perhaps what Kymlicka means is just that *good* lives have to be led from the inside. Even if that is his intended meaning, my argument suggests that the loose phrasing is not merely accidental.

[11] These problems have suggested to some that the endorsement constraint is best understood as promoting choices that better match up with the diversity of persons' natural constitutions. I explore this argument in the following section.

subjectivist accounts, it is much more problematic on objectivist accounts. For notice, the endorsement constraint does not assert that one's *life goes better if one* endorses one's ends than if one does not. That seems plausible, given that pleasure and self-respect, for example, are legitimate goods likely to be enhanced in such a life. Rather, the endorsement constraint asserts that *one's life is not improved at all* by engaging in activities one does not endorse. But unless we accept subjectivism this raises a puzzle: for if endorsing the value of one's ends does not make them valuable for a person, why should rejecting them mean their pursuit cannot enrich one's life? If we can go wrong in thinking we are leading a good life, why can't we also go wrong, *pace* the endorsement constraint, in thinking we're leading a bad one?[12]

Advocates of the endorsement constraint need to defend this asymmetry. A first response is that any good life must have its share of pleasure (or preference-satisfaction, or self-respect, etc.: I shall stick with pleasure) and that agents derive no pleasure from engaging in activities they do not endorse. The latter claim is not strictly true – one can regard sexual activity as degrading and still get pleasure in it – but this is a minor quibble. The larger problem is that persons can achieve significant pleasure in some pursuits even if they achieve little or none from their unendorsed engagement in others.[13] So long as one experiences whatever amount of pleasure is needed for a good life, it's not clear why one's life is not improved by engagement in worthwhile pursuits even if they do not yield pleasure because they are not endorsed. In fact, once we distinguish (1) whether a pursuit is seen as valuable, from (2) whether a pursuit really is valuable, the first defense of asymmetry appears even more inadequate: for just as the pleasure derived from corrupting activities might be outweighed by their disvalue, so might the lack of pleasure in unendorsed pursuits be outweighed by their objective value, thus improving the quality of a life.

As a second defense of the asymmetry, advocates of the endorsement constraint might reply that one can succeed in worthwhile pursuits only if one endorses their value. This claim can be advanced on either empirical or conceptual grounds. If advanced empirically, i.e. as a thesis about how attitude affects performance, note that it shifts the nature of the endorsement constraint significantly. Whereas previously the constraint appeared

---

[12] Wall makes a similar point in rejecting the endorsement constraint, suggesting that since one's judgment of the value of ends is always in principle fallible, one's own endorsement cannot be essential for one's life to be improved.
[13] Arneson, "Human Flourishing versus Desire Satisfaction," 140.

to posit a logical connection between endorsement and the quality of one's life, the issue now becomes the relation between an agent's mindset and her prospects for success. This empirical claim is difficult to assess, but there is no reason to think that those who undertake activities in a manner that falls short of the endorsement constraint cannot achieve a reasonable level of success. Even if persons so motivated tend to be less successful than those who endorse their ends, that lesser achievement may still contribute more to the quality of their lives than greater "success" in misguided goals they do endorse.

Defenders of the endorsement constraint may then defend the relation between success and endorsement as a conceptual point. The idea here is that the very notion of pursuing and succeeding in a goal requires satisfying the endorsement constraint to some degree. Just as being forced to recite the Lord's Prayer at knifepoint doesn't really constitute praying, it may be thought that the goals, relationships, and so forth that add value to a life can truly be pursued only if one endorses them. Ronald Dworkin provides an example along these lines, imagining an art student whose important aesthetic choices are made by his more talented instructor. This student is not really painting, Dworkin points out, and so his life is not enriched by the value in being a good painter.[14]

Such examples undeniably show a connection between intention and achieving a goal: success requires caring about one's performance and responding rightly to its challenges. But neither of these requires that one endorse one's goals. We need, in other words, to distinguish the question whether an activity was taken up in a manner satisfying the endorsement constraint from the question whether one's performance reflects the degree of intentionality that (conceptually) constitutes engagement in the activity. Even if Michelangelo had undertaken the Sistine Chapel ceiling only because of Julius' deadly threat, that would nullify neither his artistic accomplishment nor the claim that his life went better as a result of the greatness he achieved thereby. The intention to do something can be present even if one is doing that only because of outside interference (though again, enthusiastic and willing involvement makes one's life go even better). So long as value accrues to a life in part through the successful pursuit of worthwhile tasks, the conceptual defense does not establish endorsement as a necessary condition for improving one's life.

---

[14] Ronald Dworkin, *Sovereign Virtue*, 268.

Even if the endorsement constraint could withstand the objections I have raised, moving from it to a defense of liberalism via autonomy faces a final obstacle. The problem is that the constraint can be satisfied in conditions falling short of the liberal ideal of autonomy. To see why, consider someone who non-autonomously adopts a worthwhile conception of the good, who pursues that vision steadfastly, and whose life goes well as a result. This possibility is recognized even by one as sympathetic to autonomy's value as Raz, who acknowledges that persons may be wholeheartedly committed to their pursuits and experience their value fully without having autonomously chosen them.[15] Endorsement does not appear to require the conditions of autonomy as liberals understand them, so from the endorsement constraint we cannot derive the superiority of the liberal ideal of autonomy without further argument. (The natural move for the liberal here – that greater freedom with more options enhances the likelihood of endorsement – I discuss in the next section.)

Even more provocatively, the endorsement constraint does not rule out the permissibility of coercion, a fact Dworkin acknowledges. Consider Pascal's wager, which rests on the possibility that engaging in a pursuit one initially does not endorse can lead one, later, to endorse it. This rarely happens in the case of religious worship (a main reason Pascal's argument fails to convince), but in other contexts it seems more promising. For example, Lawrence Kohlberg's model of moral development suggests that persons initially abide by moral norms out of fear of punishment but come to endorse them for their own sake. Something similar goes on in formal education, where students are first motivated by incentives having little to do with the intrinsic good of education and only later come to see that value. So even if endorsement were critical to a pursuit's adding value to a life, it does not follow that such endorsement must precede one's commitment to various valuable ends.[16] Collectively, these reasons make highly dubious the attempt to ground liberal autonomy on the endorsement constraint.

---

[15] "I do not see that the absence of choice diminishes the value of human relations or the display of excellence in technical skills, physical ability, spirit and enterprise, leadership, creativity, or imaginativeness … it is a mistake to think that what is chosen is more likely to attract our dedication and involvement than what is not" (Raz, "Facing Up: A Reply," *Southern California Law Review* 62 (1989), 1227–8). For an argument that such a life would not be as good as a similar life chosen from a range of options, see Martha Nussbaum, *Sex and Social Justice* (New York: Oxford University Press, 1999), 42ff.

[16] No doubt there would be limits on when endorsement must occur if one is to lead a good life: if at the age of eighty one for the first time endorses one's life work, this seems inadequate. But neither does it seem reasonable to insist that endorsement must occur at the first moment.

THE INSTRUMENTAL CASE FOR AUTONOMY

The instrumental case hinges on three claims: that those who are more autonomous are more likely to identify and have a chance to pursue the good; that they will not face distinct obstacles in committing themselves to it; and that they are not more likely to experience significant harms that will make their lives go worse. The first claim is needed because expanding autonomy means greater liberty to choose from more options, so identifying worthwhile goals will be especially critical to how well one's life goes. The second is central because without it autonomous persons might be more likely to identify the good but less likely to pursue it with commitment and integrity. The third is important because the commitment to autonomy may generate significant costs, and the instrumental defense needs to show that whatever harms arise are outweighed by the goods that autonomy makes possible. I will argue that each claim is sufficiently controversial as to cast doubt on the overall argument.

Identifying the good

There are two main ways of defending the claim that increasing autonomy makes one more likely to identify the good. The first argues that what is good for a person is in key respects a function of particular natural facts about that person and that promoting autonomy makes it much more likely that persons will understand and then pursue their distinctive good. The best such argument, which I will call the correspondence argument, begins in the ideas that self-development is a critical good and that persons differ significantly in their natural talents, interests, and temperaments. (The latter I shall refer to collectively as one's character set.) The thought here is that the greater self-reflection implicit in autonomy, along with exposure to and experimentation in a wide range of options, allow one better to appreciate one's own distinctive character set and so to identify more accurately those pursuits that correspond to one's natural constitution, thus allowing one to develop fully in the manner that best suits the individual.

Some might wonder straight away whether the argument from correspondence does not simply recapitulate the endorsement constraint. For while it appeals to the idea of self-development and not to a subjectivist view of the good, it sanctions a de facto enthronement of an individual's own judgment both of where her good lies and what her particular nature is that will likely be rejected by those who oppose the endorsement constraint. Though it seems true that in some regards our natures seem fixed and not open to reformation through the interventions of others (think of one's sexuality, or natural curiosity), in others our nature speaks much less clearly, and discerning its direction is far from an easy task. Moreover, to the degree that one's development into a mature human being involves restructuring and reordering natural drives and tendencies so they become better integrated and more responsive to reasons, it is not clear whether social conditions should be designed maximally to accommodate our bare natures or if instead they should be structured with an eye to how they may influence those natures. Finally, to the degree that the argument from correspondence assumes that the good for a person is fundamentally a matter of developing his or her natural talents, tendencies, and so on, it is open to familiar objections that plague natural law accounts of human flourishing.

Even if those worries could be overcome, the argument from correspondence is incomplete. What it must also show is that there exists a great number of differing character sets among individuals. For even if the range of character sets displayed by persons varies greatly, the overall number of such sets might still be relatively small (i.e. there might be a limited number of different personality types). If so, then a range of options narrower than that which liberal autonomy protects might allow all persons to pursue goals appropriate to their particular make-up. Few human communities fail to recognize the value of poets, scholars, doctors, teachers, artisans, entertainers, and so on, and this range of activities will surely go some way to accommodating people of diverse character sets. The argument thus hinges on the assumption that the talents and interests of persons are inherently so diverse that they can be accommodated only under conditions of liberal autonomy.

This assumption, however, is extremely difficult to establish. To begin with, though the idea may resonate powerfully among many liberal citizens, that appeal may itself reflect the common experience of living within regimes that celebrate and call forth diverse individual expression.[17] If our confidence in the claim for broad diversity of natural character reflects particular social conditions, that claim cannot without circularity be invoked to justify those conditions. Another problem here derives from the fact that one of the ways in which people seem naturally to differ is in the degree to

---

[17] "The vast majority of individuals in any group are shaped to the fashion of that culture. In other words, most individuals are plastic to the molding force of the society into which they are born" (Ruth Benedict, "Anthropology and the Abnormal," *Journal of General Psychology* 10 [1934], 78). Liberal citizens are no exception.

which they relish self-expression, individuality, and the like. Though some find the task of fashioning a distinct self within liberal regimes an enlivening challenge, others find it a distressing and anxiety-producing burden. The claim for natural diversity thus points to serious harms that liberal regimes may cause some citizens, a topic I discuss below.[18]

But perhaps the most serious problem in deploying the argument from correspondence to defend liberal autonomy is that many persons who live without such autonomy do not believe that this lack is the chief threat to their leading good lives: they often identify more mundane factors such as the lack of food, economic prospects, health care, and so on. Granted, when such goods are provided some do clamor for liberal autonomy; but many do not. If we accept the argument from correspondence, it follows that such persons either fail to appreciate the importance of self-development corresponding to their natural constitutions or mistakenly think they are achieving it. Either response impugns the rationality of large numbers of people chiefly because they appear content with a way of life that departs from the liberal ideal, a conclusion that hardly seems consistent with the ideal of respecting others' autonomy. Perhaps, then, the range of character sets among persons is narrower than the correspondence argument suggests, or the requisite threshold of self-development lower, such that many can achieve meaningful self-development in conditions that fall short of liberal autonomy.[19]

These problems suggest the need for an alternative way of establishing autonomy's instrumental value in identifying the good. This second approach, which I shall dub the argument from revisability, downplays the claim for the idiosyncratic content of a person's good and argues instead that expanding the conditions of autonomy – maximal freedom of expression, experiments of living, a non-tutelary state, and so on – promotes more accurate judgments about the good. Often advanced in response to critics who charge liberals with embracing subjectivism or skepticism, the argument from revisability stresses how liberal regimes help citizens reason better about objectively good ends.[20]

---

[18] Brian Barry articulates this idea nicely: "Liberalism rests on a vision of life: a Faustian vision. It exalts self-expression, self-mastery and control over the environment, natural and social; the active pursuit of knowledge and the clash of ideas; the acceptance of personal responsibility for the decisions that shape one's life. For those who cannot take the freedom it provides alcohol, tranquilizers, wrestling on the television, astrology, psychoanalysis, and so on, endlessly, but it cannot by its nature provide certain kinds of psychological security" (*The Liberal Theory of Justice* [Oxford: Oxford University Press, 1973], 174).

[19] "All that self-development demands is that people develop their talents and capacities to some significant degree" (Wall, *Liberalism, Perfectionism, and Restraint*, 152).

[20] The argument from revisability is often advanced alongside the endorsement constraint. Cf. Kymlicka: "So we have two preconditions for the fulfillment of our essential interest in leading

The argument begins from the assumption, presupposed by the task of political philosophy, that authoritative values and norms are accessible to human understanding. Now if we assume, as the liberal project does, that political institutions can be justified to persons living under them, then we must believe that such persons have the capacity for reasoning coherently about political morality. If we then reject the notion of an epistemic divide between knowledge of political norms and knowledge of the good,[21] we are perforce committed to the view that persons have the capacity for reasoning coherently about the good. It then seems reasonable that the conditions characterizing liberal autonomy will generally increase citizens' knowledge of the good, because they will promote wider experimentation and a broader exchange of ideas, reflection, and experience, all of which should yield improved judgments.[22]

While this argument has undeniable appeal, it rests on a conception of rationality that many critics might reasonably reject. Consider an alternative account that stresses the serious obstacles threatening our ability to form accurate judgments of the good. (If knowledge of the good is anything like knowledge of political morality, such an account will seem plausible.) Along with the intrinsic difficulties involving judgments about value, such obstacles include the distortions created by our own biases and temptations, the fact that worthwhile activities may offer only delayed gratification in contrast to less valuable ones that tempt us more urgently, and the corrupting influence of those who would gain from our making poor choices. Some citizens, believing these difficulties sizeable, fear that without significant direction human beings are likely to err in such judgments, and so endorse measures at odds with basic liberal commitments that they believe should significantly shape the process whereby persons reach such judgments.[23]

On the latter account, the critical question then becomes whether the state should have a significant role in that process or whether instead it

a life that is good. One is that we lead our life from the inside, in accordance with our beliefs about what gives value to life; the other is that we be free to question those beliefs, to examine them in the light of whatever information and examples and arguments our culture can provide" (*Liberalism, Community and Culture*, 19–20). Ronald Dworkin's defense of liberal regimes invokes both ideas as well.

[21] Compelling reasons against such an epistemic divide are provided by George Sher in *Beyond Neutrality*, 149ff.

[22] Though neither Kymlicka nor Dworkin explicitly sets forth the argument in these terms, it seems to me the most natural reconstruction of their positions.

[23] A rich depiction of these fears, and the mindset associated with them, is provided in Eamonn Callan, "Autonomy, Child-Rearing, and Good Lives," in *The Moral and Political Status of Children*, ed. David Archard and Colin Macleod (New York: Oxford University Press, 2002), 135ff. Note that this approach represents a different understanding of the "challenge model"

should be left entirely to civil society – a choice between what Kymlicka calls state or social perfectionism.[24] Kymlicka opts for the latter on the assumption that "under conditions of freedom, satisfying and valuable ways of life will tend to drive out those which are worthless and unsatisfying."[25] In part his position rests on just the sort of rosy picture about our capacities for discrimination rejected by the critic I've imagined – a picture which, Kymlicka acknowledges, is unsubstantiated in his account. But he also argues that state perfectionism has two serious flaws: it tends to penalize those who cannot articulate clearly their own views about the good, and it creates pressure for minority groups to misrepresent their own positions so as to curry favor with the majority. Though he allows that these problems can arise in the cultural marketplace as well, Kymlicka believes they are more pronounced under state perfectionism, since the state (1) has greater power to dictate to minorities the terms within which they must make the case for their way of life, and (2) forces them to do so "in a time and place – political deliberation over state policy – in which minorities are most vulnerable."[26]

These considerations, however, are hardly decisive. To begin with, the argument threatens to beg the question. Many critics would just deny that ensuring the widest protection of minority ways of life is an obvious goal. They believe, instead, that some views of the good are deeply mistaken and that their influence should be checked. Nor should we imagine that critics object to minority ways of life *per se*: indeed, within liberal societies their view of the good is often a minority view. What they oppose are ways of life connected to ends that are worthless, corrupting, and so on.

Note also that despite Kymlicka's worries, state perfectionism can have salutary effects. Advocates of deliberative democracy have suggested that having to make one's case in a public forum imposes norms of fairness and reasonableness more easily ignored in the private realm, where no public accounting is required. Because it involves public justification before others committed to different norms and goals, political deliberation can, observes Bikhu Parekh, "deepen mutual understanding between different groups, sensitize each to the concerns and anxieties of

that Ronald Dworkin invokes in arguing against paternalism (*Sovereign Virtue*, 253ff.). Dworkin understands this challenge as involving a single person who must make the correct value judgments that lead to a good life. But one can also see the challenge as confronting a whole community and assess individual lives (in part) in terms of how far they help the community meet that challenge.

[24] Will Kymlicka, "Liberal Individualism and Liberal Neutrality," *Ethics* 99 (July 1989), 883–905.
[25] Ibid., 885.   [26] Ibid., 901.

others, [and] lead to an unconscious fusion of ideas and sensibilities."[27] Even if we think Parekh downplays the influence of less noble factors behind political discourse, the cultural marketplace may be even worse off. Not only is it dominated by self-interested agents concerned more to shape the goals and choices of citizens than to cultivate their ability to discern value, but since it takes place outside the site of collective deliberation it is both more vulnerable to forces operating behind the backs of citizens and less responsive to public reason-giving. It is more than a little ironic that advocates of the revisability argument, so fond of the idea that increased debate and reflection can help individuals identify valuable ends, should worry that the chief effects of such collective discussion in political fora will be to threaten worthwhile ways of life. If we have confidence in the private exercise of our common reason, why should we be so uncertain about the judgments we will reach in our shared and public deliberation?

Autonomy and commitment

The second claim in the instrumental argument asserts that those who are more autonomous are no less likely to be steadfastly committed to their goals. One might think this follows directly from the idea that autonomy in part involves ordering one's less important desires by one's more important goals (this is the "deep self" view described earlier), but this would assume precisely what is in question: namely, whether persons who mature in an environment built around the ideal of personal choice from a wide range of options, which celebrates critical revision remaining ever alert to the possibility that better pursuits might come along, will develop the steadfast commitment to their projects that the deep self view champions. These factors seem more likely to temper one's resolve towards any particular end and to promote the condition that Durkheim called anomie, in which individuals feel a deep sense of aimlessness, rootlessness, and lack of conviction in their own ends. Durkheim saw this malaise as a prominent feature of modern liberal societies, with their emphasis on individuality and self-creation, and its importance as a diagnosis of liberal culture helps explain the wide attention that greeted William Galston's remark that "the greatest threat to children in modern liberal societies is not that they will believe something too deeply, but that they will believe nothing

---

[27] Bikhu Parekh, *Rethinking Multiculturalism: Cultural Diversity and Political Theory* (Cambridge, MA: Harvard University Press, 2000), 307.

very deeply at all."[28] The point here is not that no autonomous person can be firmly committed to her goals, but that there are reasons to think that at some point amplifying autonomy works to undermine conviction.

The most promising reply to this worry appeals to a point Mill makes in *On Liberty* concerning the connection between knowledge and exposure to diverse viewpoints. There Mill argues that to fully understand one's own view one must clearly understand the rejected alternatives. If one fully understands the value of one's goals only through comparison with a wide variety of options, and if a deeper understanding of the value of one's goals engenders stronger commitment, we have grounds for thinking that enhancing autonomy strengthens commitment. In her perceptive study of Mill, Wendy Donner endorses this line of thought, suggesting that "unless we choose our own pleasures and activities, we cannot completely appreciate and understand their value, and we miss an opportunity to exercise our powers and in so doing to amplify them."[29] Donner's point, if sound, strengthens the instrumental case in just the right way: in increasing appreciation of one's goals, liberal autonomy fosters greater commitment.

This Millean argument, however, faces several objections. To begin with, the connection between autonomously choosing our goals and understanding their value is dubious. Imagine two individuals whose ways of life result not from autonomous reflection but simply from falling into family traditions: one lives in a small rural community and sees herself as closely connected to the land, the other excels at scholarship in the academy. Why think that neither can really understand the value of the goals they're engaged with, especially if each achieves some success? True, each may not understand the value of her goals *relative to other goals*, but why should this matter to the quality of their lives?[30]

---

[28] A concise account of Durkheim's conception of anomie is found in Mark Cladis, *A Communitarian Defense of Liberalism: Emile Durkheim and Contemporary Social Theory* (Stanford: Stanford University Press, 1992), 62–9. The Galston quotation appears in his "Civic Education in the Liberal State," in *Liberalism and the Moral Life*, ed. Nancy Rosenblum (Cambridge, MA: Harvard University Press, 1989), 101. Eamonn Callan has also noted that educating for autonomy runs the risk "that individuals will be unable rationally to adhere" to their ideals of the good. "Coming adequately to appreciate many things that make our lives good requires a certain steady resistance to distraction and a constancy that do not come easily as we grow to maturity" ("Autonomy, Child-Rearing, and Good Lives," 134).

[29] Wendy Donner, *The Liberal Self: John Stuart Mill's Moral and Political Philosophy* (Ithaca: Cornell University Press, 1991), 151.

[30] Cf. Mill's discussion in *Utilitarianism* on the importance of "competent judges" who can make comparative assessments because they have seen both sides. Note that Mill's point there is to establish a criterion for a hierarchy of values, not to suggest that one can experience one type of value only if one is aware of others.

A second objection is that the strength of commitment to one's goals is, strictly speaking, a function not of how well one understands their value, but of one's confidence that they are valuable: the truth of the belief is not relevant to strength of commitment. The argument from revisability speaks to the accuracy of judgments about the good. The objection being considered here, however, concerns the confidence with which such judgments are held. As we are dismayingly reminded, the connection between confidence in one's judgments and their correctness is all too contingent.

Finally, it's doubtful that the Millean claim can be extrapolated to ways of life given value pluralism. Mill is imagining a debate where one view is largely correct, the others mistaken. Value pluralism, however, tells us that many of the options liberal citizens are encouraged to consider are not inferior: though bypassed, they remain valuable. In contrast to Mill's case, here closer examination of other options and a better understanding of them will not work to confirm the rightness of one's choice, because it will not confirm the wrongness of the bypassed alternative. The Millean point about greater understanding of alternatives, then, does little to ease the fear that increasing autonomy makes it harder to remain committed to one's goals.

Assessing costs and benefits

To the preceding objections the defender of liberal autonomy has a ready reply. It may be, she will say, that enhancing autonomy allows and in some cases encourages persons to pursue worthless or misguided goals, and that it as well poses an inevitable threat to commitment for certain persons, who may suffer the anomie that is liberalism's distinctive malady. But such costs, the liberal will insist, are on balance outweighed by the goals enhanced autonomy brings – greater experiments of living from which persons can learn, increased freedom to pursue the goals that align with one's values and character set, stronger protection against the intrusions of a misguided tutelary state, and so on. This is the final claim in the instrumental case, viz., that the harms that may be engendered by the strong commitment to autonomy are outweighed by its benefits. Is this claim compelling?

One reason for doubt derives from the fact, noted in Chapter 2, that commitment and integrity to one's goals and projects connect to important human goods. So long as one's ends meet certain criteria, constancy in their pursuit enables one to develop talents, confers feelings of accomplishment, and contributes to a sense of oneself as an enduring and coherent personality over time. These effects amplify the worry over commitment because they raise the possibility that a person might, by pursuing with deep commitment a goal that is either not as valuable as another or not as well suited to her character set, lead a better life than if she had pursued, with less commitment, a goal that was either more valuable or to which she was better suited. If enhancing autonomy makes many persons more vulnerable to diminished commitment, dilettantism, and disabling second-guessing, then to assess the claim that autonomy's benefits outweigh its costs we must compare (1) conditions in which persons more accurately identify worthwhile pursuits (assuming *arguendo* the merits of social perfectionism) but face special challenges in remaining committed, with (2) conditions in which persons on the whole make somewhat less accurate judgments but are more likely to remain committed. Such calculations are just extremely difficult, and it is not at all clear that the superiority of (1) could be justified before skeptics with the degree of conclusiveness needed to support the liberal case. When we keep in mind that value pluralism validates as worthwhile a wider array of options that persons might reasonably choose, the threat to commitment brought about by expanding autonomy becomes even more worrisome.

The final liberal reply can also be challenged by pointing to other harms, besides those having to do with diminished commitment, likely to result from the liberal state's commitment to maximizing personal autonomy. Some of these primarily affect individuals. Along with the sense of anomie just mentioned, the emphasis on autonomy may leave persons feeling disconnected from historic or cultural traditions, more vulnerable to a creeping value subjectivism that results in a flattened normative landscape, and less likely to achieve the goods that result from participation in large-scale collective efforts to advance common ideals. Other harms affect the collective political community as a whole. The problems here have to do both with individuals' motivation to solve collective problems (likely to be hindered both by the emphasis on individualism implicit in autonomy-based liberalism and by the loss of motivation that shared substantive ends can provide) and with their abilities to do so (undermined both by the increased moral dissensus that autonomy promotes and by the lack of a common moral language with which to deliberate over shared problems and to propose terms for resolving them). And though it is difficult to gauge how far these concerns will affect groups smaller than the polity, it is worth noting that to the extent they are free from them (because the group in question unites around shared ends), that indicates the group's distance from the central value driving the political community as a whole.

To be clear, in advancing these considerations I am not arguing for the superiority of illiberal regimes. My central point is just that in citing the alleged benefits of enhancing autonomy, advocates of its instrumental value need both to acknowledge the costs such a policy incurs and show that the benefits outweigh them. Liberal theorists have not to date offered such an argument. Without it, the instrumental case for autonomy remains inconclusive.

THE INTRINSIC CASE

The case for autonomy's intrinsic value proceeds not by showing that enhancing autonomy promotes other goods, but by defending autonomy itself as having such value that any genuinely good life must achieve it. There are two general routes for establishing the claim. First, one can argue that given the great value in exercising the skills that autonomy draws on (critical rationality, choosing from options, etc.), it follows that the more robustly one exercises those traits the better one's life is. This strategy, however, faces serious problems. To begin with, it threatens to beg the critical question. The goal is to establish autonomy's extraordinary value. Doing so by appealing to the value of the elements constituting autonomy just shifts the burden of proof, for the skeptic will now ask why those elements are so important as to outweigh the goods that may be compromised by promoting autonomy. Even if a persuasive case could be made for the value of exercising autonomy's constitutive elements, those skills can be exercised in various pursuits not themselves autonomously chosen. Consider the previous examples of the scholar or farmer who take up their careers non-autonomously. They may still be called upon to exercise those capacities – critical assessment, reflection, choice, and the rest – implicit in autonomy. True, they will not have exercised them under conditions that celebrate autonomy, but if that is the critical issue, then the defense of autonomy here rests not on the value of those capacities but on the value of exercising them under those conditions, and this just begs the question.

The final problem with defending autonomy's intrinsic value via its constitutive elements involves the implicit endorsement of some goals over others. In stressing the value of rational choice, critical examination, and so forth, the argument suggests that goals involving these skills have greater value *per se* than those that do not. But this claim is problematic, and not just because it seems suspiciously self-congratulatory when advanced by philosophers theorizing about autonomy. It is also intuitively at odds with what autonomy is about: one would have thought autonomy would counsel equal respect for the various reasonable goals a person might pursue, rather than clearly championing one set over others. And even if the exercise of rationality is one of our most valuable talents, is it so clear that pursuits revolving around this capacity are always more valuable than alternatives? Are such goods as friendship, play, love, or worship intrinsically less valuable than others because they draw less on our capacity for rational thought? Human beings are characterized by not only intellectual but affective and emotional capacities as well,[31] and the argument for the supremacy of autonomy's constitutive elements risks unduly demoting the latter.

Faced with these objections, autonomy-based liberals might reply that in appealing to the value of autonomy's components they mean only that any life marked by other goods will be better the more autonomous it is, and so in this sense autonomy has universal value. But this response, even if it is coherent,[32] won't do: it simply fails to address the worry that liberal autonomy unreasonably denigrates other goods that add significant value to a life.

These problems motivate a second route for defending autonomy's intrinsic value.[33] The most promising alternative, the one that offers the surest way of defeating the vexing problem of balancing the goods and harms engendered by enhancing autonomy, is to defend autonomy not as one good outweighing others, but as a good of a different kind – as the condition of other human goods, the *sine qua non* without which they could not contribute value to a human life. The strategy here focuses not on what makes a human life good, but on what makes a life human. As articulated in Stanley Benn's influential paper, the thought is that "anyone who attaches importance to his ontological status as a person [or to anyone else's, we might add: DM] will have a reason for accepting autonomy as an ideal."[34] By connecting autonomy directly to our status

---

[31] On Mill's attention to these areas of human life, see Donner, *The Liberal Self*, 92–117.

[32] Raz, for example, thinks it is not: "As I have argued … you cannot just add autonomy, that is, free choice, to the same life … It makes no sense to say that a life with autonomy is better than the same life without autonomy" ("Facing Up," 1228).

[33] Worries over a too close connection between autonomy and critical rationality are raised by Robert Young in *Personal Autonomy* (London: Croom Helm, 1986), 10–13, and by Richard Double, who maintains that "the self-possession theme in the idea of autonomy appears to leave room for folks who are terrible reasoners, yet are candidates for autonomy. An account of *autonomy* should capture this thread" (Double, "Two Types of Autonomy Accounts," 75).

[34] Stanley Benn, "Freedom, Autonomy, and the Concept of a Person," *Proceedings of the Aristotelian Society* 66 (1975–6), 124. Where Benn speaks of being a person, I shall sometimes speak of leading

as persons, what I am calling the argument from personhood bypasses the problems of balancing the value of autonomy with other goods it may imperil.

The general idea here is similar to that advanced by James Rachels and William Ruddick in their defense of the value of liberty.[35] Instead of defending liberty in terms of its contribution to well-being, Rachels and Ruddick argue that liberty is implied in the very idea of a human life. If one is never allowed to shape one's actions in any important way (the absolute slave is their example), one does not lead a bad life so much as fail to lead a life at all; one is reduced to the status of mere object. The argument from personhood builds on this distinction between objects and brute animals on the one hand, and the capacity for authoring actions that distinguishes human beings on the other. If we regard enslavement as a great evil because it denies a person's capacity to be self-determining, i.e. to reflect on and act from reasons, then we must also combat whatever undermines that capacity and strive to secure whatever furthers it. Someone totally lacking autonomy takes on her goals without critical reflection or an adequate range of options, and so does not choose on the basis of reasons in the manner distinctive to persons. The supreme value of autonomy follows directly from our recognition of the unique value accorded to persons as opposed to other kinds of thing.

THE CASE FOR THE THRESHOLD ACCOUNT

The argument from personhood offers an elegant way to bypass the question-begging aspect of the argument via autonomy's constitutive elements. Rather than defending autonomy's value by appeal to those elements, the argument from personhood proceeds by showing how autonomy is itself a component of a more encompassing value around which there exists deep consensus, i.e. the special value in being a person as opposed to an object or brute animal. In doing so it surely captures an aspect of our lives of extraordinary value. But even granting that the argument could bear much more development and elaboration, it invites two challenges. The first is that it does not escape the problem of balancing competing goods. I have suggested that regimes that champion autonomy increase the likelihood of various ills – feelings of alienation and anomie, diminished

a human life (as opposed to the life of a member of the species *homo sapiens*). Hurka advances a similar argument, connecting autonomy to ideas of responsibility and human agency, in "Why Value Autonomy?"

[35] James Rachels and William Ruddick, "Lives and Liberty," in *The Inner Citadel: Essays on Individual Autonomy*, ed. John Christman (New York: Oxford University Press, 1989), 221–33.

commitment to one's ends, etc. How can we establish that the ideal of self-determination implicit in personhood outweighs the risk of those ills? The response to this worry is two-fold. First, at some point our judgments of value may reach a point where they cannot be supported by further argument and simply reflect what J. J. C. Smart usefully called "a disagreement in ultimate attitude."[36] Bentham, for instance, thought nothing outranked pleasure and pain, for Kant human dignity occupied the highest rung, and Mill tried to have it both ways. Faced with such debates, we can turn to thought experiments like Robert Nozick's experience machine (which confers maximum pleasure in exchange for total loss of agency) to clarify what we most value. Such examples, I believe, unequivocally establish that our capacity for rational agency is the part of us that we are least willing to give up. If an opponent insists that a life characterized by a steady succession of chemically induced pleasures (or some other good not dependent on personhood) is just as worthwhile as one involving the exercise of our capacity for rational agency, the argument is largely over (even if it is not won). The second part of the response adds that the competing goods that enhanced autonomy may threaten have only conditional value. We do not value happiness in the suffering of others, or courage in the conduct of a murderous campaign. Since we value these goods only when certain criteria are met,[37] it is reasonable to attribute special value to our capacity to discern and apply those criteria, and this is precisely the capacity emphasized in the argument from personhood.

Still, a second, deeper criticism can be brought against the argument from personhood. For if we insist that leading a fully human life requires conditions of liberal autonomy, the implication is that those who live in conditions that fall short of liberal autonomy lead lives that are somehow

---

[36] J. J. C. Smart, "An Outline of a System of Utilitarian Ethics," in J. J. C. Smart and Bernard Williams, *Utilitarianism: For and Against* (New York: Cambridge University Press, 1963), 17.

[37] Lawrence Haworth advances the general idea here with reference to the good of community: "A community, one may say, just by virtue of being a community, has no value whatever. It may be a band of Nazis with a shared purpose to annihilate Jews, or a group formed to raise money for the Heart Foundation. Living together, sharing purposes, doing one's duty – these bring value to groups and lives if the common way of life, the shared purpose, the content of the duty, are admirable. It isn't that they don't contribute everything; as such, they contribute nothing" (*Autonomy: An Essay in Philosophical Psychology and Ethics* [New Haven: Yale University Press, 1986], 207). Here I think Haworth overstates his basically sound point. Common engagement in worthless pursuits can still give rise to intrinsically admirable acts of courage, sacrifice, loyalty, and the like. Rather than insisting that community in itself contributes nothing of value, we can preserve Haworth's insight by saying that the goods related to community are more easily outweighed when the communal ends are worthless, and virtually certain to be outweighed when the latter are positively evil.

less than fully human. Given the great number of citizens who do not live in conditions conducive to liberal autonomy, this will strike many as a repugnant conclusion.

The hard-nosed response to this worry is simply to accept that many persons outside liberal societies do not achieve the degree of autonomy that constitutes full personhood. This view need not lead to a policy of indifference; it can be conjoined with a sincere commitment to improve the lives of others (along lines of the white man's burden, perhaps). Nonetheless, in viewing members of such communities as falling short of the criterion of full personhood, the hard-nosed response is troubling. I am not denying that members of certain communities – those that fall under the sway of ruthless despots, for example, or undergo massive social breakdown – may fail to lead appropriately human lives. But this seems an unreasonably harsh claim to make about the billions of people living in illiberal societies, not to mention the possibility that such a claim might lead to a diminished sense of obligation to others who, after all, are not persons like us.

We can, however, accept the argument from personhood while rejecting the repugnant implication if we allow that the notion of self-determination it relies on does not require the robust ideal of autonomy underpinning liberal states. The key move on this approach is to reject what some have called a scalar interpretation of autonomy and to opt instead for a threshold interpretation. The scalar interpretation assumes that since some degree of autonomy is needed for a human life, a life is more fully human the more autonomous it is (the greater one's liberty, the more options one chooses from, and so on). The threshold interpretation, in contrast, agrees that leading a human life requires some autonomy but insists that once an appropriate level has been reached, increased autonomy does not make one more fully human. The critical point here is that the threshold interpretation does not provide *prima facie* reasons for always increasing autonomy. The scalar interpretation does.

At first glance, the threshold account may seem a merely *ad hoc* attempt to preserve the argument from personhood while rejecting its repugnant implication. That suspicion is not entirely unwarranted, but here it is not so obviously a criticism. For most of us confidently endorse two claims – that some amount of rational self-determination is central to leading a human life, and that those living in illiberal societies are fully human – which, as we have seen, threaten to pull against each other. The threshold interpretation represents the best hope for reconciling these two claims, neither of which we are prepared to abandon.

Further support for the threshold interpretation arises from the fact that members of liberal societies differ in their effectiveness at, and interest in, exercising the components of autonomy. Though ideally all have exercised some amount of self-reflectiveness, critical examination, and the like, many either have not done this to the same degree as others or have undertaken pursuits where such aptitudes figure much less centrally. The scalar account requires that we see these others (who may be lovers, friends, or family members) as somehow not achieving the fullest degree of humanity possible, a conclusion again deeply at odds with our confident judgments.

Third, pursuing the ideal of autonomy on the scalar account entails various serious costs. In principle that account recommends ceaselessly scrutinizing one's values, continually reviewing one's commitments, remaining ever mindful that one's current projects might be replaced by better ones, and so on. But an unflinching commitment to such ideals is problematic, for reasons already given. Not only will there exist people for whom the challenge of maximal autonomy provokes anxiety and so compromises the quality of their lives, but unceasing critical reflection also can sap energy from our pursuits, compromise our commitment to them, and undermine relationships built on trust and unconditional support.[38] If we insist on the scalar interpretation, then, we are again driven to recognize autonomy as just one good to be balanced alongside others, thereby exposing the argument to the objections we had sought to avoid. Understanding autonomy via the threshold account helps tame such worries, making the ideal of autonomy more ecumenical and attractive.

Finally, and perhaps most tellingly, the notion of autonomy has built-in constraints that call into question the coherence of the scalar interpretation. Consider the idea of critical examination. Such examination never proceeds *de novo*, but is always guided by canons of evaluation not themselves chosen through critical reasoning but presupposed by any act of critique.[39] Any intelligible exercise of autonomy, then, must fall within constraints narrower than the limitless ideal implied by the scalar account. Or again, consider the idea of choosing from options. No society makes

---

[38] These and other problems with the scalar interpretation are helpfully explored in Noggle, "The Public Conception of Autonomy."

[39] Cf. Joel Feinberg's claim: "Rational reflection thus presupposes some relatively settled convictions to reason from and with. If we take authenticity [i.e. the idea of pursuing goals that are one's own] to require that *all* principles (beliefs, preferences, etc.) are together to be examined afresh in the light of reason on each occasion for decision, then nothing resembling rational reflection can ever get started" (*The Moral Limits of the Criminal Law*, vol. III: *Harm to Self* [New York: Oxford University Press, 1984], 33).

possible all goals: social space is finite, and all human beings lead their lives in conditions lacking some options. But if so, the ideal of personhood endorsed by the scalar account is one no human being can achieve. The question, then, is not whether to endorse the threshold interpretation, but where the threshold should be drawn.

The superiority of the threshold over the scalar interpretation deals a decisive blow to those who defend liberalism by invoking autonomy's intrinsic value. That defense fails not because autonomy is not critical to a good life, but because the sort of autonomy needed to lead such a life does not require the robust commitments (the harm principle and antipaternalism) that characterize liberal states. I recognize I have done nothing to address the worries over indeterminacy that arise on the threshold interpretation – how much liberty is needed to ensure the threshold, how diverse the options must be, how far self-reflection must extend, and so on. But the advantages of the threshold account argue for resolving those challenges, rather than endorsing a scalar conception that may have greater logical simplicity but is ultimately less compelling. Lest this conclusion be thought too conciliatory, keep in mind that nothing I have said implies that all illiberal societies provide adequate conditions for their citizens to achieve threshold autonomy. All I have argued is that there is no reason to deny that some of them can do so. That conclusion is enough to defeat autonomy-based liberalism.

CHAPTER 4

Liberal autonomy: the particularist case

RAZ AND PARTICULARIST LIBERALISM

Even if the universal value of liberal autonomy cannot be established with the conclusiveness needed to overcome the critics' objections, there remains a second route for defending liberalism via autonomy. Here the argument proceeds not by appealing to autonomy's value for persons everywhere, but by stressing its special importance within existing liberal societies. This particularist approach does not claim that the liberal state is the ideal model of political association for all times and places, but instead defends it as appropriate given the particular social facts of certain human communities. Will Kymlicka's influential defense of minority rights in liberal states draws to some extent on such particularist claims, as does Michael Oakeshott's defense of liberalism, with its emphasis on human conduct as always situated within a world of meanings created by inescapably social agents.[1] Here, however, I shall concentrate on the most highly articulated and, I believe, most powerful version of the particularist case in liberal theory, that advanced by Joseph Raz. If the particularist case as Raz sets it forth cannot survive the critic's objections, this gives strong confidence for thinking that no such argument can do so.[2]

Raz's argument is especially intriguing in several respects. First, while various theorists defend liberalism by appealing to autonomy, or to value

---

[1] See Will Kymlicka, *Multicultural Citizenship* (New York: Oxford University Press, 1995), esp. ch. 5, and Michael Oakeshott, *On Human Conduct* (Oxford: Clarendon Press, 1975) and *Morality and Politics in Modern Europe*, ed. Shirley Letwin (New Haven: Yale University Press, 1993). My use of the term "particularist" has no connection with the sort of moral particularism associated with Jonathan Dancy, for example, which is skeptical of general moral principles or considerations. I use "particularism" simply to contrast with the view that endorses liberalism's universal superiority.

[2] I concentrate on Raz's argument as set forth in *The Morality of Freedom*, hereafter *MF*, and amplified in subsequent essays collected in his *Ethics in the Public Domain* (New York: Oxford University Press, 1994), hereafter *EPD*, and *Engaging Reason: On the Theory of Value and Action* (Oxford: Oxford University Press, 1999), hereafter *ER*.

pluralism, or to the political culture of liberal democracies, for Raz these diverse considerations figure not as competing ways of defending liberal regimes but as complementary ideas that combine to make the most powerful case. Aside from the intrinsic interest of an attempt to fuse these distinct considerations, his argument promises to be especially powerful insofar as their disparate force can be harnessed within a single account. Additionally, Raz's argument relies on claims about value pluralism and the place of well-being in political argument broadly similar to those advanced in Chapter 2. This makes his argument especially likely to meet the criteria I have adopted here. A final intriguing feature is that Raz self-consciously distances his own account of liberalism from those which stress state neutrality towards ideals of the good. Raz recognizes the sectarian nature of the ideal of personal autonomy and nonetheless insists that liberal regimes may rightly privilege it.

This repudiation of state neutrality has led some liberals to regard Raz with some suspicion.[3] It also raises a worry for my discussion, insofar as his embrace of perfectionism may seem to recommend a model of political association that departs in important ways from my characterization of liberal regimes to this point. Despite the differences between Raz's approach and those of avowedly neutralist liberals, however, Raz's position is on the whole broadly consistent with the two features of liberal regimes I have emphasized throughout. He endorses an extensive sphere of personal liberty similar to that outlined in Mill's harm principle (his chief departures from Mill have to do with the way he justifies that principle and with the implications he draws from that route of justification for greater state activism in the economic realm). And second, while he allows that his argument implies the "ready embrace of various paternalistic measures," he stresses that such measures are justified chiefly to the extent that they enhance autonomy and the range of options it requires.[4]

---

[3] Consider just the titles of two discussions of Raz: Patrick Neal, "Perfectionism with a Liberal Face? Nervous Liberals and Raz's Political Theory," *Social Theory and Practice* 20, no. 1 (Spring 1994), 25–58, and Loren Lomasky, "But is it Liberalism?," *Critical Review* 4, nos. 1–2 (Winter 1990), 86–105.

[4] Raz, *MF*, 422. I say "chiefly" because Raz does allow that states should "discourage the pursuit of base [ends]" (*MF*, 423). I am not sure, however, that this claim is derivable simply from the requirement to protect autonomy, since the presence of worthless options *per se* does not interfere with autonomy so long as an adequate range of valuable options is present. Moreover, it is not clear how far Raz's allowance that states may discourage base ends is consistent with his objection against a state's "expressing a relation of domination and an attitude of disrespect" towards its citizens (*MF*, 418). Though that objection arises in a discussion of coercion, some would argue that a state that took strong steps to discourage ways of life that citizens value expresses disrespect towards citizens drawn to those ends.

In the main, then, he allows departures from anti-paternalism only when they enhance the ideal of individuals being maximally free to choose for themselves, without tutelage, how their lives shall go. Given the great difference between permitting states to act so that persons can effectively exercise autonomy (Raz's view) and believing that states should actively steer individuals towards particular valuable ends (as many critics claim), Raz's liberal *bona fides* remain intact.

A deeper challenge in assessing Raz's argument concerns his apparent vacillation on whether autonomy is of universal or merely particularist value.[5] The case for autonomy as a universal value is usually grounded in either the strong claim that no non-autonomous life can be good for the person who leads it, or the more modest claim that the best possible non-autonomous life is not as good as the best autonomous life. Though he rejects the strong claim (he allows that autonomy is "inconsistent with various alternative forms of valuable lives"),[6] many of Raz's comments suggest that he inclines to the modest claim. Autonomous persons, he says, are "part creators of their own moral world"; they experience more concretely such goods as personal integrity, dignity, and self-respect; they are more likely to develop "all the capacities human beings have an innate drive to exercise";[7] and they engage more fully in self-creation. Given these claims, one might think that for autonomy not to have universal value there would have to be either significant drawbacks to possessing autonomy or important benefits in lacking it. Since Raz nowhere suggests that either is the case, readers might reasonably conclude that he sees autonomy as a universal value.

Despite these temptations, there are, I think, two good reasons for seeing Raz as offering a particularist defense of the value of autonomy. First,

---

[5] This ambiguity is noted by Lomasky, "But is it Liberalism?," and by Donald Regan, "Authority and Value: Reflections on Raz's *Morality of Freedom*," *Southern California Law Review* 62 (1989), 995–1095. For example, Raz begins the section of *The Morality of Freedom* entitled "The Value of Autonomy" by saying that he will refute the "powerful reasons telling in favor of the view that personal autonomy is only one valuable style of life, valuable to those who choose it, but that those who reject it are none the worse for that" (*MF*, 390). This seems a promissory note for a defense of the universal importance of autonomy. His subsequent discussion, however, concentrates on autonomy's value in liberal societies.

In defense, Raz might respond that the promissory note is for an argument showing not autonomy's universal value, but only its value to those who might reject it. If one believes that a person can reject autonomy only if it is an option, and that it is an option only in liberal societies, then the promissory note would be for a defense of autonomy only within liberal society. But given that Raz's promissory note immediately follows his raising the question whether autonomy is "an essential ingredient of a good life," and given as well his assertion in the book's concluding section that "the moral outlook the implications of which we have explored is one which holds personal autonomy to be an essential element of the good life" (*MF*, 424–5), this defense may seem a bit too clever.

[6] Raz, *MF*, 395.   [7] Ibid., 154, 374.

despite occasional passages supporting the universalist reading, the main argument in *The Morality of Freedom* centers on autonomy's particularist value, and in a subsequent essay Raz has repudiated even the modest claim for universal value.[8] Second, the particularist reading, by enlisting the communitarian insight that the human good must be understood with reference to one's social embeddedness, appears not to rest on controversial claims about autonomy's intrinsic superiority to other ideals of the good. Its more limited goal – to show only autonomy's importance within liberal societies – gives it a chance of succeeding where the universalist argument failed. Construed this way, Raz's argument makes a less far-reaching but potentially more convincing case for a liberal state.[9]

WELL-BEING, GOALS, AND SOCIAL FORMS

Raz's defense of liberalism, indeed, his political theory *in toto,* revolves around human well-being.[10] Embracing what he calls "the humanistic principle ... that the goodness or badness of anything derives ultimately from its contribution, actual or possible, to human life and its quality,"[11] Raz suggests that political institutions and policies must be defended in the end by the contribution they make to the well-being of persons who live under them. For Raz, well-being is critically connected to one's goals, i.e. one's "projects, plans, relationships, ambitions, commitments, and the like." "Success and failure in the pursuit of our goals," he asserts, "is in itself the major determinant of our well-being."[12] One important feature of those goals, Raz stresses, is the way smaller and more immediate goals are

---

[8] In his response to Jeremy Waldron, Raz writes that he sees no reason for thinking that "people who lack personal autonomy cannot be completely well-off, or have a completely good life" ("Facing Up").

[9] Steven Wall has recently offered a careful and penetrating defense of liberal perfectionism that draws heavily on Raz's work (*Liberalism, Perfectionism, and Restraint*). After defending liberal perfectionism by invoking what he calls Raz's social forms argument, Wall asserts: "To refute the social forms argument one needs to present a way of life that is both fully good and incompatible with autonomy. This is true because if the way of life is compatible with autonomy, then it is plausible to claim ... that autonomy would make that life better" (170). This passage reveals that Wall's perfectionism differs from Raz's in two key respects. First, Raz appears to believe that there do exist "completely good lives" that lack autonomy (see n. 8 above). To the extent that Wall disagrees with this, he is advancing a defense of liberalism grounded in autonomy's universal value. Second, Wall's comment suggests that autonomy can simply be added to a life without signally changing the goals characterizing that life, and this claim, too, Raz has denied (see n. 17 below).

[10] Though Raz doubts "whether well-being can play the central role in ethics sometimes assigned to it," he maintains that "political morality is concerned primarily with protecting and promoting the well-being of people" (Preface, *EPD*, v).

[11] Raz, *MF*, 194.   [12] Ibid., 297.

nested within and explicable only through more comprehensive ones: my goal of moving quickly through a faculty meeting may be driven by my wish to see my daughter play soccer, itself part of my broader goal of being a good parent. This nestedness establishes a general order of priority among a person's goals: for the most part, well-being is a function of how successful we are in pursuing our more comprehensive goals.

Given this view, two questions become critical: how do persons come to formulate and pursue their goals, and what must be true about those goals for such success to constitute well-being? Raz answers the first with his social forms thesis. Human beings, he says, do not and cannot create important goals *ex nihilo*. More comprehensive goals are possible only because we are presented with "existing social forms, i.e. forms of behavior which are in fact widely practiced in one's society."[13] These social forms structure the possibilities for many of our most important pursuits (personal relationships, careers, leisure activities, aesthetic experience, religious worship, etc.) and are embodied both in formalized social practices and in such things as common beliefs, myths, folklore, and images drawn from the public culture. "By and large," says Raz, "one's cultural membership determines the horizon of one's opportunities, of what one may become, or (if one is older) what one might have been."[14]

Raz is quick to distinguish the social forms thesis from two ideas with which it might be confused. First, it does not assert that individuals cannot pursue comprehensive goals involving real experimentation or originality; Raz maintains only that such innovations (his example is "open" marriage) depend on the existence of socially recognized pursuits, and that innovation and deviation have the significance they do only when measured against a background of stable social forms. Second, the social forms thesis does not endorse the conventionalist view that whatever is socially approved or endorsed is thereby valuable. Well-being is achieved, Raz insists, only through success in objectively valuable goals: achieving misguided goals, even if sanctioned by one's community, is not enough. This answers the second critical question, explaining what must be the case for success in one's goals to confer well-being.

---

[13] Ibid., 308.

[14] Raz, "Multiculturalism," in *EPD*, 177. In another essay he adds, "Being social animals means not merely that the means for the satisfaction of people's goals are more readily available within society. More crucially, it means that those goals themselves are (when one reaches beyond what is strictly necessary for biological survival) the creatures of society, the products of culture. Family relations, all other social relations between people, careers, leisure activities, the arts, sciences, and other obvious products of 'high culture' are the fruits of society ... Familiarity with a culture determines the boundaries of the imaginable. Sharing in a culture, being part of it, determines the limits of the feasible" ("National Self-Determination," in *EPD*, 133–4).

In *The Morality of Freedom* Raz offers two reasons for the social forms thesis.[15] First, he argues that the very existence of some comprehensive goals depends on social practices and institutions. One cannot, he says, have as a goal being a physician in a society that does not recognize such a pursuit through various conventions, institutions, licensing agencies, and the like. In a society without these, one might be able to cure disease if one miraculously possessed innate medical knowledge, Raz says, but one would not be participating in the "complex social form" that constitutes being a doctor as we understand it. We pursue goals by imagining how we might take our place in a social world that precedes us, and our goals are a function of the options available there. The second reason for the social forms thesis involves the fact that the knowledge needed to participate in social practices and achieve many goals can be learned only through attending to the responses and patterns of behavior, often uncodifiable, displayed by persons engaged in such pursuits. By and large, such know-how is transmitted only through example and habituation. Success in one's goals requires exercising the knowledge derived from exposure to existing social practices and taking one's place within those practices.

Having argued that well-being depends on success in the valuable goals offered by available social forms, to complete his case for autonomy's great value Raz needs only to show that the social forms characterizing contemporary liberal states are deeply shaped by autonomy and that success in the goals they offer depends on the effective exercise of autonomy. These claims he takes to be fairly evident. In part the pervasiveness of autonomy derives from the fact that liberal societies "call for the ability to cope with changing technological, economic, and social conditions, for an ability to adjust, to acquire new skills, to move from one subculture to another, to come to terms with new scientific and moral views."[16] Put more positively, the prominence of autonomy reflects an ideal of self-creation that has, Raz believes, permeated the practices of liberal societies: marriage is understood as a free choice between consenting adults, revocable when warranted; children are no longer expected to pursue the careers of their parents or to live in the town of their upbringing; diversity is seen not as

---

[15] In a later essay he adds a third: "Consciousness of normality or its absence has deep ramifications for the nature of the relationship ... established practices [provide a background] against which both normality and innovative deviation can be measured" ("Liberating Duties," in *EPD*, 42). This claim does not seem to me appreciably to advance the argument about the connection between social forms and well-being (because Raz does not show how normality or deviation is critical to well-being), so I shall not consider it as a separate reason in favor of the social forms thesis. In a later section, however, I discuss the place of innovation in Raz's account.
[16] Raz, *MF*, 369–70.

a problem but as an asset; and so on. The point, Raz stresses, is not that autonomy has simply been added to pre-modern social forms: it has significantly transformed them, and thus the goals of liberal citizens.[17] The social forms thesis then completes the argument for autonomy. "Since we live in a society whose social forms are to a considerable extent based on individual choice, and since our options are limited by what is available in our society, we can prosper in it only if we can be successfully autonomous."[18]

The particularist importance of autonomy established, Raz concludes by drawing the connections among autonomy, liberal societies, and value pluralism. As he sees it, any recognition of autonomy's value commits one to value pluralism.[19] One can exercise autonomy, Raz insists, only when faced with a range of significantly different valuable options. If one choice manifestly outranked the others, one would no longer be presented with a plausible range of valuable options, but in effect with just one choice-worthy option. But this violates the requirements of autonomy. If, however, several significantly different options are choice-worthy, with none clearly outranking the others, then some form of value pluralism is true.

One might think the connection between autonomy and value pluralism is not critical to Raz's overall argument, and that his argument requires only the social forms thesis plus the fact that liberal citizens' goals are shaped by autonomy. Strictly speaking, that is correct. But Raz's discussion of value pluralism serves several important functions. To begin with, it prepares the way for a response to the anticipated critic's objection that lives led in liberal societies are not as good as those led in conditions that place less emphasis on autonomy. Given value pluralism, Raz need not assess autonomous and non-autonomous lives against one another, but only show that the former are noncomparably valuable. In addition, the case for value pluralism shows why liberal citizens who value autonomy should not just tolerate but celebrate the diversity of liberal society. Finally, the connection between autonomy and value pluralism allows for a response to those who object that liberal societies lack a

---

[17] See his reply to Waldron: "Waldron may feel that good as such non-autonomous lives can be they could always be improved if they were also autonomous. As I have argued, however, you cannot just add autonomy, that is, free choice, to the same life … It makes no sense to say that a life with autonomy is better than the same life without autonomy" (Raz, "Facing Up," 1228).
[18] Raz, *MF*, 394.
[19] "Valuing autonomy commits one to weak value pluralism" (Raz, *MF*, 398). Though he believes that the ideal of autonomy implies only weak pluralism, he suggests that his argument for incommensurability (ibid., ch. 13) demonstrates strong pluralism. On the distinction between strong and weak pluralism, not relevant here, see ibid., 395–9.

common culture and shared values: tolerance for diversity itself, Raz can say, reflects a common culture grounded in a shared commitment to the value of autonomy.

Raz's argument yields a broadly familiar picture of the liberal state. It should not strongly direct citizens towards some goals over others, lest it compromise their autonomy, nor should it interfere with an individual's choices unless needed to protect autonomy (through the prevention of harm, chiefly). Whether the harm principle really does follow from Raz's account of autonomy is, I think, a nice question,[20] but I shall not address it here because his defense of the principle, and of the liberal state overall, hinges on his argument for the great value of autonomy in liberal societies. Since I shall argue that he has not made that case in a way that should persuade the critic, the question of whether the harm principle follows from Raz's conception of autonomy can be bypassed. The serious challenges facing Raz's defense of liberal regimes lie not in the implications he draws from his defense of autonomy, but in that defense itself.

THE SPECIFICITY OF GOALS AND PRACTICES

Raz's argument invites various lines of critique. Some might object to his grounding political philosophy in well-being or to his interpretation of well-being in terms of the successful pursuit of objectively valuable goals, but on both issues Raz seems fundamentally right. In Chapter 1 I stressed the importance of well-being in political theory, and in any adequate account of well-being, active agency in valuable pursuits will figure centrally. (Imagine a perfectly satisfied person pumped with hash, or someone who successfully pursues utterly worthless goals.) I shall instead concentrate on two lines of critique that I believe present more serious problems. The first denies that the goals conducive to well-being depend on distinct social forms in the way Raz's particularist argument requires. The second argues that even if they did, the particularist argument lacks the resources to persuade the most worrisome anti-liberal. In later sections I shall take

---

[20] One potential problem here has to do with the fact that since autonomy is largely a function of being able to choose from among valuable options, the state would not appear to compromise autonomy by denying citizens access to valueless options. In Raz's words, "Since autonomy is valuable only if it is directed at the good, it supplies no reason to provide, nor any reason to protect, worthless let alone bad options" (*MF*, 411). But then why should the state allow individuals to engage in worthless options? Both answers Raz offers – that restricting choice shows disrespect to persons, and that governments by and large cannot be trusted to remove only the valueless options – are problematic, for reasons given in chs. 5 and 3, respectively.

up the second critique. Here and in the following section I concentrate on the plausibility of the social forms thesis.

Recall that Raz offers two arguments for the thesis. The first is that the very existence of many of our goals depends on shared social practices. This is the reason for Raz's assertion that someone born into a society with no medical practice but possessing innate medical knowledge "could not be a medical doctor, of the kind we have in our society."[21] Is this general claim of dependence true, and does it establish the social forms thesis? I want to argue that, read one way, the claim is trivially true and does not establish the point Raz needs, while on the stronger reading that does establish the needed point the claim is dubious, and so fails to demonstrate a close connection between well-being and available social forms.

First, the trivial truth. If being a doctor, of the kind we have in our society, is understood in terms that make reference to participating in the social practices of our society, then by definition one cannot be a doctor as we understand it in a society lacking those practices. The same holds for any number of goals specified in those terms: if being a lawyer (Raz's example) as we understand it involves attending law school, passing exams, and the like, then in a society lacking such practices one cannot have the goal of being a lawyer. Granting this, however, does not establish the point Raz needs.

To see the problem, take Raz's example seriously. Imagine someone with an innate ability to heal born into a society lacking the medical practices we are familiar with. What goals is such a person likely to develop? If we assume that hers is a society in which people suffer injury and disease, and that the ability to minister to such problems is generally valued, it seems likely that she would use her knowledge to improve the health of her fellow citizens, that she would inform others of her availability to help, and that those requiring treatment would seek her out.

Is this person not pursuing the goal of being a doctor? In terms of how that goal is constituted by the social practices of our society, perhaps not: she undergoes no formal schooling, no period of internship under experienced physicians, no licensing or exams, etc. But it is not clear why any of this is relevant to her achieving well-being. With respect to the successful pursuit of valuable goals, our hypothetical "doctor" seems engaged in the same pursuit that leads us to attribute value to being a doctor in our society. As Raz declares in a later essay, "In part (a large part) success as a doctor is success in treating one's patients and nursing them back to

---

[21] Raz, *MF*, 310.

health."[22] If the person Raz imagines can do this without participating in our distinctive medical practices, it appears that she can pursue the goal of being a doctor in a manner conducive to her well-being.

The particularist may reply that I have cooked Raz's example. His scenario imagines a society with no recognized medical practice, whereas I referred to one that values persons who minister to the unwell. But that reply just relocates the problem at a deeper level. All human communities have, and value highly, social practices for ministering to the sick. More generally, all make available a variety of goals common across cultures – teaching, trading, soldiering, policing, entertaining, adjudicating, and so on. If such important goals transcend the practices of any one society in particular, and if well-being involves success in such goals, then one's well-being will be a function of success in goals not limited to the particular social forms characterizing one's society.

Nor is this point restricted to professions. On one plausible view of the human condition,[23] many of the goals constitutive of well-being (e.g. friendship, family relations, religious worship, leisure, sociality, sport), though structured in distinct ways by different societies, are common to all. In some cases, it is true, the value inhering in a goal may be a function of how a particular society structures it: perhaps only where doctors must pass difficult exams and intern under trying conditions can they demonstrate the extraordinary diligence and self-sacrifice we associate with doctors. And there may be some goals, as I note below, achievable only through culturally distinct practices. But nothing Raz says in *The Morality of Freedom* rules out the possibility that many important goals derive from features common to all human communities and so transcend any particular society's practices. If that commonality is wide enough, it would undermine Raz's claim that "a person's well-being depends to a large extent on success in socially defined and determined pursuits and activities."[24]

In a series of recent essays, Raz has presented a forceful response to this line of critique and elaborated his case that valuable goals cannot

---

[22] Raz, "Duties of Well-Being," in *EPD*, 4.
[23] Cf. Donald Regan's claim: "Even wildly varying social practices may have such value as they have because of their content as considered under a small number of headings, such as the amount of intrinsically valuable knowledge called upon by participation in the practice, the nature and degree of identification with other people manifested in participation in the practice, and so on. If this is the case, a virtually unlimited range of social practices could be evaluated by a relatively compact set of objective standards" ("Authority and Value," 1050). Regan advances this claim against Raz's argument for incommensurability, but it also suggests why the variation in social forms across societies may be smaller than Raz imagines.
[24] Raz, *MF*, 309.

be easily distinguished from social practices.[25] To Raz, the objection I have pressed fails to acknowledge the "crucial distinction … between practices which create or sustain the existence of goods and values, and practices which are conditions for access to such goods or values."[26] While some practices are valuable chiefly because they provide access to a single common value (as medical practices serve human health, for example), others bring into being the goods they make available. In the latter cases it simply makes no sense to think individuals might pursue those goods outside those social forms. This view of sustaining practices is no endorsement of conventionalism, Raz insists, for the presence of objective values establishes constraints any practice must meet if it is to offer genuine human goods. Precisely how objective values do this is a difficult question to which Raz devotes some energy,[27] but he leaves no doubt that he thinks the world of value sufficiently plastic to allow a broad variety of human practices that make available a wide array of objective yet socially distinct goods.

Raz offers both a direct and indirect argument for the idea of sustaining practices. The indirect argument claims that the alternative, which Raz dubs Platonism, is both implausible and incoherent. As Raz sees it, Platonists are committed to the absurd view that valuable activities such as chess or opera must have existed in some form before they became instantiated as human activities. But this is ludicrous: can we really imagine that chess was found to exist in some world of Ideas, rather than created by a series of human decisions culminating in a distinct activity? Raz also criticizes Platonists for their view that unknowable goods exist somewhere beyond the world of human practice: unknowable goods cannot enrich our lives, he says, and so cannot be goods.[28]

The direct argument for the idea of sustaining practices stresses the way new activities come into being offering goods that did not exist before. Consider the invention of a new game. Such an event, Raz says, "creates not only a new good, a new object of value … *It creates a new form of the good*. There is a new activity which is good or of value, of playing the game, and a new desirable goal, of winning the game, which did not exist before."[29] Since the existence of a game depends on there

---

[25] The essays constitute chs. 6 through 9 of *ER*.
[26] Raz, "Notes on Value and Objectivity," in *ER*, 147.
[27] See, for example, Raz, "The Value of Practice," in *ER*, 210–13, and "Mixing Values," in *ER*, *passim*.
[28] Raz, "Mixing Values," in *ER*, 189.
[29] Raz, "The Value of Practice," in *ER*, 205 (my emphasis).

being a particular social practice of playing it, and since new games create new forms of the good, Raz concludes that the example of such new forms of the good establishes his point for the importance of sustaining practices

The direct and indirect arguments stand or fall together. Both hinge on Raz's assumption that particular activities (he mentions chess, opera, cricket, and impressionist painting) contribute to human well-being in ways relevantly different from other activities of a similar type. (If not, then the invention of a new game, for example, would not constitute a new form of the good.) But for this critical assumption Raz offers little argument. No doubt there is something absurd in the thought that chess existed in some Platonic realm for centuries before human beings hit on it. But Platonism is not the only alternative to Raz's account. A third, more plausible option is to say that while activities like chess or opera differ from other games or forms of performance, what makes them valuable often are not those distinguishing features but instead elements they share with similar activities across countless cultures. Seen this way, the invention of a new game or form of performance need not constitute a new form of the good but might simply offer a different way to achieve some good transcending any one culture. In the case of chess, for example, what makes it valuable (that it offers creative and adventurous exercise of the mind in a relatively secure context) may be captured in other games; as for opera, many cultures suspend the workaday world and give attention to storytelling involving words, music, and costume; and so on. The particularist might reply here that our very notion of a game or public performance reflects a social practice distinct to some cultures, but Raz suggests little sympathy with this way of thinking: his stress on the requirements of intelligibility across cultures implies that many such broad practices are common to human communities.

On the third option I am sketching, the goals whose achievement constitutes well-being, though pursued within particular practices (no one can just play a game: one plays chess, go, mancala, etc.), are nonetheless common across societies. Since the particular activities exemplify a broader type, they do not create distinct socially defined goods. As I just noted, Raz allows that significant commonalities must be present across cultures if we are to understand various activities as games, performances, works of art, and the like, but this raises the question of why the goods those activities create cannot similarly be explained by those commonalities. Though Raz locates the source of value at a more precise level of description than the third option I am presenting, he does not provide a persuasive argument for that view.[30] In its absence, his claim for sustaining practices, and for the distinctness of the goals characterizing liberal societies, is inconclusive.

The particularist might bolster her claim for the distinctness of liberal goals by arguing that even if we grant some commonality in goals across cultures, along lines I've argued for, those goals are significantly restructured by the prominence of autonomy within liberal societies. "The careers, relationships, and other pursuits in our societies are partly constituted by the fact that they have to be chosen to be engaged in as they ought to be engaged," says Raz. "The fact that they were freely chosen is part of what makes them what they are."[31] Note that Raz is claiming not that autonomy is itself one of the goals liberal citizens pursue, but that the goals such citizens pursue are shaped by that ideal.[32] The general idea is that the circumstances in which one chooses goals can significantly change their nature, and that once imported into liberal societies traditional goals will be transformed by the prominence of autonomy.

This controversial claim, however, needs more argument than Raz provides. To see why, imagine a liberal citizen who joins a community structured around ideals hostile to liberal autonomy. Is her goal significantly different from that of a member of a similar community in a non-liberal society? No doubt many aspects of their situations are different: the first will have (and know she has) the option of leaving, while the second may not; the first will be conscious of her difference from others in her society, the second may not; the first may be aware of alternative goals, the second may not; and so on. But these do not seem properly described as differences in their goals: they seem more like differences in the circumstances of two persons pursuing the same goal.

Could the particularist reply that the differences in those circumstances entail differences in the goals as well? No: that reply would cause serious problems for the idea, central to the social forms thesis, that different people within a society might pursue a common goal. Consider,

---

[30] Raz asserts that social practices orient individuals in their pursuit of goals in two critical ways: they provide standards of normality, and they acculturate persons into standards of value ("Mixing Values," in *ER*, 192). But since neither of these distinguishes his position from conventionalism, Raz must also believe that the criteria for evaluating whether practices offer genuine goods exist independently of the practices themselves. To my knowledge, Raz has nowhere explained how we arrive at these criteria. The lack of such an account significantly complicates the task of figuring out at what level of description to locate the source of value.

[31] Raz, "Facing Up," 1228.

[32] Raz, *MF*, 391. Raz is right: if autonomy requires choosing from among various options on the basis of their value, the options must be valuable for reasons other than that they offer an autonomous life. George Sher makes a similar point in *Beyond Neutrality*, 57.

for example, three persons seeking to become doctors – one who seeks the challenge the career presents, a second who feels a divine calling, a third driven by compassion for those who suffer. On the reply we are considering, the three are pursuing different goals. Even if we feel the pull of this position, the fact that it seems right to say they are all pursuing the same goal shows that Raz must provide more argument for his view that autonomy significantly changes the goals available to liberal citizens. Without that, the possibility remains that the prominence of autonomy in liberal societies affects only the circumstances in which citizens pursue their goals, not their basic content.

I have been raising doubts about the degree to which the goals available in liberal societies diverge from those of other cultures. But even if some goals do differ significantly, perhaps for the reasons Raz offers, it is still unclear that one can flourish in liberal societies only by being autonomous, as the particularist argument suggests. That further claim assumes that citizens by and large have little choice but to participate in the autonomy-structured goals of liberal society and be profoundly shaped by this experience. Is this assumption true? It would be if liberal regimes put in place measures ensuring that all citizens were exposed to a diversity of lifestyles and requiring them to choose in line with the liberal ideal of autonomy. But one aim of the particularist argument, one would have thought, is to determine whether such measures are justified: it cannot begin by assuming they are. Doing that is tantamount to intentionally infecting someone in order to defend your claim that they need antibiotics. Without such measures, many citizens might grow up unaware of various options and opt for those most familiar to them in a manner that falls short of liberal autonomy. Why should we think they cannot be successful in those goals?[33] If such goals lacked the value that would accrue to them if chosen autonomously, this might offer Raz some response here, but in responding to critics he has strongly denied that being autonomously chosen adds to the value of many important personal goals.[34] The possibility of success in such non-liberal pursuits thus raises a serious obstacle to those who would apply the social forms thesis in defense of liberal autonomy.

THE ELEMENTS OF SUCCESS

Raz's second argument for the social forms thesis begins from the idea that success in any field requires understanding its standards of achievement,

---

[33] Bikhu Parekh makes the same point in *Rethinking Multiculturalism*, 93.
[34] Raz, "Facing Up," 1227.

displaying the relevant skills, and acquiring that know-how through immersion in existing practices. Raz is very helpful in reminding us how much our behavior is guided by a kind of knowledge that both defies explicit accounting and can be learned only through an informal process of habituation. As he points out, there are at least two reasons for this: the relevant knowledge often cannot be captured in general formulae, and even if it could be, part of what is involved in certain relationships (think of being a friend or spouse) is that one's actions result not from consciously applying a formal rule to one's circumstances, but from a more spontaneous response to the particulars of a situation.[35]

These considerations suggest a second argument for the social forms thesis.

1. One can pursue and succeed in only those goals one can conceptualize for oneself and whose relevant skills one has developed.
2. Such goals are defined by the social forms that characterize one's society.
3. Well-being requires success in one's goals. Therefore,
4. well-being involves achieving success in goals shaped by the social forms of one's society.

The argument is valid. Are the premises true?

There are, I think, good reasons to agree with the first premise: we learn to do things well only by first doing them, just as we can intentionally pursue only what we know of or can imagine by conjoining different aspects of what we know. The third premise is also uncontroversial (so long as we keep in mind that well-being requires not only success in one's goals, but also that those goals be valuable). The problem in the argument lies with the second premise. Against it, I want to suggest two ways in which persons can form and pursue goals that differ significantly from those offered by the social forms dominant in their society. Though Raz acknowledges both, I do not believe he recognizes the serious problems they present to his account.

First, one might learn of and be drawn to a goal reflecting social forms that do not characterize one's own group. Raz allows this possibility when he suggests that "the question of the degree to which the practice has to be shared and the question of whether it has to be shared by one of the groups in the midst of which an individual lives, or of which he is

---

[35] On the second point, see Michael Stocker, "The Schizophrenia of Modern Ethical Theories," *Journal of Philosophy* 73, no. 14 (August 12, 1976), 453–66.

a part, or if it is enough if it is a practice of a group he is familiar with, though not a member of, admit of no straightforward answer ... It is very much a matter of degree in most cases."[36] This is a significant admission. If individuals can pursue goals connected to the social forms of groups and cultures to which they do not belong, this threatens the connection the particularist requires between well-being and the distinct character of one's society. To be sure, a social form exists only where there is agreement among persons on beliefs, expectations, meanings, and the like. But in leaving open the question how far this agreement must extend through one's society, and allowing that habituation is compatible with individuals pursuing goals derived from social forms marginal within their society, Raz suggests an alternative to the stringent social forms thesis his argument needs.

There are two explanations, consistent with Raz's account of habituation, of how individuals can pursue such marginal goals. Either (1) goals that appear to diverge are rooted in a common social practice, for which habituation in any society prepares one (for example, seeking to be a good Buddhist, Hindu, or Catholic may all be goals made possible by habituation into the common social form of religious worship), or (2) human beings are able, notwithstanding the influence of habituation into their own community's social forms, to pursue goals drawn from alien social forms. Either explanation raises problems for Raz's position. The first suggests that the goals made available by apparently diverging social forms are not, in the end, all that different from one another, and so reinforces my earlier claim that significant commonality characterizes human goals across societies. The second explanation allows, *pace* Raz, that habituation does not limit individuals to goals drawn from the social forms that dominate their community, but prepares them to pursue goals afforded by other social forms.

The availability of social forms of other communities constitutes one of the two main ways in which individuals can pursue goals different from those embodied in the social forms of their society. The other involves radically departing from existing social forms and creating new ones. Raz attempts to defuse this second problem for the social forms thesis in two ways. First, he suggests that such innovations always derive from and so piggyback on existing social forms. But this general claim requires more argument than Raz gives and seems implausible on its face. Take the example of couples who live together without getting married, or families

---

[36] Raz, *MF*, 310.

who live communally and share collective responsibility for the raising of children. Why think these pursuits logically depend on particular social forms involving cohabitation in marriage or the nuclear family? Even if they constitute variations on human practices, the relevant practices (seeking ongoing proximity to the object of one's love, rearing children) may be common across societies, and so the fact of piggybacking would not strengthen the social forms thesis.

Raz's other response to the possibility of persons radically departing from social forms is that "the distance they have traveled away from the shared forms is, in these cases, the most significant aspect of their situation. It more than anything else determines the significance of their situation and its possibilities for those people."[37] While this may be true in some cases, it is unconvincing as a general claim. Why think that those who opt to lead lives far afield of the dominant forms of liberal society (think of the sexually experimental subculture, or those who commit themselves to hierarchical communities built around illiberal ideals) do so primarily to express their rejection of dominant practices and not out of a belief that such alternatives offer distinct human goods? To suggest that the appeal of such alternatives lies mainly in their being rejections of dominant models verges on the suggestion that such people are moved by the adolescent drive to be different for the sake of being different, and this seems uncharitable. Though it is (tautologically) true that the pursuit of experimental or unusual goals is a departure from the mainstream, it does not follow that the motivation for such pursuits is the desire to depart from the mainstream.

To be clear, I am not denying that habituation takes different forms in different communities. Though all pass on lessons about how to negotiate the practical world, they differ both in the extent to which they tolerate and/or encourage significant innovation and experimentation, and in how welcoming they are to the pursuit of non-dominant goals. It is possible, then, that the phenomenon of persons pursuing goals outside their dominant social forms is especially pronounced in liberal societies, with their emphasis on individuality, self-expression, and experimentation. But even if my account of habituation relies on a dynamic that is especially pronounced in liberal societies, and operates in others with much less force, this fact would not strengthen the particularist argument in the way Raz needs. For his chief concern is with the goals members of liberal societies pursue: even if my discussion applies chiefly, or even exclusively, to

---

[37] Ibid., *MF*, 312–13.

liberal regimes, it nonetheless targets precisely those societies with which a particularist like Raz is concerned.

Defenders of the particularist approach may remain unmoved by the objections I have offered. They may believe that I have underestimated the connection between goals and particular social practices, or have overestimated most persons' capacities for innovation and originality in forming goals. Even if the claims I have advanced are conceptual possibilities, they may say, it is still the case that the overwhelming number of persons pursue goals structured by their community's dominant practices, and this sufficiently confirms the social forms thesis.

But even if some version of the social forms thesis could be made good, I want to argue now, the particularist argument still does not have the resources to convince the critic who thinks the emphasis on autonomy in liberal society either directs attention away from genuinely important goods towards those that are insignificant or corrupting (e.g. concern for the common good gets replaced by narrow self-interest, family closeness by the drive for professional success), or seriously compromises existing goals (e.g. marriage becomes increasingly contract-like, religious affiliation devolves to a vapid and undemanding spirituality).[38] Critics who see liberal society as a discouraging spectacle in which large numbers of citizens pursue misguided goals will have little reason to find Raz's argument persuasive, for that argument depends on the assumption that existing social forms make valuable goals available in ways that motivate citizens. This is just what such critics deny.

Faced with this objection, Raz might offer several responses. First, he might cite the fact that many in liberal society are already committed to goals built around autonomy, and so undermining autonomy threatens the pursuit of their goals in ways that will damage their well-being.[39] This response does not succeed, however, for the critic broadly denies the value of the goals characterizing liberal society, and the failure to reach valueless goals does not, Raz allows, compromise well-being. Even if some are

[38] At one point Raz expresses sympathy with this worry. See his caveat against assuming "that those who believe, as I do, in the value of personal autonomy necessarily desire the extension of personal choice in all relationships and pursuits. They may consistently with their belief in personal autonomy wish to see an end to this process, or even its reversal" (*MF*, 394).

[39] The fact that mature individuals are always already involved in the pursuit of various goals is offered by Raz as a reason for liberal states to proceed cautiously in assimilating non-liberal communities (*MF*, 424).

harmed by curtailing autonomy, the critic may see such costs as an acceptable price to pay for creating social conditions more conducive to citizens' overall well-being. Alternatively, Raz might defend autonomy as a vital component in any fully good life or argue that a diminished commitment to liberal autonomy unacceptably exposes liberal societies to a range of harms. The former asserts autonomy's universalist value, while the latter echoes the position widely known as the liberalism of fear. I have already criticized the universalist claim, and in Chapter 7 I take up the liberalism of fear. But those discussions are irrelevant here, for if either claim succeeded there would be no need for the social forms argument: the particularist liberal could just appeal to those claims directly.

The particularist thus has no alternative, I believe, but to contest the critic's negative assessment of the value of the goals liberal citizens pursue. There are various ways he might do this. One is to embrace some form of subjectivism about the good and then argue that liberal societies do the best job of satisfying preferences. But this move adopts a highly dubious claim that is rejected not only by critics but by many liberals as well, Raz included. Alternatively, the particularist might concede that while liberal societies make available various misguided goals, they allow for many that critics of various sorts value (shared religious worship, continuity with cultural traditions, familial closeness, etc.). But this strategy is problematic too: not only is it incompatible with Raz's claim that autonomy cannot simply be added to existing goals without significantly altering them, but it fails to engage the critic's concern that the emphasis on autonomy tends to steer individuals away from valuable goals, with serious consequences to their well-being.

To rebut the critic, I believe, the particularist has no alternative but to engage in the messy business of assessing the objective value of the pursuits to which liberal citizens are committed.[40] While this sort of strategy may be anathema to neutralist liberals, a perfectionist like Raz need not shun it. Nonetheless, there are at least two reasons for doubting his chances of success. The first involves Raz's general reluctance to offer a clearly articulated account of the objective value of various goals.[41] Without criteria for determining the value of goals and assessing relative

---

[40] Wall recognizes a similar requirement in his defense of perfectionism: "A full defense of the social forms argument would need to show that the social forms of modern western societies do not give rise to pathologies that offset the values they support and sustain" (*Liberalism, Perfectionism, and Restraint*, 173, n. 20). Wall acknowledges that he does not offer such a defense.

[41] A good example is Raz's unargued claim that the life of a farmer is more valuable than that of a gambler (*MF*, 298–9). As Patrick Neal delights in pointing out, "Bart Maverick is, on my perfectionist calculus, ranked higher than any farmer known to me" ("Perfectionism with a Liberal

well-being, any such response will be incomplete. The other problem here derives from the fact that the culture of contemporary liberal societies is, in various respects, a dismaying spectacle. If the particularist case rests on showing the objective value of the goals that liberal societies in particular make available, critics may well believe the evidence favors their side. I am not saying the point the particularist requires cannot be established – just that the argument needs to be made.[42] That it needs to be made shows that Raz's particularist approach, which sought to defend liberalism without weighing the liberal ideal of autonomy against other accounts of the good, cannot deliver on its promise.

Some might think I have misidentified what Raz must do to defeat the critic's objection. He need not compare liberal visions of the good with competing conceptions, they might say, but can instead invoke the incommensurability of plural values. If the value of an autonomous life is incommensurable with that of a non-autonomous life, and citizens in liberal societies do much better at achieving autonomy, then the particularist case is not weakened even if the commitment to autonomy engenders costs absent from non-liberal societies. For while the lives of citizens in liberal societies may be no better than those in non-liberal societies, they are no worse, and so the critic's case collapses.

But this response does not escape the critic's worry. To see the problem, consider what is perhaps Raz's strongest claim for the value of autonomy: "Since autonomy is morally valuable, there is reason for everyone to make himself and everyone else autonomous."[43] At first glance this passage seems at odds with Raz's commitment to incommensurability: if a good life without autonomy is incommensurable with a good autonomous life, why does someone leading a good non-autonomous life have any reason to make herself autonomous? To reconcile the two, we must interpret the quoted sentence above as claiming that the value of autonomy constitutes only a *prima facie* but not a conclusive reason to become autonomous. Given Raz's view that one can lead a fully good life without

---

Face?," 58, n. 73). Even if Neal needs to meet more farmers, his point is sound: one wishes Raz would do more to explain his claims about value. Raz may believe it is not possible to justify such judgments – at one point he allows that "pervasive and unshakeable features of human practical thought need no justification" – but if so, it's not clear how he would proceed against critics whose basic judgments diverge from his own (*MF*, 288–9).

[42] Raz has flatly asserted: "It is reasonable to surmise that just about all societies have an adequate range of acceptable options available in them" ("Duties of Well-Being," in *EPD*, 24). Raz gives no argument for this claim, but even if it is true, the critic may still question the relevance of the *availability* of such options if large numbers of citizens forgo them.

[43] Raz, *MF*, 407.

being autonomous, we can also infer that autonomy is incompatible with certain goods the non-autonomous person experiences. For if not, a fully good life would be characterized by those goods plus autonomy.

But now the full force of the critic's objection becomes clear. For the critic need not deny that autonomy is objectively valuable. He simply believes that the liberal emphasis on autonomy generates a host of ills whose collective cost to human well-being outweighs its *prima facie* value. So even if a good autonomous life is incommensurable with a good non-autonomous one, that does not speak to the critic's objection: most citizens of liberal societies, he claims, do not lead good lives of autonomy. Raz allows that we can sometimes make relative value judgments in the presence of incommensurables,[44] and this is what the critic is doing: judging the autonomous life with its attendant ills inferior to the non-autonomous life without them. The fact that a good autonomous life is incommensurable with a good non-autonomous one is thus irrelevant to the critic's objection that the emphasis on autonomy in liberal society undermines the value of a host of human activities and generates significant ills. The particularist approach alone cannot give liberal autonomy the defense it needs.

MINORITY CULTURES

My discussion has proceeded at a fairly abstract level. I shall conclude by considering one area of practical controversy where the issues I have discussed are especially prominent, i.e. the question of how a liberal regime should regard non-liberal communities within its borders who are neither territorially separate nor economically independent. This case shows with special clarity some of the general worries I've raised against Raz's argument.

In a discussion admittedly brief and speculative, Raz explores this issue by asking how liberal societies should treat a minority community whose culture is inferior to the dominant liberal one. He answers: "The perfectionist principles espoused in this book suggest that people are justified in taking action to assimilate the minority group, at the cost of letting its culture die or at least be considerably changed by absorption."[45] Though Raz acknowledges that "this is easier said than done," and that wrenching people out of their social contexts may cause real harm, he defends the principle of assimilation by liberal society, at least with regard to inferior non-liberal communities.

[44] Raz, "Mixing Values," in *ER*.   [45] Raz, *MF*, 424.

The first question raised by Raz's account here concerns the grounding for his assumption that such a community might be inferior to that of liberal society. There are two possible readings. On the first, the judgment of inferiority reflects an intrinsic shortcoming in that community. Jeremy Waldron, for example, suggests that Raz may judge the community's culture intrinsically inferior because it is not autonomy-endorsing.[46] Or it may be that the culture has inferior standards of achievement, or flawed moral norms. Such attempts to identify an intrinsic shortcoming, however, are at odds with comments Raz has subsequently made. For not only has Raz denied, as we have seen, that autonomy is a universal value, but he has also insisted that cultures cannot be compared in terms of relative value, "that none of them can be judged superior to the others."[47]

These problems motivate an alternative reading of Raz's judgment of inferiority: that the minority culture is inferior not intrinsically, but only insofar as it exists within a liberal society whose social forms reflect the prominence of autonomy. On this second reading, then, the inferiority of the community reflects no intrinsic shortcoming, but instead its failure to prepare its members for the autonomous lives they must lead in liberal society, with ensuing damage to their prospects for well-being.

Raz's case for assimilating such minority cultures thus hinges on the question of how far their members can avoid leading lives characterized by liberal autonomy. The problem for the particularist approach, however, is that the answer depends on how robustly the state champions the liberal ideal of autonomy. For example, if it takes steps to restructure minority cultures, perhaps by enforcing liberal educational and social norms, or insists that participation in the wider liberal society must be carried out under terms showing little tolerance for the traditions of those cultures, then members of such cultures will have to adapt more strenuously to liberal norms.[48] But whether such steps are justified in the first place is precisely the question we want answered. If liberal regimes have already made such inroads into those cultures, reshaping them along lines just mentioned, it seems problematic to justify the continuance of those policies by pointing out that they are already in place. That sort of argument threatens to offer retroactive justification to policies that initially constituted wrongful intrusion into another culture.

[46] Jeremy Waldron, "Autonomy and Perfectionism in Raz's *Morality of Freedom*," *Southern California Law Review* 62 (1989), 1123, n. 99.
[47] Raz, "Multiculturalism," in *EPD*, 183.
[48] Think, for example, of cases where adherents of a religious faith are prohibited from wearing traditional items of dress, or where non-mainstream religious observance is not accommodated.

If we do not begin by assuming the legitimacy of a liberal state's promoting autonomy, then, the critical question – at least with respect to those communities neither territorially separate nor economically independent – becomes whether members of such communities might interact with various aspects of liberal society (its economy, housing markets, health care systems, etc.) without endorsing the broader goals associated with liberal autonomy. Though Raz appears to think that such interaction will significantly alter the goals of such communities, there is ample evidence that they can achieve some degree of integration with liberal society without compromising their characteristic social practices: think of Orthodox Jews in New York City, Muslims throughout France, or Hindu communities in London. How far that integration may be achieved compatible with preserving a culture's distinct practices will in large part be a function of how accommodating liberal regimes will be. But the particularist defense seems unable by itself to offer guidance on that question.

In contrast to the assimilationist position, with its vision of a liberal state promoting the liberal ideal of autonomy, we have here something like a self-fulfilling argument for deferring to cultures that reject that ideal. The more tolerance liberal societies show for the practices of such groups, the less likely their members will be forced to select goals that are deeply shaped by the liberal ideal of autonomy; the less they are forced to do that, the greater the case for liberal tolerance. In an essay subsequent to his discussion in *The Morality of Freedom*, Raz has endorsed the logic of this line of thought. "Multiculturalism requires a political society to recognize the equal standing of all the stable and viable cultural communities existing in that society ... There is no room for talk of a minority problem or of a majority tolerating the minorities."[49] But this admission, if we grant the viability within liberal regimes of cultural communities who reject liberal autonomy, effectively renounces the claim that liberal states (at least in multicultural societies) should privilege that ideal. That spells defeat for the particularist case for autonomy-based liberalism.

---

[49] Raz, "Multiculturalism," in *EPD*, 174. Raz specifies in this essay that his endorsement of multiculturalist neutrality applies to cultures that are neither geographically nor economically separate from the main institutions of society, indicating that he has moved away from his claim in *The Morality of Freedom* that communities who interact with liberal society will tend to abandon their distinctive social forms in favor of those characterizing liberal society broadly.

CHAPTER 5

Political liberalism

THE MOVE TO *POLITICAL LIBERALISM*

A different form of particularist argument for liberal states is offered by those who defend political liberalism. They too ground their case for the liberal state on features of existing societies – in this case, the norms that characterize the public political culture of such societies and the standards of political justification they believe those norms imply. The foremost advocate of this strategy is John Rawls, and I shall concentrate on the argument advanced in his book *Political Liberalism.*[1] To understand that argument, however, it will be helpful first to examine the relation between it and his earlier *A Theory of Justice.*[2]

Though some readers view the explicitly particularist aims of *Political Liberalism* as a significant departure from the position advanced in *Theory*, that view should not be overstressed. Though the later book more forthrightly declares that its argument is aimed at liberal pluralistic societies, the argument of *Theory* had similarly relied heavily on the considered judgments of the liberal citizens to whom it was addressed, and in an essay appearing shortly after *Theory* Rawls acknowledged that its argument presupposed certain liberal ideals.[3] Furthermore, what has clearly

---

[1] John Rawls, *Political Liberalism* (New York: Columbia University Press, 1993). A version of political liberalism closely related to Rawls's has been advanced by Charles Larmore in his *Patterns of Moral Complexity* (Cambridge: Cambridge University Press, 1987) and *The Morals of Modernity* (Cambridge: Cambridge University Press, 1996). Similar views are also defended in Thomas Nagel, "Moral Conflict and Political Legitimacy," in *Authority*, ed. Joseph Raz (New York: New York University Press, 1990), 300–24; Joshua Cohen, "Moral Pluralism and Political Consensus," in *The Idea of Democracy*, ed. David Copp *et al.* (Cambridge: Cambridge University Press, 1993), 270–91; J. Donald Moon, *Constructing Community: Moral Pluralism and Tragic Conflicts* (Princeton: Princeton University Press, 1993); and Stephen Macedo, "Liberal Civic Education and Religious Fundamentalism: The Case of God v. John Rawls," *Ethics* 105 (April 1995), 468–96.
[2] John Rawls, *A Theory of Justice*, rev. edn. (Cambridge, MA: Harvard University Press, 1999).
[3] In responding to criticisms by H. L. A. Hart, Rawls allows that "the basic liberties and their priority rest on a conception of the person that would be recognized as liberal and not, as Hart thought, on considerations of rational interests alone" (*Political Liberalism*, 290).

not changed between the two books is the conception of the liberal state Rawls defends. That conception asserts that deliberation over fundamental political matters should exclude substantive ideas of the good and comprehensive frameworks of value of the sort the critic wishes to introduce.[4] From that exclusion, Rawls then derives both a commitment to a broad sphere of liberty, along the lines of the harm principle, and a prohibition on state paternalism.

Where the two books differ most profoundly, of course, is in the nature of the argument by which Rawls defends that conception of the state. Rawls says that the "important differences" between the two books arise from his attempt in *Political Liberalism* "to resolve a serious problem internal to justice as fairness, namely … that the account of stability in Part III of *Theory* is not consistent with the view as a whole." The serious problem, Rawls elaborates, involves "the unrealistic idea of a well-ordered society as it appears in *Theory*."[5] Rawls appears to have concluded that his argument in *Theory*, because it takes stands on issues hotly contested in liberal regimes (including views about the relation between the self and its ends, the importance of autonomy and individuality, and the source of the authority of moral principles), cannot reasonably expect to win the consensus of citizens in a pluralistic state whose comprehensive frameworks differ significantly. *Political Liberalism* thus seeks to avoid such controversial claims and appeals instead to ideals and norms widely recognized as authoritative in liberal societies by citizens committed to diverse comprehensive views. To show how the liberal state defended in *Theory* could be vindicated by the "freestanding argument" of *Political Liberalism*, to use Rawls's term, would thus both satisfy the justificatory requirement and give liberals better grounds to think that such a state can win widespread support under conditions of normative diversity.

But *Political Liberalism* can also be read as filling a gap that had marred Rawls's argument in *Theory*. In *Theory* Rawls had tried to show

---

[4] An anonymous reader has rightly pointed out that matters are more complicated than I let on here. Ideas of the good may be more or less substantive; they may differ from value frameworks; such frameworks may be more or less comprehensive; and so on. The sort of critic I have in mind understands human well-being as marked by certain substantive goods, valuable activities, virtues, and so on, all of which are rooted in some related framework of value where they broadly hang together. But the critic may have difficulty in distinguishing among those elements and in understanding their interrelatedness. For this reason I shall refer, variously and indiscriminately, to ideas of the good, conceptions of the good, comprehensive ideals, frameworks of value, and so on. While philosophers concerned with conceptual clarity will properly be interested in the distinctions among such elements, I am chiefly interested in their (often undifferentiated) role in the mind of the critic.

[5] Rawls, *Political Liberalism*, xv–xvi.

that citizens behind the veil of ignorance would reject even a moderate principle of state perfectionism. He offered two main reasons: the parties lacked the necessary information to identify perfectionist criteria, and they could not foresee how the normative frameworks and ideals of the good to which they were committed would fare with respect to such a principle. Neither reason, however, was fully persuasive as stated. Against the first, it seemed possible either that knowledge of basic facts of human nature and psychology (which Rawls allows behind the veil) might vindicate at least some perfectionist criteria, or that the parties might agree while behind the veil to allow perfectionist principles to be selected after the veil was removed, once they engage in fully aware deliberation about the goods that characterize a fulfilling life.[6] Against the second, some critics pointed out the oddness of insisting that one's conception of the good be accorded status equal to all others regardless of its actual value: if not irrational, that view seemed to rest on a controversial subjectivism or skepticism about the good. Rawls's argument against perfectionism also implied that standards of excellence were either too indeterminate or too subjective to play a useful role in political debate, and this again invited a range of objections.[7]

These weaknesses in *Theory*'s case against perfectionism promise to be remedied by the argument advanced in *Political Liberalism* – in particular, by the prominence in that work of two ideas: the liberal principle of legitimacy, and the idea of the reasonable citizen. But despite the strengths of Rawls's revised argument, it fails to defend the liberal state against the critic who believes that the exercise of reason can yield knowledge about the objective values central to well-being.[8] Political liberalism must be compatible with this belief not just because of its intrinsic plausibility, but because many liberal citizens reasonably hold it. But as I shall argue here, no reconstruction of Rawls's argument can secure the liberal commitments

---

[6] Raz makes this point in *MF*, 126.

[7] Rawls asserts that criteria of excellence are "imprecise ... their application to public questions bound to be unsettled and idiosyncratic," and that they tend "to be influenced by subtle aesthetic preference and personal feelings of propriety" (*A Theory of Justice*, 330–1). For problems with these and other claims in Rawls's rejection of perfectionism in *Theory*, see my "Knowing About the Good: A Problem with Anti-Perfectionism," *Ethics* 110 (January 2000), 311–38.

[8] To be more precise, I am interested here in the response to Rawls's argument from critics who believe that reason affords substantial insight into the nature of the good, that such claims can be justified to others, and that the content of the good is in important respects not dependent on an agent's subjective attitudes, preferences, life-plans, etc. Objectivism about the good defended through non-discursive means (by appeal to grace, personal revelation, and so on) presents a different and, I think, less troubling case for political liberals than does objectivism of the sort I discuss, for reasons I discuss in note 13 below.

Rawls seeks against such a critic. Notwithstanding the increased ecumenicism that he claims for *Political Liberalism*, it remains fundamentally at odds with the reasonable comprehensive views of many liberal citizens. For this reason, we cannot conclude that Rawls's account would win their uncoerced endorsement in the way his own commitments require.

JUSTIFIABILITY AND REASONABLE CITIZENS

Rawls's defense of political liberalism revolves around two fundamental norms which he claims are implicit in the public political culture of liberal regimes: the liberal principle of legitimacy, and the idea of the reasonable citizen. The former states that "our exercise of political power is fully proper only when it is exercised in accordance with a constitution the essentials of which all citizens as free and equal may reasonably be expected to endorse in the light of principles and ideals acceptable to their common reason."[9] This a straightforward endorsement of what I have called the justificatory requirement, i.e. the claim that the terms of political association should be justifiable to citizens through their shared capacity for reason.

The importance of the idea of the reasonable citizen becomes clear once we distinguish two interpretations of liberal legitimacy, corresponding to two senses in which a claim can be said to be justified to another. The first I will call justifiability in practice, the second justifiability in theory.[10]

---

[9] Rawls, *Political Liberalism*, 137. Cf. Larmore's suggestion that the defining feature of liberalism is "the idea that the fundamental principles of political association, being coercive, should be justifiable to all whom they are to bind" ("Pluralism and Reasonable Disagreement," in *The Morals of Modernity*, 152). Rawls makes a point of saying that this principle refers to constitutional essentials and matters of basic justice, and he appears uncertain whether public reason-giving in general should also forgo appeals to comprehensive doctrines. At one point he seems inclined to think that the constraints of liberal legitimacy should apply at less basic levels as well (*Political Liberalism*, 215). Later, however, he states that citizens may be guided by their comprehensive views when voting on non-basic issues (235). It is hard not to see Rawls's equivocation here as reflecting a difficulty in the distinction between basic and non-basic issues. The stricter constraint seems the appropriate position for Rawls, given his emphasis on the state as the author of ultimate coercive power. Since the liberal principle of legitimacy relates to the state's coercive power over individuals, it's not clear why it makes a difference whether that exercise concerns matters of basic justice or other matters.

[10] Rawls does not devote much energy to the distinction. At one point, for example, he asserts that "since justification is addressed to others, it proceeds from *what is, or can be,* held in common" (*Political Liberalism*, 100, my emphasis). Larmore seems more strongly committed to the view that justification depends on there being in fact common ground (not just the potential for it); according to him, the search for common ground with other citizens involves appealing to "what they already believe in" ("Political Liberalism," in *The Morals of Modernity*, 135). This may be why he allows that public decisions may rely on those conceptions of the good on which there is unanimous agreement among citizens (*Patterns of Moral Complexity*, 67).

A claim is justifiable in practice if, given another person's existing set of beliefs, reasoning abilities, exposure to appropriate evidence, and the like, a line of reasoning can be laid before her that will lead her to see the claim as warranted by good reasons. In contrast, a claim is justifiable in theory if it is grounded in reasons that would persuade an appropriately competent interlocutor, even if in practice one may not be able to justify that claim to some other person – perhaps because of his shortcomings, or because the claim relies on intricate and complex reasoning, or because he lacks the appropriate evidence. For example, an astrophysicist trying to justify to me some claim about the passage of time relative to a fast-moving object would not get very far. The concepts she would invoke and steps of reasoning leading to her conclusion are just beyond my abilities. But my obtuseness should not shake her confidence in the soundness of her claim. While her claim is not justifiable in practice to most people, this should not lead her to doubt that it is correct and so is, in some important sense, justified. Our belief in the truth of many claims is of just this sort.

Now if the principle of liberal legitimacy is interpreted in terms of in-theory justifiability, the argument for political liberalism cannot persuade the critic imagined here. For the critic believes that reason can yield knowledge about the objective human good, i.e. that claims about the good are warranted by good reasons. Since whatever are good reasons for leading one person to regard a claim as warranted must also be good reasons for another (at least one with similar epistemic capacities), then on the critic's view claims about the good meet the criterion of justifiability in theory. Allowing them into political argument would thus satisfy liberal legitimacy on the in-theory justifiability interpretation. Liberal legitimacy can exclude them, on this interpretation, only if we assume that such knowledge is not accessible through reason, i.e. only if the critic is wrong and subjectivism or skepticism is true.

To avoid having to make that assumption (which the critic will rightly see as biasing the argument against him), political liberalism appears driven to interpret liberal legitimacy in terms of what is justifiable in practice to citizens committed to diverse comprehensive views. But why, one might ask, is this the appropriate criterion for political argument? How does such a move not abandon important considerations about value that can be rationally vindicated simply to secure the agreement of citizens, some of whom may not be fully rational?

One answer is that the criterion of in-practice justifiability offers the likeliest way to achieve political stability, an important good in any society. While Rawls's discussion of stability in *Political Liberalism* has led some to believe that this is his central concern, that defense of the in-practice interpretation faces various problems. First, it is not clear how much weight to give the good of stability (what if the greatest stability could be achieved with the fewest people leading good lives?) and so not clear how far that good justifies the emphasis on in-practice justifiability.[11] Second, and more important, Rawls himself does not regard uncoerced stability as the sole desideratum for political principles. He is concerned with principles that provide both stability and justice, and we cannot conclude from the mere fact of uncoerced stability that a society is just. The Victorian society Mill described in *On the Subjection of Women* may have exhibited uncoerced stability, but Rawls would probably agree that it was characterized by significant injustices to women – injustices made more insidious, not less, by the fact that many women consented to their condition. In Rawls's formula, the goal is not just stability but "stability for the right reasons."

A final problem with in-practice justifiability arises from the fact that liberal societies contain various citizens (e.g. Nazis, White Supremacists) whose belief systems are such that no liberal principles can in practice be justified to them. Since Rawls does not want to concede that liberal states lack authority over such people, there must be some limits to what in-practice justifiability requires, and identifying these moves us some way towards the in-theory interpretation. But as I have argued, that interpretation excludes considerations of the good from political deliberation only by denying the critic's claim that such issues are open to reason. So while the norm of justifiability at the heart of liberal legitimacy must be given either an in-theory or an in-practice interpretation, neither seems able to do the work Rawls want it to.

To escape this dilemma Rawls invokes the idea of the reasonable citizen, a notion he claims is implicit in the public political culture of liberal democracies and so can be invoked without privileging any particular comprehensive framework. Reasonable citizens share two features. First, they desire to live under fair public principles that recognize others' freedom and equality. This solves the problem of the state's authority over Nazis or White Supremacists. Since such citizens are unreasonable (in failing to recognize the equality of all citizens), and the liberal standard of justification applies only to reasonable citizens, their rejection of liberal terms does not undermine the liberal state's legitimacy.

---

[11] For further objections here, see Raz, "Facing Diversity: The Case of Epistemic Abstinence," *EPD*, 69ff., and Sher, *Beyond Neutrality*, 85ff.

The second feature of reasonable citizens is that they realize that various complicating factors which Rawls calls the burdens of judgment – including difficulties in interpreting and weighing evidence, conceptual vagueness, and inescapable background assumptions – will lead others to reach comprehensive views different from their own, and they therefore agree to abide by a canon of public reason acknowledging those burdens.[12] This second feature, which explains how reasonable persons will come to disagree in their views of the good, shows why excluding objective claims about the good is neither a concession to pragmatic necessity nor a denial that reason can vindicate such claims. For if the burdens of judgment mean that citizens will reasonably endorse a range of comprehensive views, while liberal legitimacy mandates that principles of political association be acceptable to all reasonable citizens, then those principles should not privilege any one view over others. Thus does political liberalism yield the anti-perfectionism that grounds distinct liberal commitments while accommodating the critics' claims about the good.

This is a powerful argument. Both the liberal principle of legitimacy and the idea that we should not decide important political matters by appeal to judgments about the good over which citizens reasonably disagree are deeply attractive. But despite its appeal, the argument remains vulnerable to a powerful objection from the critic. The objection targets Rawls's use of the idea of reasonableness. That idea can be given either a weak or a strong interpretation, but neither can do the job political liberalism requires. While the weak interpretation may plausibly be said to be implicit in the shared political culture of liberal regimes, it does not yield the anti-perfectionist conclusion political liberals want. And while the strong interpretation does secure that conclusion, it is highly controversial within liberal regimes. Indeed, many citizens who believe that reason can yield knowledge about the good and who for that reason oppose defining liberal commitments – the very critics political liberalism must convince – have good grounds for rejecting it.

---

[12] Though he expresses some reservations about Rawls's account, Larmore agrees that one of the burdens Rawls identifies – in Larmore's words, "the great variety of life experiences created by modern society, with all its complex divisions of labor and its rich heritage of many different cultural traditions" – provides the key to explaining reasonable disagreement over comprehensive views ("Pluralism and Reasonable Disagreement," in *The Morals of Modernity*, 170). The burdens of judgment may also explain the distinction Larmore draws between what he calls proof ("the logical relations among a set of propositions") and justification ("a proof directed at those who disagree with us to show them that they should join us in believing what we do," one that "can fulfill this pragmatic role only by appealing to what they already believe in") ("Political Liberalism," in *The Morals of Modernity*, 135).

On the weak interpretation, to say that citizens are reasonable is to say only that they embrace certain political norms relatively uncontroversial within liberal democracies: for example, they accept the need for public and rational justification of the terms of political association, recognize the interests of others as meriting equal respect, endorse the norm of reciprocity, and so on. It does seem that agreement to such beliefs is part of the notion of a reasonable citizen operative within liberal regimes: this is why we so confidently classify as unreasonable the Nazi, the Klan member, and the fanatic who grounds his claim to political authority on divine revelation. But the broad model of liberal politics, and, in particular, the prohibition on ideals of the good in political deliberation, does not follow from agreement to these modest norms. What must further be established, and this is the strong interpretation, is that any citizen who accepts the modest norms just mentioned also accepts that ideals of the good have no place in political deliberation.

Can this stronger interpretation of the reasonable citizens be, as it were, read off from the public political culture of liberal regimes in the same way the more modest claims can? There are good reasons to doubt it. Consider first a citizen who sees her own views of the good as rationally warranted. Confronted with others who endorse conceptions of the good that are worthless, corrupting, and trivial, the citizen must believe that others either are not reasoning in as competent a way as she or have not been confronted with the evidence needed to reach a correct judgment.[13] If she did not believe either of these, she would not be able to see her own claim about the good as founded solely on good reasons and would instead have to see it as a function either of what she simply takes (perhaps mistakenly) to be good reasons, or of some combination of reasons and a leap of faith. But seeing her claim as grounded in either of these ways is inconsistent with believing that its truth is warranted

---

[13] It bears repeating that my emphasis is on reason and discursive argument as a way of justifying claims about the good. As a contrast, consider the claim that one knows the good through some personal transcendent experience. Political liberals do not always distinguish between these two groundings for knowledge claims, but, given the priority of reason-giving in liberal theory, the distinction is critical. Where citizens' claims are grounded in transcendence alone, they do violate liberal legitimacy if they seek to incorporate those views into political deliberation. The assertion of inner experience as a warrant for truth carries no epistemic authority for authors, for it cannot be distinguished from mere belief. Providing reasons, in contrast, claims a public authority that distinguishes it from mere belief. Both Nagel, in "Moral Conflict and Political Legitimacy," and Cohen, in "Moral Pluralism and Political Consensus," are helpful on this issue. Nagel is especially careful to distinguish reason-based claims from faith-based claims, arguing only that the latter be excluded from political argument as failing to meet standards of liberal justification. For this reason, his criterion is potentially more inclusive in allowing views about the good into political argument than is Rawls's.

by the exercise of reason. She must, then, regard the views of those who disagree as epistemically inferior.

Two clarifications are in order here. First, I am not claiming that believing something is the same as knowing it to be true. My point is just that one cannot claim to know something through the proper exercise of reason in conjunction with facts of the world and at the same time see opposing views as equally warranted responses to the same evidence. Nor, second, am I denying that persons may reasonably hold wrong beliefs.[14] This is perhaps one way to characterize Othello. Though his conclusion about Desdemona's infidelity is wrong, he may be reasonable in reaching it: after all, his best and trusted friend of countless years has planted damning evidence in such a way as to make the conclusion quite plausible. My point concerns the way Othello has to see his own beliefs: he cannot consistently see them as correct and accept that a different belief has just as much warrant on its side. So even if we employ the idea of reasonableness to characterize the process whereby persons come to hold beliefs and extend it to describe those persons themselves, we can still ask a separate question about the epistemic weight their beliefs carry.[15]

The possibility that some persons might reasonably hold wrong beliefs brings us to the central question raised by the strong interpretation of the reasonable citizen: how should political deliberation proceed when some citizens reasonably hold beliefs that are wrong, and wrong in ways that have serious consequences for the well-being of themselves or others?[16] In light of the role played by the burdens of judgment in Rawls's conception of the reasonable, to defend the exclusion of the critic's claims about the good Rawls must maintain that it violates liberal legitimacy to allow into political deliberation beliefs that some citizens, influenced by the burdens of judgment, reasonably reject. I want to argue now, though, that this reading of the reasonable citizen places liberals in a dilemma: if hewed

---

[14] Here I correct a thoughtless mistake in my "Knowing about the Good." There I asserted that one cannot regard as reasonable another who holds beliefs one knows to be false. That assertion ignored the difference between a person's reasonably holding a belief and the belief's being true. I am indebted to Kai Draper for correcting me on this.

[15] Berys Gaut's distinction between the merely and the maximally reasonable roughly parallels the one I am drawing here between a belief's being reasonable, meaning that someone's coming to hold it is understandable given their circumstances, and its having epistemic authority ("Rawls and the Claims of Liberal Legitimacy," *Philosophical Papers* 24 [1995], 1–22).

[16] The problem is nicely captured by J. Judd Owen: "[In Rawls's conception] reasonable persons are not moved by the general good as such: they are willing, it seems, to subordinate the good of the community to their sense of fair cooperation with others ... Yet can an action taken in knowledge that it is bad for all concerned possibly be reasonable?" (*Religion and the Demise of Liberal Rationalism* [Chicago: University of Chicago Press, 2001], 115).

to consistently it endangers a host of central liberal positions, while if relaxed in the way needed to preserve those positions it cannot in principle disallow claims about the good that undermine liberal commitments to the harm principle and anti-paternalism.

To see why, recall that the burdens of judgment include such things as difficulty in interpreting and weighing evidence, conceptual vagueness, and the fact that, as Rawls puts it, "the way we assess evidence and weigh moral and political values is shaped by our total experience, our whole course of life up to now; and our total experiences must always differ."[17] Consider in this context three objectionable beliefs: that most cases of poverty result from the fecklessness of the poor; that on the whole races differ in intelligence; and that homosexuals are morally corrupt. How do these beliefs stand with respect to the burdens of judgment? Notice first that it is not hard to imagine a process of belief formation and moral development that would lead a person to hold such beliefs; on the contrary, it's all too easy. If such views satisfy the burdens' criterion of reasonableness, it constitutes an unacceptably low threshold for liberal public reason. Liberal states cannot remain agnostic on such questions. They must determine how much public aid the poor deserve, apportion money efficiently to support researchers of different races, and make public appointments where moral character is relevant, and the beliefs in question are relevant to each task. If, however, the liberal state rejects those views as failing the burdens' criterion of reasonableness, despite the fact that some liberal citizens endorse them, then why assume that all views about the good satisfy it? If we can know about the good, and if the burdens of judgment do not simply validate false views by acknowledging their origins in some intelligible process of belief formation, then we can recognize the influence of the burdens on citizens' views about the good while still distinguishing, on the basis of good reasons, between true and false views. And if we can override mistaken judgments in one case, why not in the other?[18]

At this point political liberals might defend their position by insisting that beliefs of the sort just cited can be shown to be unreasonable without invoking the sorts of judgments to which the burdens apply, and that this

---

[17] Rawls, *Political Liberalism*, 57.
[18] Similar arguments, showing that the effect of the burdens cannot be limited to ideas of the good in the way Rawls wants, have been offered by Bruce Brower ("The Limits of Public Reason," *Journal of Philosophy* 91 [January 1994], 5–26) and Simon Caney ("Liberal Legitimacy, Reasonable Disagreement and Justice," in *Pluralism and Liberal Neutrality*, ed. Richard Bellamy and Martin Hollis [Ilford: Frank Cass, 1999], 19–36).

distinction explains why ideals of the good in particular must be kept out of the political realm. For surely, they might say, with respect to the beliefs just cited empirical evidence is relevant, and may be so compelling that to maintain dissenting views is, even allowing for the burdens' influence, clearly unreasonable. One can continue to believe that poverty results largely from laziness, say, or that races differ in intelligence, only by remaining willfully ignorant of the relevant data.

This response, however, is unlikely to resolve the worry I have raised, for three reasons. First, in controversial cases the import of empirical evidence is itself likely to be hotly disputed. Partly this will be for reasons Rawls acknowledges: such evidence is often complex, conflicting, and difficult to interpret, our assessments often inescapably shaped by our differing experiences. But such disputes are also complicated by controversies over what counts as evidence: the very criteria for evidence invoked by adherents of one view may, in the eyes of adherents of another, already prejudge the case against them.[19] Second, with respect to many controversial issues facing liberal states it is just not clear what empirical evidence is relevant, or how one might obtain it. What evidence would help us resolve whether murderers should be executed on retributive grounds? How might one prove empirically that homosexuals tend on the whole to be morally on a par with heterosexuals?

The final problem with the response is that it threatens to beg the question against the critic, who may simply deny that knowledge about the human good is (as the response implies) intrinsically any less objective or knowable than a host of other issues upon which liberal regimes take a stand every day (including the causes of crime, the threat of global warming, the reasons for poverty, and so on). So even if political liberals could explain why the three obnoxious beliefs mentioned above fail to meet the criterion of reasonableness, any such explanation would, in the critic's eyes, open the door to just the sorts of claim they want to exclude. For if we ask how the argument proceeds on a more stringent reading of

---

[19] This is a problem familiar from debates over the degree to which evidence can support and disconfirm religious claims. As Basil Mitchell puts it, "The situation [between believers and nonbelievers] is not one in which there is clear agreement among all concerned as to what would constitute evidence for a particular conclusion, as there is agreement, for example, as to what would constitute evidence for the existence of a new planet" ("Introduction," in *The Philosophy of Religion* [Oxford: Oxford University Press, 1971], 9). Mitchell's point is that the relation between evidence and what he calls one's "conceptual scheme" does not run in only one direction, a claim reinforced by much work in contemporary philosophy of science. Though Mitchell concentrates on the status of evidence in the context of religious beliefs, the problem he identifies has broader scope.

the burdens of judgment, the answer, presumably, is through such steps as marshaling evidence, offering reasons, invoking similar cases, and demonstrating consensus among those whose opinions should be dispositive in the matter.[20] But these are steps to which the critic may appeal as well. He may argue that strong evidence shows that a life on the whole goes better when characterized by such goods as aesthetic appreciation, the pursuit of scholarship, spirituality, and civic involvement, and that the consensus among those familiar with such goods (the only competent judges) vindicates such claims. Are we really any less sure, he will ask, that engagement with beauty and higher learning enriches a life, that coarseness and lack of civility corrupts our culture, that spirituality is an especially deep and important aspect of human experience, than we are that the races are equal, that the poor are not lazy, that homosexuals are not morally corrupt? Is dissent from any of the former claims any more reasonable than dissent from any of the latter? Interpreting the burdens more stringently thus does not exclude the ideals of the good that the critic wants to insert into political deliberation.

If we return to the central question raised earlier, i.e. whether to allow knowledge of the good some role in political deliberation when doing so might lead to improvements in people's lives, we see that the burdens of judgment can secure political liberalism only by setting too low a criterion for reasonableness. Such a move threatens to replace epistemic warrant with psychological causation in a manner to which many critics will reasonably object. Conceptions of the good matter to many citizens not because they see their holding them as predictable given their idiosyncratic backgrounds, psychologies, conceptual frameworks, and the like, but because they see them as true, as confirmed by reason reflecting on facts of the world. Some political liberals may believe such confidence misplaced and so may view debates on such matters as just "a bare confrontation between incompatible personal points of view."[21] Citizens who understand their views of the good as matters of faith may even characterize them this way. But those who believe they know about the good will not. They will want those views of the good to shape political argument and thereby help promote good lives. For them to accept anything less would demonstrate the selfishness and indifference to other citizens'

---

[20] The last of these appears to be Brian Barry's explanation of why teaching evolution over creationism in American public schools does not violate neutrality: "For the purposes of teaching and research, the consensus of the scientific community is precisely what government within a neutral constitutional system should defer to" (*Justice as Impartiality* [New York: Oxford University Press, 1995], 161, n. a).

[21] The phrase is from Nagel, "Moral Conflict and Political Legitimacy," 316.

welfare that liberalism is so often accused of engendering. And once those views of the good are allowed into political deliberation, there is no assurance that the distinctive shape of the liberal state, with its defining commitments to extensive liberty and anti-paternalism, will remain in place.

THE PRAGMATIC RESPONSE

Proponents of political liberalism can offer two broad responses to the critique I've offered. First, they may reply that the argument I've advanced is dangerously utopian and quite ignores the pragmatic needs of political theory in the real world of liberal democracies.[22] Though this pragmatic concern is not, I noted above, Rawls's central motivation for the shift to *Political Liberalism*, it nonetheless points to a legitimate concern that is of a piece with Rawls's worry that his argument in *Theory* had failed to respond properly to the depth of pluralism in liberal societies and so could not expect to secure wide consensus. Such a failing would be especially problematic in liberal regimes which depend in distinctive ways on citizens voluntarily doing their part to support their common life.[23] For this reason, a critical factor affecting their stability is the extent to which citizens regard their governing principles as consonant with their own deep judgments on such matters as the source of moral authority, the nature of the good, and the norms that should structure a human life. If citizens of liberal regimes have any realistic hope of reaching consensus on the principles governing their common life, it will be said, political argument will have to exclude considerations on which they are deeply and permanently divided, and this is reason enough to rule out the critic's claims for the relevance of ideals of the good.

This response on behalf of political liberalism is, however, open to various objections. The first questions the alleged pragmatic advantages of appealing to ideals alleged to be implicit in the public political culture of liberal regimes. The political liberal seems to believe that since citizens differ in their comprehensive frameworks and ideals of the good, the way to achieve political consensus is to bypass those views and appeal instead to shared norms implicit in the political culture. But pointing to the need for consensus on such norms is not an argument that such consensus exists, and there is, in fact, continuing disagreement over the degree

---

[22] I am grateful to Susan Moller Okin for stressing the importance of this pragmatic response.
[23] Charles Taylor makes this point in "Cross-Purposes: The Liberal-Communitarian Debate," in *Liberalism and the Moral Life*, ed. Nancy Rosenblum (Cambridge, MA: Harvard University Press, 1989), 159–82.

to which the state should adopt the positions political liberalism recommends. That disagreement might stem from various factors. One factor, which Rawls on occasion appears to assume, is that citizens recognize both the norms that should shape their common political life and their great importance, but fail to discern the political implications that follow from them. This reading may explain why Rawls's idea of an overlapping consensus often seems to involve getting citizens to understand the positions to which their deepest moral beliefs already commit them. Leaving aside the question of how the argument of *Political Liberalism* will help bring this about (few citizens, after all, read Rawls), one may wonder whether that explanation of disagreement doesn't reflect its own share of troubling utopianism, assuming away the problem to which it is a response.

Let me instead suggest two alternative explanations for the continuing disagreement within liberal regimes. One is that citizens agree that certain norms do broadly inform their political culture but see them as both inconsistent with and subordinate to the requirements of their own comprehensive views. Where Rawls speaks of a shared or common political culture, these citizens will instead speak of a dominant one. In their eyes, an appeal to the political culture of liberal regimes figures not as a reason in any argument but as a refusal to register their objection. A second explanation is that continuing discord within liberal regimes reflects disagreement over either the norms embodied in their political culture or the implications of agreed-upon norms. Either of these seems a plausible account of the conditions in liberal regimes, and if either is true, appealing to ideas implicit in the public political culture will merely displace and not resolve disagreement.

A second weakness with the pragmatic response concerns the problems that the strictures insisted on by political liberals create as liberal democracies seek to resolve the challenges they face. For example, few within liberal regimes deny that all citizens deserve fair and equal treatment from the state. Disputes arise over competing interpretations of what fairness and equality require. Such interpretations, however, are often rooted in deeper normative frameworks that specify how to weigh competing human interests and how to understand concepts like desert, responsibility, and rights.[24] For this reason, excluding such views may result in a

---

[24] A similar argument is made by Nicholas Wolterstorff in his exchange with Robert Audi on the relation between religion and politics. See their *Religion in the Public Square: The Place of Religious Convictions in Political Debate* (Lanham, MD: Rowman & Littlefield, 1997), 162ff. It should be noted, though, that Audi's conception of public reason seeks to allow religious conceptions a substantial role in a citizen's deliberation.

relatively paralyzed political association in which citizens cannot collectively address serious issues. David Paris has made a similar point, arguing
for a relation of inverse proportion between the acceptability of principles
of justice and their power to adjudicate actual disputes: principles will be
more widely acceptable the thinner they are, but the thinner they are the
less helpful they will be to resolving actual disputes.[25] If political debate is
to resolve in some determinate way the various disputes over justice that
arise in liberal democracies, there may be no alternative to the untidy
spectacle of public debate in which citizens make the case for the deep
norms and values that drive their position. But as this seems almost a
definition of politics, we should not be surprised that political argument
cannot dispense with it.

A third problem with the pragmatic response involves its claim that
allowing ideals of the good into political deliberation, as the critic wants,
must compromise the overall stability of liberal regimes. Note that on the
pragmatic response, such ideals should be excluded not because they are
intrinsically inappropriate (as the argument from liberal legitimacy and
the idea of the reasonable citizen implied), but because including them
unacceptably endangers consensus and stability. But this line of argument gives no reason for excluding those ideals that do not threaten stability, and there seems no way to identify these until one actually engages
in political argument and considers their level of support or opposition
among citizens. The degree to which such considerations are destabili-
zing will be a function of numerous factors related to the particular ideals
in question, including how many citizens endorse them, how many are
opposed, how strong these feelings are, and the extent to which citizens
see other such considerations allowed some role in political argument.
While these are complicated questions, there is no reason to believe either
that they are insoluble or that they must result in a blanket condemna-
tion of the considerations the critic wants to introduce. What seems more
likely is that while some such considerations may be ruled out, others may
be allowed in. Such judgments, however, cannot be made *in advance* of
political argument involving those considerations, but will require attention to particular contexts.[26]

---

[25] David Paris, "The 'Theoretical Mystique': Neutrality, Plurality, and the Defense of Pluralism,"
American Journal of Political Science 31 (November 1987), 924ff.
[26] I suspect that political liberals tend to connect stability with the exclusion of ideals of the good
because they recall the horrors of religious conflict in the early modern period and, like Rawls,
see the progress of liberalism as a broadening of religious toleration to encompass diverse views
about the good. But it is not at all obvious that religious claims and conceptions of well-being
must be either similarly divisive or similarly resistant to rational argument. Religious beliefs by

The final problem plaguing the pragmatic response on behalf of political liberalism is that the worry over stability is both indeterminate and unpersuasive against the critic who values stability but does not see it as worth any price. To begin with, how shall we measure such stability? Overall law-abidingness? Recurrent peaceful transitions of power? Political participation? And is it so clear that liberal regimes lack appropriate stability? Compared to whom? Even if such questions could be answered, citizens have different thresholds for acceptable levels of stability, shaped in many cases by their own views about the good. Those who, for example, doubt the authority of objective goods and accept the sovereignty of individual preference-satisfaction may not see the stability of the liberal state as carrying any special price. For citizens I have dubbed critics, however, that stability carries a distinct cost, for it means that true and worthwhile ideals of the good are not being promoted as effectively as they might be. These citizens may thus be willing to tolerate lower levels of stability, and if they are, it is not clear how the argument of political liberalism should persuade them.

It is important not to misunderstand this point. I am suggesting that critics may be willing to tolerate greater instability not because they believe that those conditions advance their own interests, but because they think people's lives will go better if correct ideals of the good inform political decisions. This point can be obscured, and critics made to seem self-serving, when liberals describe them as seeking a privileged place for their own ideals. Such critics want those views to influence political deliberation, in a manner that may oppose defining liberal commitments, not because they are the beliefs they happen to hold, but because they think they are true.[27]

THE RESPONSE FROM EQUAL RESPECT

The other response from political liberals will be that the objection I have advanced ignores the principle of equal respect upon which their

---

their nature seek to explain matters that lie beyond human experience in this world. But claims about well-being are in principle more accessible to inspection by others. This is not to deny that claims about the good are often controversial. My point is just that they are more likely to satisfy the criterion of rational justification that liberal legitimacy mandates. For contemporary attempts to outline objective elements of the human good, see, for example, Thomas Hurka, *Perfectionism* (Oxford: Oxford University Press, 1993); Sher, *Beyond Neutrality*, ch. 9; and John Finnis, *Natural Law and Natural Rights* (Oxford: Oxford University Press, 1990).

[27] Gerald Dworkin makes a similar point in "Non-Neutral Principles," in *Reading Rawls: Critical Studies on Rawls'* A Theory of Justice (Stanford, CA: Stanford University Press, 1989), 124–40.

argument is, either explicitly or implicitly, based.[28] Political liberalism excludes comprehensive ideals and substantive views of the good, they will say, not because it denies that reason can vindicate such views, but because establishing political institutions on the basis of such judgments, and allowing governments to act for reasons deriving from them, privileges some citizens' views over others and so violates the requirement of showing equal respect to all citizens. This is a point, they will say, that hinges not on any controversial view about objective frameworks of value or our ability to know them, but simply on the overriding requirement that the state treat all persons with equal respect.

One way for the critic to reply would be simply to concede that the position he advances does violate the norm of equal respect but maintain that this is not a serious drawback. I shall not pursue this strategy, because political liberals seem to me right in suggesting both that the norm of equal respect is hugely important and that it is (in underlying the liberal emphasis on JR) central within the public morality of existing liberal societies. The problem in their response, I believe, lies elsewhere. For that response to be compelling, political liberals must do two things: (1) identify the capacity in human beings that merits their being treated with equal respect, and (2) show that allowing substantive claims about the good to influence political argument is incompatible with the respect owed to human beings by virtue of that capacity. My claim is that if we allow both that knowledge of the good is possible and that the burdens of judgment do not (for reasons given earlier) rule out assessing the relative accuracy of such views, then on the most plausible account of the respect-meriting feature of persons, allowing substantive ideals of the good into political argument either does not violate the principle of equal respect or does so in a manner that political liberals must accept.

For political liberals, persons merit respect due to their capacity for rationality.[29] Because we are rational we ought not to be treated merely as things, but are instead owed explanations and justifications for actions

---

[28] The importance of equal respect figures explicitly in Larmore's argument (as a self-evident requirement of morality) and implicitly in Rawls's (exemplified both in the liberal principle of legitimacy, which insists that political power be endorsable by each person over whom it is exercised, and in the overall design of the original position). For an argument that Rawls's argument in *A Theory of Justice* rests centrally on the norm of equal respect, see Ronald Dworkin, "Justice and Rights," in *Taking Rights Seriously* (Cambridge, MA: Harvard University Press, 1977), 150–83. In *Political Liberalism* the importance of such respect derives from Rawls's conception of citizens' higher-order interests in exercising their two moral powers, described below.

[29] Rawls locates the relevant exercise of rationality in the two moral powers of citizens: "a capacity for a sense of justice that enables them to understand, apply, and to act from the reasonable

that affect us.[30] Since the free exercise of reason has led to a plurality of frameworks of value and related views of the good, privileging any one view in political argument fails to respect the rationality of citizens who endorse others. Equal respect for others' rationality requires that political deliberation appeal only to what can be justified on neutral grounds to all, independent of the particular conceptions of the good some rational agents may hold, and this requires that such conceptions be rigorously excluded from political deliberation.

This reliance on the idea of justification through neutral grounds cannot, however, do the work political liberals require. The problem, to adapt a point Margaret Moore has made,[31] is that the justification of beliefs on neutral grounds does not entail neutrality between competing beliefs. If your belief is warranted by good reasons, but mine is the result of personal prejudice, neurosis, or an unwillingness to confront the relevant facts, then a move to neutral rational grounds will not be neutral towards our beliefs but will vindicate yours. In such a situation I could not reasonably object that the move to neutral ground privileges your belief and fails equally to respect mine, for the superiority of your belief is a conclusion *resulting from* the move to such grounds and the accompanying exercise of impartial rationality: it does not distort that process from the start. Nor does appealing to the burdens of judgment show why citizens' wrong beliefs should be respected equally: as I argued earlier, that move imperils too many defining liberal commitments. But if liberal regimes can properly judge some beliefs as more warranted than others, then the principle of equal respect does not imply a commitment to treat all views as equally well grounded. Why, then, is equal respect especially imperiled when those views involve judgments about the good?

principles of justice that specify fair terms of social cooperation ... [And] a capacity for a conception of the good: a conception of the ends and purposes worthy of our devoted pursuit, together with an ordering of those elements to guide us over a complete life" (*Political Liberalism*, 103–4). Larmore stresses the second, suggesting that "we owe one another [equal respect] as beings capable of affirming a vision of the good life" ("Political Liberalism," 136). But as his discussion proceeds, it becomes apparent that the capacity for reason-giving in public debate is, with respect to political philosophy, the critical way in which our rationality manifests itself. For this reason, I read his suggestion that "the distinctive feature of persons is that they are beings capable of thinking and acting on the basis of reasons" as referring to our capacities both to form and to pursue conceptions of the good and to justify our actions to others (ibid., 137). Jeremy Waldron has asserted that "liberalism is ... bound up in large part with respect for rationality" ("The Theoretical Foundations of Liberalism," 132–3). Political liberalism is no exception.

[30] As Larmore puts it, equal respect is the concept "that however much we may disagree with others and repudiate what they stand for, we cannot treat them merely as objects of our will, but owe them an explanation for those actions of ours that affect them" (*Patterns of Moral Complexity*, 62).

[31] Margaret Moore, "On Reasonableness," *Journal of Applied Philosophy* 13 (1996), 167–77.

To see the issue here, consider whether you fail to treat me with respect when you act towards me as your beliefs suggest despite my lack of consent. It is true that you fail to respect my beliefs on the matter, but the norm political liberals stress is respect for persons, not their beliefs.[32] Then perhaps you are not respecting my ability to reason. That may or may not be so. If you offer no reasons for acting as you do and treat me as a mindless object, then you do not respect my rationality. But if you offer good reasons whose power I fail to appreciate, it is not clear how you have failed to respect my capacity for rationality. To the contrary, your attempt at justification presupposes and manifests such respect.[33] And if in the end I remain unpersuaded by your reasoning, then from my standpoint, it is true, your action may appear inconsistent with the respect I am owed. But on any plausible view of what equal respect requires, the subject's perspective alone cannot be the final criterion for whether an action satisfies that norm. That question must be determined at least partly through the force of good reasons, as seems only reasonable given that the ground of respect is our capacity for rationality.[34]

For how else, we might ask, can political liberals justify coercion, as on occasion they must, when a citizen does not see the reasons justifying it? If they agree that coercion in such cases shows lack of respect for that person, then they recognize instances where respecting others is not required. If instead they claim that such coercion demonstrates lack of respect not for that person but only for his judgment about a particular matter of justice, and that this is morally acceptable, then the critic who

---

[32] Rawls stresses this distinction in "Fairness to Goodness," *Philosophical Review* 84 (October 1975), 536–54.

[33] As William Galston suggests, "We show others respect when we offer them, as explanation, what we take to be our true and best reasons for acting as we do" (*Liberal Purposes* [New York: Cambridge University Press, 1991], 109). Cf. Brian Barry's claim: "It is perfectly consistent with everything that Larmore says about equal respect that we should believe that the explanation required is an explanation of the superiority of our conception of the good. If we are convinced that nobody could reasonably reject our explanation, we would seem to have done all that 'equal respect' can demand of us" (*Justice as Impartiality*, 176).

[34] The problem here is similar to that faced by Kant's categorical imperative phrased in terms of treating people as ends in themselves. This is usually read as stressing the importance of persons' consenting to how they are treated, but however we interpret that requirement, problems arise. If persons must *in fact* consent, then sentencing unwilling criminals would be immoral: this seems crazy. If what matters is what they *would* consent to if fully rational, this opens the door to disputes over what full rationality entails. Given this choice, the only viable approach for a Kantian is to opt for the latter and engage in the messy business of explaining what is involved in being fully rational. Political philosophers who stress the principle of equal respect must make a parallel move in explaining the contours of the reasonable. One of way of putting my objection, then, is that many citizens who wish to insert claims about the good into political argument may (reasonably) endorse a conception of the reasonable at odds with that which political liberalism requires.

suggests departing from liberal commitments by appeal to claims about the good can make the same argument: such inclusion, he will say, shows disrespect not to other citizens but only to their judgments on particular matters of value. Nor can political liberals object that the critic here ignores the critical distinction between political matters and questions of well-being, because the normative salience of that distinction is the conclusion they want to defend: it can't be a premise in that argument. However political liberals reconcile coercion with the principle of equal respect, then, the objectivist who believes that claims about the good have a place in political argument can make a parallel answer.

Political liberals may assay one final attempt to get from equal respect to the liberal state. The principle of equal respect, say Rawls and Larmore, implies that all citizens meet some minimal threshold in their capacities for reasoning. If this claim extends to citizens' capacities to make judgments about the good, it would rule out the assumption of differential reasoning abilities that figured in the argument above squaring illiberal positions with equal respect. Neither Rawls nor Larmore offers much argument for this claim about minimal rationality,[35] but even if it is granted, we still need to distinguish two possibilities: the first is that all citizens meet some minimal threshold in their ability to work out a generally coherent plan to reach whatever ends they regard as worth pursuing; the second is that they meet it in their ability to identify ends that are in fact worth pursuing. Here is where the critic's objection bites, for even if he grants the first claim, he may have ample reason to doubt the second. One need not be among those critics who see contemporary liberal society as a modern-day Sodom and Gomorrah to doubt that all persons can adequately discern what is important, good, and rewarding in life. Among the hardest questions we face, there is little reason to assume all citizens stand equally prepared to answer them (and more than a little evidence to suggest they don't). As we saw when discussing the merits of social versus state perfectionism in Chapter 3, some citizens

---

[35] Rawls simply asserts that citizens "possess the two moral powers to the requisite degree" (*Political Liberalism*, 109; cf. also 79). Perhaps he is not making an empirical claim and is offering only a definition: if so, the question arises whether the definition is adequately instantiated. While Larmore recognizes that some people have the capacity for working out a coherent view of the world to a greater degree than others, he too suggests that "respect is something that others as persons are due just by virtue of having that capacity, so it should be given equally to all" (*Patterns of Moral Complexity*, p. 64). As it stands, this requires more argument: if respect is owed because others possess some capacity, it seems at least *prima facie* plausible that those who possess this capacity to a greater degree merit more respect. The latter seems a more accurate explanation of how respect for others arises in normal human interaction.

believe that the ability to make informed judgments on such matters depends on a careful process of training and guidance that begins early in life and receives continued support throughout it. The critic might, then, believe that all persons are naturally able to reason properly about the elements of well-being if they have been raised under conditions conducive to epistemic adequacy, but he might doubt that they can do this after they have been subject to conditions that systematically distort and corrupt.

Is the critic's position here, i.e. that our capacity for rationality develops properly only with certain background conditions in place, consistent with the idea of equal respect underlying JR? There are two reasons to think it is. Consider first the example of a man raised in a virulently racist environment who comes to deny that the interests of all persons matter equally. His rejection of liberal principles does not, I noted earlier, compromise JR in any worrisome way. Nor need we see him as somehow less rational by nature: he has simply grown up under conditions that impede his ability to reason correctly about what morality requires. In this case we explain his reasoning having gone astray by noting conditions that thwart its appropriate development and at the same time believe that overriding his overall framework of value violates no important notion of equal respect. But this is just what the critic claims also. And if the liberal insists here that overriding is acceptable on some basic moral norms but not on central judgments of value that relate to well-being, this just begs the question against the critic.

The other reason for seeing the critic's position as consistent with JR connects to an idea Kent Greenawalt develops in defending realism about moral claims. What is critical in the realist account, he suggests, is that "the truth or falsity [of a claim] must be available to some degree to common human understanding." Even if such truths can now be grasped "only by people with a particular training or cultural background," the central realist assumption is that there exist "reasons capable (at least eventually) of persuading others who now lack their training or background." What a moral realism committed to general accessibility rules out, on Greenawalt's view, is the idea that moral knowledge is revealed only to "a selected few who have no common ground with other people to persuade them of the truth they have learned." If we accept this construal of what it means for principles to be generally accessible, and understand JR in terms of such accessibility, then the critic's position is not at odds with JR but instead represents one interpretation of that criterion – one that understands the exercise of reason to be dependent on a certain structure, marked by various illiberal elements, collectively maintained by other human knowers.[36]

There is, however, a quite different way of getting from the norm of equal respect to the idea that the state should exclude from political deliberation substantive claims about the good, in a manner likely to uphold the liberal commitments. If one believes that there is a range of ways of leading a good life, built around uncombinable and noncomparable ideals, virtues, goals, and the like, one thereby has some grounds for thinking political deliberation should respect equally citizens committed to those diverse ways of life, and so has the beginnings of an argument for the liberal commitments to extensive personal liberty and anti-paternalism. This last approach is one political liberals must abjure, however, for it involves an embrace of value pluralism and so rests on just the sort of controversial value claim they wish to avoid.[37] But though political liberals cannot pursue this strategy, many believe that it offers the best way to defend the distinctive features of liberal regimes. Whether they are right is the focus of the next chapter.

---

[36] Greenawalt, *Private Consciences and Public Reasons*, 26. On Greenawalt's view, the critic I am imagining would have to have (similarly accessible) reasons explaining why others have failed to grasp the truths in question.

[37] Larmore comes close to endorsing some form of value pluralism when he asserts that "the ideals of autonomy and individuality effectively blind us to the real merits of many ways of life" ("Political Liberalism," in *The Morals of Modernity*, 130).

CHAPTER 6

Pluralist liberalism

PLURALISM AND CHOICE

None of the preceding attempts to deliver the liberal project overcomes the critic's objections, whose cumulative force is amplified by the fact of value pluralism. Given such worries, liberal theorists have increasingly sought to turn value pluralism to their advantage, arguing that it offers the best defense of the liberal state. As was the case with argument from autonomy, pluralist liberalism can be advanced in both universalist and particularist versions. I shall begin with the universalist attempt.

There are two main routes for the universalist defense. The first is to argue that value pluralism establishes the extraordinary importance of individual choice and that choice is widest and most powerfully protected in liberal regimes. The basic idea is famously expressed in Isaiah Berlin's "Two Concepts of Liberty." Two passages reveal his line of reasoning:

The world that we encounter in ordinary experience is one in which we are faced with choices between ends equally ultimate, and claims equally absolute, the realization of some of which must inevitably involve the sacrifice of others. Indeed, *it is because this is their situation that men place such immense value upon the freedom to choose*; for if they had assurance that in some perfect state, realized by men on earth, no ends pursued by them would ever be in conflict, the necessity and agony of choice would disappear, *and with it the central importance of the freedom to choose*.[1]

One page later we are told:

The necessity of choosing between absolute claims is then an inescapable characteristic of the human condition. This gives its value to freedom as Acton conceived of it – as an end in itself, and not as a temporary need, arising out of our confused notions and irrational and disordered lives, a predicament which a panacea could one day put right.[2]

---

[1] Berlin, "Two Concepts of Liberty," 168 (my emphasis).   [2] Ibid., 169.

The fact of pluralism means that human beings must often choose among noncomparables, Berlin is claiming, and the inescapability of this condition validates the special importance attached to personal liberty. The superiority of liberal regimes then follows directly from the extraordinary value of liberty.

Some have charged that Berlin's argument here commits a clear *non sequitur*.[3] The fact that the human condition is one in which we must choose between noncomparable goods, these critics claim, says nothing about whether choice-making itself is either one of those goods or one that we have special reason to protect. The inescapability of choice in human affairs is one thing, its special value another, and Berlin's argument illegitimately derives the second from the first.

Though his argument may invite this critique, I do not believe the objection adequately identifies the main thrust of Berlin's argument or its central problem. In the rest of his essay, and in a subsequent response to critics, Berlin does more than argue that choosing among noncomparables is inescapable. He also stresses that the exercise of choice is partly constitutive of being human, that our very distinctiveness from other creatures is inextricably bound up with our capacity for choosing under conditions of freedom.[4] This, one might think, makes an airtight case for the importance of personal choice: it simply is necessary to lead a human life.

While this reading fills the apparent *non sequitur* between the inevitability of choice and its extraordinary value, it does not defend choice in the way liberal theory needs. To see why, consider again Berlin's suggestion that only the pluralist account of value adequately explains the importance of individual choice. Even if we grant that pluralism vindicates the great value of choice, it does not follow that monist theories cannot do the same. True enough, some monist theories – think of the commitment to pleasure satisfaction that drives the brave new world – fail to register the importance of choice. But that is a problem with those particular theories, not with monism generally. After all,

---

[3] See John Gray, *Isaiah Berlin* (Princeton: Princeton University Press, 1996), 160–1, and George Crowder, "Pluralism and Liberalism," *Political Studies* 42 (1994), 293–305. Crowder has since argued that pluralism does support liberalism (*Liberalism and Value Pluralism* [New York: Continuum, 2002]). I discuss this more recent argument below.

[4] Berlin claims there is "a minimum area of personal freedom" which "a man cannot give up without offending against the essence of his human nature" ("Two Concepts of Liberty," 126). Cf. "there is a minimum level of opportunity for choice – not of rational or virtuous choice alone – below which human activity ceases to be free in any meaningful sense" ("Introduction," in *Four Essays on Liberty*, lii).

many philosophers have attributed great value to both the idea of self-direction and the acts of choice through which that idea is realized. If, as Berlin alleges, most of them have failed to grasp the truth of pluralism, it would seem to follow that one needn't endorse pluralism to recognize the importance of choice.

This conclusion is strengthened when we realize that there is no reason to think the distinctively human exercise of choice requires noncomparable options. In many circumstances we deliberate over reasons, determine which has greatest weight, and choose on that basis. Even in the absence of noncomparables, the depth and complexity of this process qualify it as an exercise of choice-making distinctively human: it's hard to see how the presence of noncomparables adds to that fact. Perhaps choosing among noncomparables is something further (i.e. in addition to choosing on the basis of conclusive reasons) that only humans can do. But even if this is true, we don't ascribe value to everything that only humans can do: some of those things are indifferent, some rather awful. We still need some argument, then, as to why choice from among noncomparables is especially important.

There is a final reason, noted in Chapter 3, for doubting that our humanity involves choosing among noncomparable options in a way that only liberal regimes protect. The problem can be put as a dilemma. Either members of illiberal communities also have opportunities for such choice, or they do not. If we agree that they do, the grounds for the superiority of liberal regimes collapses. But if we deny they have such opportunities, we must also deny, on the argument we are considering, that such persons lead fully human lives. Not only is such a denial troubling in itself, but it is also sharply at odds with Berlin's manifest aim to expand our conception of the human and our sense of the variety of social worlds human beings can create.

These considerations point up the limitations in William Galston's recent attempt to defend the primacy of liberty by invoking Berlin.[5] In challenging pluralists who believe that Berlin's pluralism undercuts the claim for superiority of liberal regimes, Galston insists that no regime should be tolerated that does not secure "a measure of negative liberty" for its inhabitants. Galston surely is right that any community that accords no value at all to individual choice and self-direction is deeply flawed and offends against a vital element of our humanity. He is right as well to declare: "Political communities cannot rightly be prisons, figuratively or

---

[5] William Galston, *Liberal Pluralism* (Cambridge: Cambridge University Press, 2002), ch. 5.

literally."[6] But these claims do not demonstrate the superiority of liberal regimes: to think they do assumes too narrow a vision of the political options. The world does not divide into two sorts of communities, those that celebrate the maximal protection of individual choice and those that allow for no meaningful choice at all. Such a dichotomy leaves out regimes that, while perhaps constraining liberty or advancing particular values in ways incompatible with basic liberal commitments, still allow sufficient freedom for persons to make choices in a manner that distinguishes a human life.[7]

Berlin himself implies the possibility of such intermediary regimes and raises doubts whether the liberal state alone is an acceptable form of political community. When he mentions the liberal goal of "maintaining conditions making possible the widest possible choice," he notes that these must be adjusted to other needs, such as social stability, predictability, and order. That this is only a partial listing of such competing goods becomes clear in the following passage:

> The fathers of liberalism – Mill and Constant – want more than this minimum [i.e. the minimum needed to be a human being]: they demand a maximum degree of non-interference compatible with the minimum demands of social life. It seems unlikely that this extreme demand for liberty has ever been made by any but a small minority of highly civilized and self-conscious beings. The bulk of humanity has certainly at most times been prepared to sacrifice this to their goals: security, status, prosperity, power, virtue, rewards in the next world; or justice, equality, fraternity, and many other values which appear wholly, or in part, incompatible with the attainment of the greatest degree of individual liberty, and certainly do not need it as a precondition for their own realization.[8]

Though Berlin does not take sides in the debate he recounts, the overall thrust of his argument undermines the claim for the intrinsic superiority of the liberal model. There is no social world without loss. Any political arrangement privileges some goods and subordinates others. I have argued in previous chapters that the critic has reasonable grounds to believe that in championing goods like self-expression, individuality, and choice, liberal regimes do less well in fostering others – cultural continuity within normative frameworks, aesthetic coherence across the community,

---

[6] Ibid., 56.
[7] A similar suggestion, i.e. that states must be either liberal or tyrannical, appears in Fernando Teson's account of "Kantian International Liberalism," in *International Society: Diverse Ethical Perspectives*, ed. D. Mapel and T. Nardin (Princeton: Princeton University Press, 1998), 103–13, esp. 107–9.
[8] Berlin, "Two Concepts of Liberty," 161.

fraternity with fellow citizens, moral integrity, and so on. If ways of life built around these goods are truly noncomparable, as pluralism suggests, then there is no reason to regard the liberal model of political association as superior to all others.

ARE MORE VALUES BETTER?

The other way of mounting a universal case for liberalism via pluralism appeals not to the extraordinary importance of choice, but to other values said to flow directly from the diversity and freedom that are so pronounced within such regimes. Within liberal states committed to extensive liberty and anti-paternalism, individuals will pursue a broad range of ideals, virtues, and ways of life, and pluralists, it is thought, must endorse this situation over one in which fewer such goods are available. The intuitive idea here is nicely captured in Bernard Williams's claim that "if there are many and competing genuine values, then the greater the extent to which a society tends to be single-valued, the more genuine values it neglects or suppresses. More, to this extent, must mean better."[9] The argument can be captured thus:

1. There exist various uncombinable and noncomparable virtues, ideals, ways of life, etc.
2. Citizens in liberal states pursue and achieve a greater range of those goods than citizens in illiberal states.
3. Given value pluralism, it is better if citizens can pursue and achieve a greater range of goods. Therefore,
4. Liberal regimes are superior to illiberal ones.

How good is this argument? The first premise is just a description of value pluralism and so unobjectionable. The second, stressing the diverse ways of life liberal regimes offer, also appears persuasive when one considers factors like the range of religious diversity within liberal societies, the numerous private associations through which citizens pursue a variety of ends, the broad tolerance for individual experiments of living, and so on.[10] The third premise is thus the critical one. It is, however, both controversial and unclear.

[9] Bernard Williams, "Introduction" to Isaiah Berlin, *Concepts and Categories* (New York: Viking, 1979), xvii.
[10] Against the second premise, some have objected that the protection of diversity in liberal regimes implicitly promotes a distinct view of the good, Millean in character, according to which the best life for any individual is whichever one he fashions for himself from among various options.

For starters, we can ask what is more important: that as many values as possible be instantiated in the world, or that individuals lead good lives? Assume the former. As many pluralists now agree, it is likely that in liberal societies certain values will tend to lose out, and certain ways of life offering distinctive goods will become harder to sustain. But if this is true, then the claim that we want as many values instantiated in the world as possible argues for preserving illiberal societies (indeed, it would urge their creation if they did not already exist), for without them the distinct values they promote would disappear.[11]

In addition, we might wonder about the overall coherence of the view that what matters is that the world instantiate as many values as possible. How should we understand this idea? We don't want to say that it is better for the world, or better for the values involved (or just better in itself?) that as many values as possible be present. If any of those is meant, the third premise abandons the assumption of humanistic well-being and verges into mysticism. In a different context Philippa Foot has observed that it makes no sense to talk of "the best state of affairs from an impersonal point of view," if by that we mean something like the viewpoint of the universe, and if we interpret the third premise in any of these ways it approaches the incoherence Foot cautioned against.[12] Finally, note that this reading of the third premise reflects a sympathy with the goal of maximizing values, and so charting them quantitatively, that is difficult to square with pluralism's stress on uncombinability, incommensurability, and noncomparability.

These worries drive us to the other reading of the third premise, i.e. to the idea that the lives of human beings are likely to go better in a society where a greater number of values are realized. Defending this claim will require showing two things: first, that the greater diversity of values enhances the lives citizens lead; second, that these enhancements are not

---

Even if the state's protection of diversity rests on that view, however, the point becomes an objection only through a *non sequitur*. From the fact that the liberal state is committed to protecting individuals in their chosen ways of life it does not follow that the visions of the good that citizens endorse imply that the value of any goal derives from its being the object of choice. Many citizens reject this view and see goals as having value independent of an individual's choosing them. And even if some do believe that a life can be good only if one has freely chosen it, this does not imply that any freely chosen life is a good one.

[11] Gray makes this point in *Isaiah Berlin*, 152.

[12] Philippa Foot, "Utilitarianism and the Virtues," in *Consequentialism and its Critics*, ed. Samuel Scheffler (New York: Oxford University Press, 1988), 232. As Daniel Weinstock notes, "The instantiation of value *per se* is not a good thing. It is only good to realize values if human beings can in some way or other benefit from them" ("The Graying of Berlin," *Critical Review* 11, no. 4 [Fall 1997], 493).

offset by any harms such diversity may bring about. This second point is often overlooked by advocates of diversity, but its importance is clear from earlier arguments. In allowing some to flourish through commercial entrepreneurship, liberal regimes may make avarice more prominent and promote a market mentality which sees all human goods as exchangeable. Extreme openness to free expression may lead to a decline in the quality of the cultural marketplace and a broad inability to discriminate the beautiful from the base. Celebrating personal autonomy and self-creation may undermine extended families and communal connectedness. And so on. Since assessing such costs is a daunting task, many liberals proceed by showing the extraordinary importance of the benefits deriving from diversity, assuming that if these benefits are large enough, the balance likely falls in their favor.

Two routes for demonstrating such benefits can be distinguished. The first invokes the idea of natural diversity, suggesting that a wide range of options allows more persons to achieve their distinctive good. I criticized this idea in Chapter 3 and shall not repeat those objections here. The second way of showing the benefits of diversity appeals to the value of truth. As Bernard Williams presents that argument (attributing it to Berlin), liberal regimes more accurately track the structure of value in the world than do illiberal regimes. In calling upon citizens to choose among uncombinable and noncomparable goods, and thus create worthwhile lives in the face of more values than one person can ever achieve, liberal societies more authentically respond to the basic challenge characterizing the human condition and so "express more than any others a true understanding of the pluralistic nature of values."[13] Illiberal societies constitute an "evasion" of this fundamental fact. Liberal regimes courageously confront it.

Keeping in mind that the critical question concerns the relative well-being of persons living in communities where more values are realized, we can reconstruct the argument from truth thus:

1. In liberal societies characterized by deep diversity, citizens must choose from noncomparable values, not all of which can be realized.
2. Those who choose under such conditions are more likely to recognize the truth of value pluralism.
3. Understanding the truth of value pluralism is a good important enough to offset whatever disadvantages might be created by the distinctive commitments of liberal regimes. Therefore,

---

[13] Williams, "Introduction," xviii.

4. Liberal societies significantly advance the well-being of citizens in ways illiberal regimes do not.

As before, let's grant the first premise. The real questions concern the second and third. To begin with the second, is it true that citizens of liberal regimes are more likely to recognize pluralism? One reason for doubt lies in the unambivalent willingness to expand liberal institutions, even at the cost of indigenous ways of life, that many liberal citizens display. Even if liberal regimes are on balance superior, many within them appear to regard the transition from illiberal to liberal society as an unqualified gain, in which nothing of significant value perishes. (Not for them the idea that any social world involves loss!) So even if such citizens recognize the diversity of goods within liberal regimes, their unqualified support of liberal expansionism bespeaks not a recognition of value pluralism, but the endorsement of a narrower range of ideals centered on individuality, self-creation, authenticity, and the like. That view is not so much a competitor to monism as itself a form of monism in which the liberal ideal of autonomy is accorded supreme value.

Another objection to the second premise has to do with the dynamic that Joseph Raz calls competitive pluralism. By this Raz has in mind the process whereby a person, in living out her commitment to a particular way of life and investing significant energy and time towards those ends, naturally tends to elevate the value of the related goals, virtues, and the like over those she has forsworn. Raz's point is not that someone who has already committed to a particular goal has special reasons to continue in that pursuit (this he acknowledges elsewhere), but that an initially pluralistic conception of values tends to narrow over time. Significantly, Raz does not present competitive pluralism as a marginal phenomenon. Though his comments are speculative, he calls competitive pluralism "a very common kind of pluralistic morality," ultimately declaring: "It is possible that all viable forms of pluralism are competitive."[14] It may be, then, that even in conditions of diversity there are real limits to how far citizens will embrace the truth of pluralism.

---

[14] Raz, *The Morality of Freedom*, 404, 406. For Raz, the fact of competitive pluralism explains why tolerance of what is deemed valueless is so critical in liberal societies. The ground of that tolerance is to be found, he suggests, in respect for autonomy. This does present Raz with a serious challenge, however: since autonomy on his view requires the presence of valuable options, it is not clear how autonomy is circumscribed (or if it is, why that is objectionable) if worthless options are removed. The challenge he faces is to show why someone who denies the value in some goal or activity nonetheless has a reason, grounded in respect for others' autonomy, for preserving access to it. For Raz's attempted solution, see *The Morality of Freedom*, ch. 15.

Irrespective of the pervasiveness of competitive pluralism, liberal regimes are in any case bound to contain citizens whose value systems do not acknowledge value pluralism, and the wide tolerance liberal regimes provide ensures that such citizens will remain a sizeable force within such regimes. We saw in the previous chapter that Rawls's decision to recast his argument grew out of his recognition that under free institutions there were bound to exist large numbers of citizens who rejected the Kantian presuppositions of the argument in *A Theory of Justice*. But it is just as unreasonable to demand that free citizens endorse value pluralism as it is to expect them to endorse Kantian autonomy. If Rawls is right in thinking many citizens within liberal regimes will continue to endorse a wide variety of ethical and meta-ethical positions, then we can expect that many will not, *pace* premise 2, endorse value pluralism.

The third premise, which asserts the value of endorsing value pluralism, is no less problematic. Why should we think that recognizing pluralism is a good of such significance that it thereby vindicates the superiority of liberal regimes? One quick answer is that knowledge just is intrinsically valuable in itself. Put this way, the case seems weak. Even granting the intrinsic value of knowledge, it is not true that we always improve someone's life by adding to the things they know. Sometimes knowing more may impinge on the quality of our lives. Learning about the anti-Semitism of our favorite poet may make it impossible for us to appreciate his poems, which before we had valued highly. Here our gain in knowledge seems not to outweigh what we lose in aesthetic enjoyment. The point extends to more urgent cases as well. Though it is true that gaining knowledge is often more valuable when what is learned has more significance (compare knowing general facts about the structure of the universe with knowing what your spouse ate for lunch yesterday), confronting more significant truths can also more seriously threaten our well-being. Think of how confidence in a hospitable world anchored by belief in God can be shattered by the experience of losing one's faith,[15] for example, or of how one's relations to one's parents or friends may be damaged by learning of some previously unknown and disturbing episode involving them.

[15] The most vivid description of this loss remains that uttered by Nietzsche's madman reflecting on the death of God in *The Gay Science*: "How could we drink up the sea? Who gave us the sponge to wipe away the entire horizon? What were we doing when we unchained the earth from its sun? Whither is it moving now? Whither are we moving? Away from all suns? Are we not plunging continually? ... Are we not straying as through an infinite nothing? Do we not feel the breath of empty space?" (*The Gay Science*, trans. Walter Kaufmann [New York: Vintage, 1974], 181). Even if Nietzsche believed that atheism might ultimately bring into view previously unimagined vistas of human excellence, he nowhere suggests that endorsing atheism must improve the quality of one's life.

To strengthen the third premise against such worries, advocates of the argument from truth will stress that the kind of knowledge involved (viz., the truth of value pluralism) is especially critical to human well-being. This view is tempting. After all, value pluralism is an important claim about the normative structure of our world, and given the connection I have stressed between well-being and the pursuit of genuine goods, recognizing such a claim seems highly conducive to leading a good life.

To see what's wrong with this line of thought, consider a person whose guiding ideals, goals, and virtues derive from one of the world's major religions. Assume as well the falsity of various claims made by such religions (about the creation of the world, the causes of suffering, the dispensation of the soul, and so on). Many pluralists want to claim that such believers can lead lives no less valuable than the lives of secular self-creation that, for example, Millean liberals celebrate. Indeed, providing a conceptual framework whereby one can defend such claims is one of pluralism's great attractions. But this raises a serious challenge to the third premise: if persons can lead noncomparably good lives while being mistaken about important religious beliefs, why can't they lead such lives while being ignorant about value pluralism? If they can, premise 3 must be rejected.

To this objection, an advocate of the argument from truth might respond that however good one's life is, it would be even better were it not marred by holding a false belief, and so any life is improved by coming to recognize pluralism. This response, one might think, is perfectly consistent with recognizing the value in various ways of life, because unlike other substantive values (think of the values of autonomy and individuality, or tradition and communal rootedness), the value of truth is not threatened by any worthwhile form of life: while those other substantive values may be in tension with one another, truth is compatible with all. Indeed, given that a good life involves the pursuit of goals, ideals, and virtues that are objectively valuable, it might seem that truth is not just compatible with any worthwhile form of life but necessarily conjoined to them all.

This response, however, misconstrues the relationship between people and their religious commitments: it assumes a distinction between what is wrong with such beliefs (the creation myths, beliefs about the dispensation of the soul, and so on) and what is right about them that cannot, in the end, stand up. In many cases the ideals, virtues, and goals that adherents of some religious faiths find compelling cannot be sheared off from those dubious claims but are closely intertwined with them. It is in part because of their spiritual beliefs that Native Americans adopt their commendable attitude of respect for the natural world, in part because

Christians believe Jesus was divinely inspired that they champion the ideals of compassion and mercy he advocated, and so on. The impossibility in such cases of separating out a commitment to worthy ideals from the broader religious view within which they are rooted suggests that one cannot simply displace the mistaken beliefs and expect to leave intact the worthy ideals.

The problem here shows why the recognition of value pluralism cannot just be added to those religious values that pluralists claim to validate.[16] Many religions not only do not recognize the truth of value pluralism, but are in fact predicated on the idea that there is one right way to live in the world, connected to a relatively narrow list of goods and virtues. If pluralism is true, those ways of life reflect a (partly) mistaken vision of the good. But then it is wrong to think that the truth can just be added to such lives: if those conceptions are mistaken, persons cannot lead *those lives* in full awareness of the truth.[17] For pluralists to acknowledge the noncomparable value of such lives is thus perforce to acknowledge limits to the value of recognizing important truths. But if it is not true that a life lived in recognition of value pluralism is significantly better than one that is not, we must reject the third premise in the argument from truth. That outcome, coupled with the serious doubts about the second, renders the overall argument highly suspect.

THE WORRY OVER PATERNALISM

The position I'm defending has, I must concede, a puzzling implication. It seems odd that a theorist would think pluralism true but not wish that others also see it as true – odder still when one considers the great efforts many theorists have made in arguing for pluralism. Steven Wall captures the worry here: "Proponents of the pluralist objection might argue that it is not necessarily a good thing for people to come to accept the doctrine of value pluralism. But this would be a strange claim for them to make, since they spend much energy urging others to accept the doctrine."[18] To the degree that it smacks of paternalism, the objection here can seem

---

[16] Stuart Hampshire goes even further, arguing that monotheistic accounts of the world are intrinsically at odds with value pluralism (*Justice is Conflict* [Princeton, NJ: Princeton University Press, 2000], ch. 2).

[17] Here I borrow a point from Raz ("Facing Up," 1228).

[18] Wall, *Liberalism, Perfectionism, and Restraint*, 177. Daniel Weinstock makes the same point against John Gray, arguing that Gray is in the "uncomfortable" position of believing both that value pluralism is an important truth about morality and that it does not much matter whether people believe it (Weinstock, "The Graying of Berlin," 491).

especially damaging, as though theorists who recognize value pluralism are reluctant to disturb the dreamworld of monists who lack the strength and maturity to handle this disquieting truth about value.

Wall is right – the claim is strange – but the strangeness does not point to a serious problem in the position I've defended. There is nothing inconsistent in both recognizing pluralism and having doubts about whether it is good for some other person to embrace it. The aim of moral theory is largely to explore and reveal the nature and structure of values in the world. Whether a claim advanced by a moral theorist is true is a question quite separate from the question how knowledge of that truth will affect people's lives. Since I've already suggested that value pluralism is incompatible with various fulfilling lives that persons lead, there is nothing surprising in believing pluralism to be true while denying that it follows naturally that all others would be better off if they too recognized it.

Still, Wall is correct in noting that many who endorse pluralism believe that recognizing it can lead to sounder positions on important political issues and so write with the aim of persuading others of pluralism's truth. It might seem, then, that either my argument or such pluralists must be mistaken in some way. To see why neither is, we need to understand the target audience at which theorists who advocate pluralism are aiming – who it is they seek to persuade. For many of them (e.g. Berlin, Gray, Hampshire), that audience consists largely of political and moral theorists within liberal regimes who have an interest in how those regimes conduct themselves. Certainly pluralist foes of universalist liberalism think it would be good for such readers to recognize pluralism, but that is because they think such recognition will move these readers towards greater respect for (some) illiberal groups and practices. Nor is it incidental to note that this target audience by definition will tend to have certain traits – an unusual level of comfort with uncertainty and critique, marked commitment to the value of rational reflection, an uncommon openness to challenging ideas – that will enable them both to appreciate value pluralism and to deal more effectively with its challenge than those committed to tradition-based monist views of the good.

My point here is that the arguments offered by theorists who defend pluralism are not obviously directed to all citizens within liberal states, many of whom subscribe to some form of monism, and are most likely to influence persons unusually receptive to critique and revision. So even if one insists that no one can consistently argue for a view without believing that it is good for others to endorse it, it is wrong to assume that theorists who defend pluralism seek to persuade all persons to their view. They seek to persuade their readers, but need not be committed to the global replacement of monism by pluralism. Indeed, in contrast to the "strangeness" Wall sees in the pluralist's willingness to leave monism in place, it would be somewhat self-contradictory for the pluralist to seek universal subscription to his view, since such a goal would entail the destruction of valuable forms of life predicated on monism.[19]

Nor, finally, does this position smack of an objectionable paternalism. Against that charge, the pluralist critic I have in mind can respond that in rejecting universalist liberalism she shows greater respect for other communities, and their distinct models of social organization, than do those who seek to export the liberal model everywhere. True enough, the pluralist critic acquiesces to a state of affairs in which others lack knowledge she has, but that is not obviously objectionable if, as she suspects, the intrusion of liberalism into another community would threaten its distinctive goods to a degree that outweighs the benefits of recognizing pluralism.

What lends initial credibility to the charges of inconsistency and paternalism, I suspect, is an assumption about the great importance that the knowledge of pluralism carries. That assumption, however, is undermined by taking pluralism seriously: after all, why should the value of moral knowledge be immune to the truth of value pluralism? No doubt knowing the truth is often of value, but as I have tried to show, it is not the only thing of value, nor is being mistaken in some aspects of one's moral outlook (as monists are) always an impediment to leading a good life. This conclusion may not be easy for philosophers to accept, committed as they are to the truth above all else, but it is neither inconsistent nor paternalistic. Nor, finally, does it amount to an embrace of irrationalism. It is simply a truth of the world that in some instances there are values more important than knowledge of the truth. Philosophers may be reluctant to acknowledge this fact (for reasons perhaps best explained by competitive pluralism), but it is no less true for that.

TRACKING VALUE IN THE WORLD

We have, however, reached a puzzling conclusion. Throughout I have stressed the importance to well-being of identifying and pursuing goals that are objectively valuable. But in rejecting the argument from truth,

---

[19] As Galston puts it, "To demand that every acceptable way of life reflect a conscious awareness of value pluralism is to affirm what pluralism denies – the existence of a universally dominant value" (*Liberal Pluralism*, 53).

and more generally the importance of grasping value pluralism, have I not severed the vital connection between accurately tracking the world of value and leading a good life? How can I allow that persons can make correct choices about the goals, ideals, and virtues worth pursuing while being in other respects quite wrong about the structure of value in the world (as those who reject value pluralism are)?[20]

To see the answer, we need to ask why understanding the world of value is important in leading a good life. Some may regard such knowledge as intrinsically valuable, but for reasons just given this move does not get us very far. A better answer, one that connects to our interest in seeing that our choices accurately track what has value, is to say that the more our judgments of value are correct, the more our choices will be for genuinely worthwhile goals, ideals, virtues, and so on. While not denying the intrinsic value of knowing the truth of pluralism, this answer speaks more directly to our guiding idea that leading a good life involves success in objectively valuable goals. In doing so, it helps us see how monists about the good can nonetheless lead lives no worse than those who are pluralists, and so explains the puzzling conclusion.

Central to that explanation is the distinction between two ways in which mistakes about values can arise.[21] We can be mistaken in our first-order claims about particular goals, ideals, and virtues worth pursuing in a life, and we can be mistaken in our second-order claims about the general structure of values in the world. Correspondingly, a conception of the good can be mistaken in two ways: it can endorse goals, virtues, and ideals that are not worth pursuing, and it can reflect or proceed from an incorrect account of the overall structure of values in the world. An example of the first sort of error is the vision of the good life built around the acquisition and conspicuous display of expensive consumer goods. An example of the second (given value pluralism) is any monistic theory of value, or any version of subjectivism that denies the existence of objective values. Armed with this distinction, we can then ask a variety of questions about a conception of the good. Are the values it champions worthwhile (a first-order question)? Does it acknowledge value pluralism (a second-order question)? And what logical relations hold between its first- and second-order claims?

---

[20] Cf. George Crowder's claim: "A willingness to acknowledge the true nature of human values, including their pluralism if that is the case, contributes to any good life for human beings" (*Liberalism and Value Pluralism*, 181).

[21] These are the two levels of pluralism referred to in Susan Wolf's essay "Two Levels of Pluralism," 785–98.

What's especially important here is the distinction between consequences that ensue from mistakes at the first-order level and those that ensue from mistakes at the second. When a conception of the good misfires at the first-order level, the costs to those who embrace it will be significant. They will pursue goals, cultivate relationships, endorse traits of character, and abide by principles that are not really valuable, in the process missing out on important goods they might have achieved. In this way the quality of their lives will suffer. But when a conception of the good misfires at the second-order level, i.e. makes errors not in the substantive goals and values it specifies but in how it understands either the general structure of value or the source of value in the world, there need not be any significant costs in human well-being so long as the values specified at the first-order level are worthwhile.[22]

To see this, consider again the case of the Amish in the film *Witness*, discussed in Chapter 2. Assume that Amish tradition specifies worthwhile goals and virtues (e.g. closeness to the land, self-sacrifice, non-violence, steadfast loyalty) such that the women and men who pursue them can lead fulfilling lives. This means that at the first-order level the Amish conception accurately tracks what is of value in the world (though it may not accurately track *all* values). Now consider what kind of second-order claim the Amish make about the world of value – in particular, whether they endorse monism or pluralism. Perhaps they are pluralists: though themselves committed to non-violence, they recognize the value in the city cop's view that allows violence under certain circumstances. If so, their conception of the good is correct at the first- and second-order levels. But what if the Amish are monists, believing that their way of life and codes of conduct are intrinsically better than any other? In this case their conception of the good is mistaken at the second-order level: while they are correct to think that the values and ideals specified by their conception of the good constitute a way of life inferior to none, they are wrong to view their way of life as better than any other. (That we can make this distinction is just what noncomparability allows.)

---

[22] Here I make the crucial assumption that the intrinsic value of goals, virtues, and the like is not available only to those who pursue them because of their alleged connection to a particular source of values (e.g. the fact that God commanded them) – i.e. that if the values are intrinsically worthwhile, then persons do well to pursue them regardless of how they understand their grounding. This assumption, it should be noted, is compatible with recognizing value in conceptions of the good that reject the assumption itself. For example, even if the adherents of some conception of the good believe that leading a good life depends on endorsing a particular view about the ultimate source of value, pluralists can reject that belief while still acknowledging that conception as an authentically valuable way of life.

The critical question is then this: if their first-order judgments accurately track what has value, what does it matter *to the quality of their lives* if the Amish go astray in their second-order judgments and fail to recognize pluralism? One response, grounded in an appeal to natural diversity, I have already rejected. Another is that failure to recognize pluralism will circumscribe the tolerance of the Amish, both for those outside their community and for members who may seek to depart from Amish traditions in various ways. This invocation of tolerance is unlikely to persuade the critic, however, for several reasons.

To begin with, whether liberal regimes should be as tolerant of personal choice as they are is itself one of the central issues on which the liberal and the critic disagree. Pointing out that endorsing pluralism tends to increase tolerance thus threatens to beg the question in favor of the liberal position. And in any case, it is not at all clear how far increased tolerance will result from the diversity brought about by the liberal state's commitments. The phenomenon of competitive pluralism constitutes at least one complicating factor, and I have as well raised questions about the idea that conditions of freedom in liberal society will engender broad recognition of value pluralism. Even if they do, we should not conclude that monistic theories of the good generally breed intolerance. Various research indicates that some who describe themselves as religious conservatives (not, one imagines, a group inclined to value pluralism) are often as well strong advocates of tolerance.[23]

Finally, even if the argument from liberal diversity through value pluralism to tolerance could be made good, such that members of illiberal societies tend to be monists and also less tolerant, they may again score better with respect to other goods precisely because of their embrace of monism. Agreement on a narrower range of goods may pave the way for features of well-being often stressed by communitarian theorists (e.g. widely shared standards of taste and beauty, participation in a shared culture, greater feelings of solidarity with fellow citizens). Even more importantly, the liberalism-pluralism-tolerance dynamic being assumed here threatens the virtues of integrity and commitment whose great importance I discussed earlier. The problem here is nicely conveyed by the quotation from Schumpeter with which Berlin closes his "Two Concepts" essay: "To realize the relative validity of one's convictions, and yet stand for them unflinchingly, is what distinguishes a civilized

---

[23] The study, cited in Galston's *Liberal Pluralism*, is detailed in Alan Wolfe, *One Nation, After All* (New York: Viking, 1998).

man from a barbarian." Whatever one thinks of the coherence of this view – whether one views such unflinching conviction as moral maturity or simple dogmatism – Schumpeter's remark implicitly reveals the degree to which the realization of value pluralism tends to undermine commitment to one's own ideals. For the civilized man's attitude is laudable precisely because he has reconciled two ideas that naturally oppose each other: recognition of the contingency of one's own ideals, and steadfast commitment to them. Schumpeter's praise makes sense, that is, only if diminished commitment is the natural outcome of recognizing that one's ideals are not objectively superior but reflect to some degree the arbitrariness of one's position. If commitment to one's (worthwhile) goals is an important value in any life, then, the recognition of value pluralism poses a potentially serious obstacle to well-being that will not be faced by monists.[24]

THE PARTICULARIST CASE FROM PLURALISM

Faced with these problems, the pluralist liberal may turn to a particularist defense. Even if he cannot establish the liberal state as intrinsically superior to illiberal models, various factors within particular communities – in particular, deep normative diversity among liberal citizens, and the presence of strong cultural, legal, and political traditions reflecting liberal norms – may recommend the liberal state over any alternative. The fact of deep diversity means that there is no clear consensus on which view of the good, or normative framework generally, should structure the community's political life, while the truth of value pluralism means the state can have no good reason to endorse any particular view over others. Excluding such ideals, in the way liberalism recommends, thus seems both the fairest and most rational approach. That diversity also means that citizens will reasonably believe their interests are threatened by a state that commits its power and resources to competing ideals, and concern for their well-being argues against creating obstacles to the goals they already endorse. As for the existence of ongoing traditions suffused by liberal norms, the particularist can grant that even if ideals of choice, individuality, and experimentation do not have the supreme value some liberals claim, they are nonetheless likely to have deeply shaped not just

---

[24] The dynamic that Schumpeter acknowledges may help explain, perhaps even justify, competitive pluralism: to the degree that awareness of the contingency of our values can diminish our commitment, the good that results from remaining committed can unwittingly motivate us to narrow our sense of what has value.

the views of the good held by various citizens but their sense of the appropriate scope of state authority. A state that either takes on a paternalist role or constrains liberty on relatively new grounds is thus likely to be perceived as overstepping its bounds and departing from political norms that enjoy the authority of custom. To the degree that the justificatory requirement recommends that the office of the state be largely responsive to its citizens' norms of political morality, the prominence of liberal traditions within a society counts in favor of its continued robust protection of liberty and its rejection of paternalism.[25]

While these considerations are weighty, the particularist case for pluralist liberalism is open to two important objections. The first concerns the uncertain support that pluralism provides for both the harm principle and anti-paternalism. Defenders of liberalism sometimes argue as if the only alternative to the liberal state were a perfectionist one narrowly committed to a specific view of the good life. Consider, for example, the contrast drawn by one advocate of liberal neutrality: "Perfectionist political theories are those which demand that the state promote a particular conception of the good, while a neutral state takes no position on the question of the good life and restricts itself solely to the enforcement of principles of the right."[26] This claim suggests that states must either adopt the defining liberal commitments and exclude from political deliberation substantive ideals of the good, or invoke a particular monist conception. But such a dichotomy omits a third option: a state might reject neutrality without committing itself exclusively to any single conception. It might recognize a wide variety of such conceptions as distinctively rewarding and take special steps to protect and support these. We might call this position pluralist perfectionism.[27]

Given the importance of human well-being in political theorizing, the recognition of value pluralism would *prima facie* recommend pluralist perfectionism over both monist perfectionism and the liberal state committed to Millean liberty and anti-paternalism. For though pluralism recognizes strong diversity in genuine goods, in acknowledging objective values it deems some goals and pursuits misguided, base, or inferior. So even if pluralism provides no conclusive reasons to endorse,

---

[25] In raising questions in the previous chapter about Rawls's claim that all reasonable citizens endorse certain ideas prominent within the public political culture of liberal regimes, I did not deny that many endorse those ideals.

[26] Colin Bird, "Mutual Respect and Neutral Justification," *Ethics* 107 (October 1996), 66.

[27] A similar view is outlined by John Kekes in *The Morality of Pluralism* (Princeton: Princeton University Press, 1993), ch. 12.

say, aesthetic achievement over scholarly pursuits, family life, friendship, or other noncomparable human goods, it permits the state's taking steps to discourage ways of life that exemplify brutishness, stupidity, and misanthropy, and to promote those especially worthwhile. The life of the pornographer and the cult groupie may not offer goods worth protecting and should perhaps be sharply constrained. Spirituality, family life, and aesthetic engagement may be important values that the state should promote. Pluralism thus leaves open the possibility of a state that, while not aligning itself exclusively to any conception of the good, departs from the firm commitments to the harm principle and the anti-paternalism that distinguish the liberal state.

It may be that such pluralist perfectionist policies will not constitute a substantial departure from the practice of many contemporary states regarded as liberal. Consider, for example, the various ways in which the restriction of liberty on perfectionist grounds meets with general approval within existing liberal democracies. Few persons sympathetic to the priority of liberty are disturbed by constraints on the liberty to consume dangerous narcotics, or to engage in bestiality, prostitution, or the selling of babies. Though these activities may have undesirable extrinsic effects, support for such restrictions also reflects a sense that they are just not appropriate activities for human beings, that they violate ideals people should honor even if they do not want to. Note also that with respect to activities judged worthless or corrupting the state might not impose an outright ban on them, but may simply make them far more difficult or costly. If pornography undermines important goods and coarsens the level of public culture, states can restrict the areas where it is available or create other obstacles to its production and dissemination. If commercial interests and advertising lead to a crass and despoiled public culture, states can establish standards to counteract that. Between outright prohibition and the extensive tolerance of the harm principle lie a range of policies that can strive to balance individual freedom with the protection of valuable ideals and goals. And though I won't detail the case here, the prohibition on anti-paternalism is also in many ways qualified in existing liberal democracies, with many supporting the special value of such pursuits as religious worship, aesthetic engagement, and advanced learning.

Some may say these considerations show that pluralist perfectionism is largely compatible with various features of existing states viewed as liberal, and that the contrast I have drawn is illusory. I rather believe that the general support for the pluralist perfectionist policies just described shows how out of step with many citizens' common-sense judgments a robust construal of the defining liberal commitments really is. The fact is that few liberal citizens accept, and few liberal states act on, a principled embargo on substantive ideals of the good drawn from (a range of) particular normative frameworks. The key question, then, is which of those ideals the state should rely on and which it should not. But once this question is posed, the substantive claims about the good that the critic thinks belong in political deliberation cannot in principle be ruled out. Nor, equally importantly, can we exclude the possibility that those arguments might properly carry the day. Having reached this concession, in other words, the critic may feel he's won the case: he can now turn his attention to political victory.

It may be, however, that liberal theorists do not trust other citizens to make the discriminations on which pluralist perfectionism relies, and that while substantive claims of the good drawn from particular comprehensive frameworks cannot in principle be ruled out, there are overriding pragmatic reasons, having to do with potential abuse by the state, to exclude them from political debate in the manner specified by the two defining liberal commitments. These reasons concern either citizens' low motivation to identify and enact correct political positions, or their general inability to discern what really has value. The concern over motivation I take up in subsequent chapters, when I take up the liberalism of fear (Chapter 7) and the importance of the civic virtues (Chapter 9). The claim that citizens are not likely to make accurate judgments of value, however, brings us to the second challenge facing the particularist case from pluralism, and at the same time raises deep questions about the liberal project as a whole.

A PROBLEM WITH JUSTIFICATION

Earlier I noted that many pluralists accept that persons committed to monist visions of the good can lead lives whose value is noncomparable to that of persons who endorse pluralism.[28] I also noted that in liberal societies a significant number of citizens can be expected to endorse such monist visions. Now the particularist case under scrutiny proceeds on the assumption of pluralism. It appeals to the diversity of the legitimate values that characterize a good life and on that basis argues for a liberal state broadly committed to robust personal liberty and anti-paternalism. The conjunction of these claims, however, reveals a troubling asymmetry

---

[28] This view is endorsed, for example, by Galston, Gray, and Raz.

that undermines pluralist liberalism even in its particularist version. The pluralist cannot proceed from a claim that is reasonably rejected by many of the citizens she aims to persuade: doing so violates the justificatory requirement (JR). But the truth of value pluralism is itself such a claim. No argument resting on it can thus be expected to persuade the critic who rejects it, and this means that no state grounded in such an argument can legitimately claim authority over such a citizen.

The problem here parallels a flaw in William Galston's pluralist argument. Though Galston's argument can be used to defend a universalist case, it's more likely to succeed on a particularist reading, since it draws heavily on a principle of expressive liberty most likely to be endorsed by citizens of liberal regimes. That principle refers to "a robust though rebuttable presumption in favor of individuals and groups leading their lives as they see fit, within a broad range of legitimate variation, in accordance with their own understanding of what gives life meaning and value."[29] Granting the value of expressive liberty, the key question here is how far to construe "the broad range of legitimate variation" Galston mentions. Galston defends an expansive reading of that range by appealing to value pluralism.

I need not dwell on the relationship between expressive liberty and moral pluralism. Suffice it to say that if moral pluralism is the most nearly adequate depiction of the moral universe we inhabit, then the range of choiceworthy human lives is very wide. While some ways of life can be ruled out as violating minimum standards of humanity, most cannot. If so, then the zone of human agency protected by the norm of expressive liberty is capacious indeed.[30]

But as I have argued throughout, the real challenge of liberal theory is not to convince pluralists that they should accept such a capacious zone: it is to convince the critic who embraces a narrower conception of human goods and well-being. The latter will see many fellow citizens as clamoring for freedom to pursue misguided goals that fall outside the zone of legitimate variation. Galston recognizes this, and one of the main goals of his argument is to legitimize the existence within liberal regimes of communities that subordinate the value of choice to other,

---

[29] Galston, *Liberal Pluralism*, 3. Galston defends expressive liberty as a precondition for leading a good life, echoing the endorsement constraint. But as I suggested earlier, the critic can accept endorsement as a necessary condition of a fully good life without seeing it as sufficient. And since paternalism and constraint can shape the goals people adopt, the critic can accept the value of expressive liberty without endorsing a liberal regime committed to the defining liberal commitments.
[30] Ibid., 37–8.

higher ends.³¹ Why then should we expect that such citizens will accept the pluralist argument, even in its particularist version, for an expansive range of legitimate variation in the worthwhile goals people may pursue?

To get around this problem, pluralist liberals may seek to narrow their conception of the reasonable citizen who is owed justification. This approach is not unique to the pluralist case: political liberals, as we saw, sometimes attempt a similar move, first asserting that a reasonable citizen treats others with equal respect and then advancing the question-begging claim that equal respect entails not seeing one's own view as meriting any special place in political deliberation. In the pluralist case, the proposal would be that anyone who rejects value pluralism falls below the threshold of rationality needed for JR to apply. If so, the fact that monists would reject the pluralist argument does not mean the argument violates JR. But this move carries too high a cost. To begin with, excluding monists from the class of citizens owed political justification seems deeply at odds with the overall pluralist impulse to validate diverse ways of life as genuinely worthwhile and not just lamentable failures of human reason. In addition, given the great numbers of liberal citizens who endorse some version of monism, the proposal implies that far too many are not owed political justification. Not only is this troubling in itself, but such a move directly indicts citizens' general ability to reason about values, undermining the broad confidence in their rationality that underwrites the liberal project. Defenders of the proposal would thus have to provide some reason for thinking that citizens by and large can reason clearly about the principles governing their political association (in the manner JR assumes) but not about the various goods available in a human life. But as I suggested earlier, these issues seem epistemically comparable, especially since we cannot assume from the outset that judgments about political life can be neatly insulated from judgments about the proper ideals to govern a human life. A final problem concerns the fact that value pluralism is widely judged a recondite position in value theory, one that philosophers themselves for a long time failed to grasp. To insist on recognizing it as a criterion for reasonableness seems not just arbitrary but unreasonably demanding.

Indeed, it's not clear whether strengthening the criteria for the reasonable citizen in this way doesn't simply do away with JR altogether. George Crowder's recent defense of pluralist liberalism squarely faces the logic

³¹ "Many forms of life do not give choice making an honored place. It is also true that from time to time individuals and groups have chosen to create and live in these nonchoice societies ... In a wide range of circumstances, it would be wrong to intervene in such societies to compel them to recognize the authority of negative liberty over their own constitutive values" (ibid., 54).

here and adopts precisely this approach. Responding to Charles Larmore's objection that pluralism is too controversial a basis in which to ground liberalism, Crowder first replies that the emphasis on reasonable disagreement at the heart of political liberalism itself presupposes pluralism, and so his own approach is no more controversial than the position Larmore endorses. But as Crowder recognizes, showing this is not enough: even if pluralist liberalism is no worse off than political liberalism, both may be seriously flawed. To strengthen his case, Crowder argues that liberals should abandon their emphasis on "justification based on consensus" and instead offer an argument that will "challenge consensus, asking people to reflect on and question their beliefs, and draw out the implications of what they can believe for good reason." Pluralist liberalism can succeed, Crowder concludes, so long as we accept that "truth rather than consensus is the goal."[32]

Crowder's approach has the simplicity of Alexander facing the Gordian knot: rather than resolve the thorny debate over the in-theory/in-practice conceptions of justification, Crowder dismisses the in-practice strand and concentrates on philosophical justification. Few political philosophers will deny the appeal of this move. But while the concern with truth must not be sacrificed, neither should we abandon the distinctively liberal commitment to the idea that all persons are naturally free and equal, and so properly subject only to political arrangements that could be justified to them as the actual persons they are, not the rational deliberators with full philosophical knowledge that they might be. Though the liberal state defended by Crowder does secure the freedom and equality of all subject to it, it is not grounded in an argument that respects those ideals in the manner captured by the liberal principle of legitimacy. The centrality of that principle reflects the fundamental error liberalism identifies in alternative conceptions of political authority, viz., their failure to reconcile the natural freedom of all persons with the existence of authoritative political institutions. Whatever its strengths, Crowder's approach also fails to do that, and for this reason cannot be deemed a success in terms of the liberal project.

The problems that arise in trying to defend liberalism via value pluralism, even in its more modest particularist version, point to a deep tension that runs throughout the liberal project. On the one hand, its emphasis on justification before all citizens presumes a confidence both

---

[32] Crowder, *Liberalism and Value Pluralism*, 176–8. Though I discuss him in the context of the particularist case, Crowder offers a universalist argument for pluralist liberalism. Larmore's argument appears in "Pluralism and Reasonable Disagreement," in *The Morals of Modernity*, 152–74.

that citizens can reason intelligently on the principles that should govern the political community and that such reasoning will converge on a single set of principles as authoritative. On the other hand, citizens living under the conditions liberalism protects continue to endorse a wide range of normative frameworks that spell out differing norms as properly structuring a human life, and value pluralism implies that many of these are reasonable answers to the question of how one should live. Given these facts, the only way to achieve unanimity on political principles would be somehow to immunize the process of political theorizing from those diverse judgments of the good by showing their irrelevance to that process. But the conclusion of the preceding chapters is that no argument for that view succeeds. Without it, the liberal project cannot succeed.

PART III

Modus vivendi liberalism

CHAPTER 7

The case for modus vivendi liberalism

The argument to this point has been chiefly critical. I have tried to show that value pluralism corroborates the critic's objections to the liberal state but also that liberals cannot turn pluralism to their advantage, since that idea is both controversial and rejected by many of the citizens they need to persuade. Some may object that my argument employs a bait and switch – Chapters 3 through 5 invoking pluralism to defeat liberalism, Chapter 6 invoking monism to the same end. But that objection ignores the fact that the liberal project aims for an argument that is both rationally compelling and compatible with the justificatory requirement (JR). The earlier chapters showed how value pluralism undermines the persuasiveness of liberal arguments. Chapter 6 argued that pluralist liberalism cannot meet JR. Since liberals are committed to success on both axes, failure in either respect defeats their project as traditionally conceived.

At this point liberals might make various moves to defend their position. One approach is to insist that only those who recognize value pluralism qualify as reasonable citizens, to whom justification is owed. As I argued in the previous chapter, that move sets the epistemic threshold too high. Alternatively, liberals could deny value pluralism any role in assessing political arrangements. Though this move might weaken the critic's objections, it deprives political philosophy of an important truth in value theory and so calls into question the soundness of any conclusions so reached. The dilemma appears inescapable: invoking all relevant considerations creates a problem regarding JR; not doing so compromises normative soundness.

Given my emphasis on considerations of human well-being in evaluating political arrangements, some might recommend that the liberal simply drop the concern with justification. Several factors count against that strategy, however. To begin with, regimes that satisfy JR will be more conducive to citizens' self-respect and less likely to leave them feeling alienated from their political community, both important components of well-being. Such citizens are also more likely to support common institutions, to follow shared rules, and to make necessary sacrifices when asked, all important goods in a polity. Moreover, even if we accept well-being as central in political argument, justification still figures as an additional moral ideal: any defense of political arrangements that satisfies it will *ceteris paribus* be stronger than one that does not. Finally, abandoning the emphasis on justification ignores the liberal commitment to the natural freedom and equality of all persons, opening the door to potentially elitist conceptions of political authority.

The upshot is that anyone who is concerned to protect the diverse ways of life that characterize liberal societies, but who at the same time holds to the goal of offering an argument that can be endorsed by the critic I've imagined throughout, has reason to pursue an alternative defense of liberalism.[1] The alternative I shall defend, which I call modus vivendi liberalism (MVL), falls within an approach to political theorizing that might be described as anti-utopian. Such approaches abandon the idea that political arrangements can be defended by appealing either to the nature of the human good or to some supreme moral value any rational agent must recognize. Accepting instead that many citizens endorse normative frameworks which recommend as ideal some illiberal model of political association, anti-utopianism grounds political life not via its consonance with citizens' deepest moral ideals but instead as something diverse citizens can agree to as an acceptable compromise. In this respect MVL shares important similarities with another anti-utopian account, the so-called liberalism of fear given canonical expression in Judith Shklar's influential essay.[2] It is important to distinguish the two, however, since the case for MVL I advance differs in key respects from Shklar's account, and noting those differences strengthens the appeal of MVL. As I shall argue now, though the liberalism of fear rightly seeks to defend liberal states from a position outside the normative contestation that divides liberal citizens, at key moments it relies on premises that are either implausible in themselves or too controversial to secure the assent of many reasonable citizens.

Now Shklar's account, it must be said, is painted in very broad strokes. Doubtful that any precise system of codifiable principles could adequately

---

[1] Note that the desire to defend the liberal state may be motivated by an acceptance of value pluralism. It does not follow, though, that the persuasiveness of any such argument must hinge on pluralism. This distinction explains how MVL avoids the problem facing pluralist liberalism.
[2] Judith Shklar, "The Liberalism of Fear," in *Liberalism and the Moral Life*, ed. Nancy Rosenblum (Cambridge, MA: Harvard University Press, 1989), 21–38.

capture moral conduct, and disinclined towards the sort of political theory "that analyzes concepts and fits specific ideas or practices to an established grid or model," Shklar's political thought neither fits within one neat architectonic nor carries clear institutional recommendations.[3] Nonetheless, in "The Liberalism of Fear," and in *Ordinary Vices*, where she first explored what she saw as the distinctively liberal commitment to "put cruelty first," she conveys clearly enough the backbone of her case.

That case hinges on three claims. The first is that cruelty – "the deliberate infliction of physical, and secondarily emotional, pain upon a weaker person or group by stronger ones in order to achieve some end, tangible or intangible, of the latter" – constitutes the greatest evil in human affairs. Though liberalism does not identify a *summum bonum* towards which individuals should strive, "it certainly does begin with a *summum malum* ... That evil is cruelty and the fear it inspires, and the very fear of fear itself."[4] The second claim is that in virtually all communities the greatest threat of cruelty lies in the state and its officers. "The fear and favor that have always inhibited freedom," she writes, "are overwhelmingly generated by governments, both formal and informal. And while the sources of social oppression are indeed numerous, none has the deadly effect of those who, as the agents of the modern state, have unique resources of physical might and persuasion at their disposal."[5] Third, she maintains that liberalism constitutes the surest way to limit the state's power and is thus the best safeguard against the most worrisome source of cruelty.

I will take these claims in reverse order. To begin with, do liberal states offer the best protection against state-sponsored cruelty? Accepting for now Shklar's conception of cruelty, her claim seems historically plausible. A comparison of regimes in terms of the degree to which they engage in the kinds of cruelties chronicled by Amnesty International, for example, shows that state-sponsored cruelty of the kind Shklar has in mind occurs with disproportionate frequency in illiberal regimes. Though this fact by itself does not establish liberal regimes as on the whole preferable to non-liberal ones, it does bolster the view that if the single desideratum in politics is protecting citizens against cruelty from the state, liberal regimes are superior.

But, of course, the state and its officers are not the only sources of cruelty. As Shklar stressed, the drive to cruelty is an all too human

[3] Judith Shklar, *Ordinary Vices* (Cambridge, MA: Harvard University Press, 1984), 228. Shklar's doubts about codifying appropriate conduct are laid out in *Legalism* (Cambridge, MA: Harvard University Press, 1964).
[4] Shklar, "The Liberalism of Fear," 29. [5] Ibid., 21.

disposition, one that finds expression in a variety of acts not confined to officers of the state. Indeed, critics from various quarters have faulted Western political philosophy generally for concentrating so heavily on the dangers the state presents to citizens and neglecting the numerous ways in which cruelty gets enacted by private individuals. When we consider issues like domestic violence, abuse in the workplace, corporal punishment in schools, and rape against women,[6] we see that there exist sources of significant cruelty other than the state. Any politics that puts cruelty first must reckon with this fact.

Doing so quickly leads to doubts about Shklar's second pivotal claim, i.e. that the main goal in designing political institutions and practices is to minimize the state's capacity for cruelty. Surprisingly, Shklar says little to defend this emphasis and its relative discounting of the cruelty private agents can inflict.[7] But even if we accept the urgency of combating the state potential for cruelty, the fact remains that private cruelty constitutes a significant evil in human affairs and so is a subject about which a politics that puts cruelty first should have something to say. Once we accept that private cruelty is a serious problem, there seems no reason to deny that the appropriate response to it might involve granting the state significantly greater authority over individual lives and liberties than liberals have traditionally allowed.

This point has implications for the liberal commitments to both maximal liberty and anti-paternalism. As for the former, it cannot be denied that many of the freedoms liberal regimes protect make private acts of cruelty harder both to detect and to prevent. Some have even argued that certain kinds of protected expression – that of pornographers, or racist hate groups – create an ideological climate in which acts of cruelty are much more likely to come about. However one sees those claims, it cannot be denied that a host of liberal rights deriving from the primacy of personal liberty – e.g. privacy in communication, freedom of association and movement, resistance to the government's tracking our purchases and whereabouts – give citizens greater leeway to conceive and carry out acts of cruelty. John Kekes may go too far in suggesting that a concern to limit cruelty should align one with conservatism, but he seems right to

---

[6] Claudia Card, for example, has argued that rape should be considered a terrorist institution tolerated by liberal regimes. See "Rape as a Terrorist Institution," in *Violence, Terrorism and Justice,* ed. R. G. Frey and Christopher Morris (New York: Cambridge University Press, 1991), 296–319.

[7] Jared Diamond has claimed that citizens under even the most horrific regimes (the Nazis, Pol Pot) faced less of a threat of violent death than did citizens in societies lacking a state. (This does not, I realize, deny that such state-backed abuses are morally far more troubling.) See Diamond, "Vengeance is Ours," *New Yorker,* April 21, 2008, 74ff.

insist that such concern raises strong doubts about preserving intact the robust personal liberties that liberals cherish.[8]

To see how the concern over private cruelty might weaken anti-paternalism, imagine that some robust program in civic or moral education worked to instill virtues and habits of mind antithetical to cruelty. If the state mandated such an education, on what grounds could someone who puts cruelty first object? True, any such program has a potential for abuse. But this is true of many legitimate functions of a state (e.g. overseeing courts, staffing a military, collecting tax revenues), and the proper response is not to eliminate such programs but to provide oversight limiting their abuse. Shklar offers one familiar objection to such programs, declaring that "since good character depends on being self-made, the interference of coercive authorities is inherently self-defeating and destructive,"[9] but this claim is both obscure and controversial. Obscure, because, as I argued in Chapter 3, the basic norms and values we rely on in any task of self-making are taken over from others before we are capable of independent reflection, and so before we have made ourselves into anything at all. Controversial, because on one construal talk about the self-making of character threatens to align Shklar's view with the ideal of liberal autonomy and so position her within just the debate that her approach, and anti-utopianism generally, seek to avoid. Alternatively, if Shklar does not mean to invoke that ideal, there is no reason to deny that substantial self-making is compatible with the directed education just mentioned.[10]

It may be that Shklar believes that any such paternalist program is destined to fail.[11] If so, further argument is needed. One might accept such a claim if one failed to distinguish (1) the idea that state-sponsored coercion or incentives cannot influence belief or character in a predictable direction, from (2) the idea that state-sponsored coercion or incentives are assessable mainly in terms of behavior and not through access to belief or

---

[8] John Kekes, "Cruelty and Liberalism," *Ethics* 106 (July 1996), 834–44.

[9] Shklar, *Ordinary Vices*, 234.

[10] I defend this point in Chapter 9. See also George Sher and William Bennett, "Moral Education and Indoctrination," *Journal of Philosophy* 79 (November 1982), 665–77.

[11] Cf. Amy Gutmann's assertion, endorsing Locke's argument in his *Letter Concerning Toleration*, that "the government should stay out of the business of making people virtuous because the virtue business, managed by the state, is bound to bankruptcy" ("How Limited is Liberal Government?," in *Liberalism Without Illusions: Essays on Liberal Theory and the Political Vision of Judith Shklar*, ed. Bernard Yack [Chicago: Chicago University Press, 1996], 66). For problems with the bankruptcy thesis as it figures in Locke, see Jeremy Waldron, "Toleration and the Rationality of Persecution," in *John Locke: A Letter Concerning Toleration in Focus*, ed. John Horton and Susan Mendus (London: Routledge, 1991), 98–124. On the general role states can play in promoting virtue in citizens, see Robert P. George, *Making Men Moral* (Oxford: Clarendon Press, 1993), esp. ch. 7.

character. The second is broadly true. The first, however, seems unwarranted. Why doubt that broadly backed social policies can shape the norms and values citizens come to hold, especially when communicated through educational programming? If we allow this possibility, the question for the liberalism of fear becomes whether dispositions that would counteract cruelty might be so promoted. It's hard to see either why this question must be off the table or why the answer must confirm strong anti-paternalism.

As a last-ditch effort, the liberalism of fear might offer a slippery-slope argument to the effect that any departure from robust liberal commitments increases the capacity for state cruelty and so should be rejected. But that reply does not succeed for reasons given earlier: there exist many features of the liberal state (any conceivable state, in fact) that increase its ability to act cruelly but against which no sensible objection can be made. Maintaining a police force, a national army, and prisons, for example, makes states more powerful and so increases their capacity for cruelty, but no one seriously argues against them. What the liberalism of fear needs to show is that departing from both the harm principle and anti-paternalism increases the potential for state cruelty in a manner that outweighs the overall threat of cruelty that would otherwise exist. But establishing this as a general claim, given the various ways in which private cruelty can get enacted, is an extremely difficult task, and Shklar's account provides no glimpse as to how such an argument might go.

Even if Shklar could satisfactorily address the worries so far raised, her first claim – that cruelty and the fear it inspires are the worst evil, the prevention of which ought to be the chief desideratum in politics – is problematic as a grounding for liberalism. To see why, consider Yael Tamir's objection that Shklar "takes an overly narrow view" of fear.

Fear has many faces: some have to do with the fear of suffering, of experiencing physical pain or torment; others concern more social fears, like the fear of being marginalized, silenced and ignored. Each of these fears leads in a different political direction. Individuals do not fear only bodily torture and cruelty, they fear social oppression, marginalization and, worst of all, invisibility.[12]

Invoking concerns familiar from debates over multiculturalism, Tamir stresses "the fear of being without status, of lacking recognition both as individuals and as members of a valuable and autonomous human group."[13] One way of taking Tamir's point here is that in concentrating on

---

[12] Yael Tamir, "The Land of the Fearful and the Free," *Constellations* 3 (1997), 302.
[13] Ibid., 301.

the fears that constrain individuals in pursuing their aims and projects, Shklar has ignored the prior goods – self-respect and self-esteem, the sense of membership within a respected cultural group – that enable individuals to see those aims and projects as worth pursuing in the first place. Such attitudes, Tamir suggests, are significantly shaped by interactions occurring in civil society and so not guaranteed by the liberal state Shklar recommends. Tamir thus concludes that any politics grounded in attention to our worst fears should attend to the relative status of various groups within the polity and to the ways marginalization and disrespect threaten human freedom and agency.

Tamir's critique challenges the liberalism of fear on two fronts. First, if politics properly centers on preventing cruelty because of its great threat to human freedom, it may be that familiar liberal commitments should be weakened when doing so would promote the confirmation of social identity Tamir stresses. It is not impossible to derive some support for this position in Shklar's assertion that "the basic units for political life are … the weak and the powerful," for if recognition, status, and the like are central goods over which citizens struggle, perhaps states should take some steps to ensure they are the subject of a fair fight.[14] So long as such measures are not grounded in claims about the intrinsic value of any particular group's ideals, they may be broadly compatible with the familiar liberal ideal of state neutrality. Their implications for defining liberal commitments, however, are uncertain. For example, the claims of groups who find certain forms of expression or behavior especially distressing to their way of life would gain added weight, as would their claims to have their young educated in a strongly paternalist fashion. Though this worry is fairly speculative, it suggests the liberalism of fear may not be able easily to accommodate Tamir's worry.

The deeper problem raised by Tamir's critique concerns its implicit criticism of any approach that seeks both to be grounded in a single value (preventing cruelty) and to accommodate the deep moral diversity of liberal states. For the more we reflect on the various goods and harms that can occur in a life, and on how these are weighted differently within competing normative frameworks, the stronger grow the suspicions that any attempt to identify a single worst evil must presuppose some particular framework and that the degree to which cruelty is bad may thus vary depending on the framework in question. This holds whether we consider the perspective of the recipient or of the dispenser of cruelty. To

---

[14] Shklar, "The Liberalism of Fear," 27.

receive cruelty is no doubt very hard, but is it always worse than exile, say, or the abandonment of one's deepest spiritual commitments, or the conclusion that one's life has no value? From the other side, too, it seems that on some approaches cruelty may be justified by the benefits it brings about either to the recipient or to others. Shklar seems to deny this possibility, but one need not be a moral monster to think that the infliction of physical and emotional pain is warranted for reasons relating either to punishment (retributivist or deterrent-based) or to the benefits of those who receive the cruelty.[15]

The worry here echoes an argument John Kekes has advanced against the liberalism of fear. Though he raises various criticisms, Kekes's deepest objection to building politics around the prevention of the worst evil is that there is no one such thing.

Just as there is no *summum bonum*, so there is no *summum malum* either. There is no doubt that cruelty is very bad, but it is not the worst thing. The worst thing is what causes the most evil [Kekes thinks this is mere tautology: that's his point]. In different circumstances different things will do that. There always is a worst thing, but there is nothing that is always the worst thing.[16]

Kekes's conclusion follows straight from value pluralism.[17] Noncomparability in diverse goods implies noncomparability in diverse evils. This point holds regardless of whether an account of the good determines what is evil, whether the relationship runs in reverse, or whether the two exist in some non-vicious relation in which neither is prior to the other. This might not be a serious problem for the liberalism of fear (granting *arguendo* that liberal regimes best protect against cruelty) if liberal states best protected against the other serious evils, but Shklar provides no such argument, and the heterogeneity of evils makes the point difficult to defend. Added to the doubts already mentioned, this final worry suggests that the anti-utopian defense of liberalism must go a different route.

---

[15] In *Rethinking Multiculturalism* Bikhu Parekh mentions monks who undergo torture and humiliation for reasons of spiritual growth. While their consent makes such cases less troubling, they consent because of what they see as independent reasons recommending such treatment in those contexts.

[16] Kekes, "Cruelty and Liberalism," 843.

[17] Kekes also suggests that the problem follows from strictly deontic considerations as well, since moral judgments always reflect a difficult weighing of "the agent's states of mind, the agent's actions, and the way the actions affect other people." If cruelty is construed in terms of just one or two of these axes, then less cruel acts that do much worse on another axis may be even worse ("Cruelty and Liberalism," 843).

MVL AS SECOND BEST

MVL is a particularist liberalism rooted in two considerations. First is the recognition that many citizens endorse normative frameworks that recommend as ideal illiberal models of political association. Those frameworks may imply, for instance, that persons should be prohibited from pursuing certain misguided goals, or that the state be more active in directing citizens towards specific virtues and goals. Such citizens also understand, however, that many of their fellow citizens do not endorse the particular illiberal vision of the state recommended by their own frameworks. The second consideration is that many citizens see the existence of the state either as an unchangeable fact of modern life or as something that contributes vitally important goods. Persons inhabiting a common world frequently make conflicting claims, face joint tasks, participate in an interdependent economy – in numerous ways come into contact and conflict with each other. If these encounters are to be manageable, stable, and productive, some consistency and uniformity in rules and overall decision-making is necessary. This means that citizens have ample motivation to establish laws and institutions all can agree upon, even if they do not match the ideal arrangements specified by many of their own normative frameworks.

MVL suggests that agreement to liberal terms might thus emerge as a compromise among citizens who recognize the value of ordered political life but realize that the political vision recommended by their distinct normative frameworks cannot be achieved. Here the liberal state appears as a second-best option, grounded on the fact that it offers terms for peaceful social coordination while protecting what William Galston calls citizens' expressive liberty, i.e. their freedom to lead their lives "in accordance with their own understanding of what gives life meaning and value."[18] MVL thus rests on a wager: that citizens will tolerate others' having broad liberties and accept that state power will not be used to advance their particular normative framework, in exchange for the assurance that their own liberties will be protected and that neither they nor their children will be subject to paternalist measures reflecting norms they reject. The wager is not a sure thing. But if it fails, it seems unlikely that agreement can be reached on any other political arrangement, liberal or otherwise.[19]

---

[18] Galston, *Liberal Pluralism*, 3.
[19] One factor increasing the odds of winning this wager is firm protection of a significant realm of discretion in private associations. The implications of this point I pursue in the following two chapters.

For some time MVL has been something of a poor cousin within the liberal family, the result, I suspect, of two factors. One is its association with Hobbesianism – in particular, Hobbes's absolutism and his strong reliance on egoism in his defense of the state.[20] Rejection of these aspects of Hobbes's thought does not, however, undermine the general case for MVL. Regarding absolutism, we should not confuse MVL's account of the central office of the state – i.e. securing terms of peaceful coexistence advantageous to all citizens – with Hobbes's idiosyncratic views on the kind of authority sovereigns must claim to achieve that end, and defenders of MVL can endorse the former while rejecting the latter. The other Hobbes-inspired concern, that MVL rests on egoism, is harder to dispatch, and I shall engage it more fully below. For now, it is enough to note that while Hobbesian contractors appear largely motivated by self-interest, the critic's desire to see political institutions informed by the value framework he endorses reflects not a concern for his own welfare but his belief that those ideals make anyone's life go better. There are no grounds for attributing egoism to the critic from the outset.

If its association with Hobbes is the first factor explaining MVL's relative marginalization within the liberal tradition, the second is the prevalence of a conception of political theory according to which fundamental political principles must be independent of such brute considerations as the existing levels of diversity in a community, specific values of the citizens in question, their willingness to compromise, and so on. To be sure, particularist liberalisms with their attention to social contingencies already depart to some degree from that picture of political theorizing. But MVL goes much further. In its frank reference to the compromises citizens are willing to accept and its inability to show that liberal principles are unconditionally vindicated as a requirement of reason, MVL risks appearing a confession of failure with respect to the task of liberal political philosophy, rather than a position within it.

---

[20] On the subject of absolutism, M. M. Goldsmith has argued that Hobbes's position reflected a mistake in working out the logic inherent in the idea of sovereignty ("Hobbes' 'Mortall God': Is There a Fallacy in Hobbes' Theory of Sovereignty?," *History of Political Thought* 1 [1980], 33–50). Regardless of that theoretical question, the history of ordered states with divided and limited powers strongly undermines Hobbes's claim that anything other than undivided and absolute sovereignty unacceptably risks the return to the state of nature. On the problematic nature of the assumption of egoism, see Thomas Christiano's aptly titled essay "The Incoherence of Hobbesian Justifications of the State," *American Philosophical Quarterly* 31 (January 1994), 23–38. Says Christiano: "Hobbesians do suppose that human beings are self-interested and assume that this is the ultimate basis of normative justification … Hobbesians understand human beings to be primarily, if not exclusively, self-interested. Humans pursue actions which benefit themselves and not other people" (24).

A main goal of my argument below is to challenge that judgment and rehabilitate modus vivendi liberalism as a viable option in political theory. For though dissatisfaction with the liberalisms discussed in my earlier chapters has of late spurred greater interest in the idea of defending liberal states via modus vivendi reasoning, MVL largely remains, as Patrick Neal has suggested, "the creation of its critics," mentioned most often chiefly to show the superiority of some other view.[21] This chapter seeks more constructively to outline an attractive version of modus vivendi liberalism.

Before turning to that, however, I must address an important ambiguity in the very notion of modus vivendi liberalism: should MVL be understood chiefly as a distinctive way of defending a familiar vision of the liberal state, or does the modus vivendi approach instead generate a liberal state that in important ways differs from that which other liberals have advanced? If we concentrate on the twin structural commitments advanced in Chapter 1 as distinctive of the liberal project (i.e. the harm principle and the prohibition on state paternalism), MVL appears simply as a different way of defending the familiar social world endorsed by liberals. But with respect to a range of other matters MVL has implications that sharply depart from other liberal theories – in terms both of what it demands (in particular, greater tolerance for the norms and practices of diverse groups in various contexts) and of what it leaves to citizens to work out through political deliberations (most notably, MVL does not by itself yield any highly articulated account of social justice). Adequately treating all such points of departure is an important project I shall not undertake here, though in Chapters 8 and 9 I shall trace out the implications of MVL in two specific areas of public controversy. In this chapter I want to present only the broad conceptual outlines of the MVL model. I shall do this by taking up in turn the three most urgent questions it raises.

1. What are the limits of toleration for MVL, and what sorts of reasons can it invoke to answer this question?
2. Does MVL recommend delegating authority in ways that allow smaller groups to override distinctive liberal commitments, or does it call for universal adherence among all citizens to those commitments?
3. How far is MVL consistent with the liberal ideal of justification captured in JR?

---

[21] Patrick Neal, *Liberalism and its Discontents* (New York: New York University Press, 1997), 191. Along with Neal's book, recent approaches sympathetic to the modus vivendi account are offered by John Gray, *Two Faces of Liberalism* (New York: New Press, 2000), Chandran Kukathas, *The Liberal Archipelago* (New York: Oxford University Press, 2003), and Stuart Hampshire, *Justice is Conflict* (Princeton: Princeton University Press, 2000).

THE LIMITS OF TOLERATION AND
MINIMAL UNIVERSALISM

Any state must establish the boundaries of acceptable conduct and so draw limits to toleration. We can distinguish two ways it might do this. First, it might consider solely the requirements of civil order and forgo appeal to moral ideals: only behavior or practices that significantly disrupt social order may be constrained or prohibited. The other approach (which need not exclude considerations relating to civil order) limits the tolerable by appealing, in part at least, to independent moral norms. The version of MVL I am advancing follows the second route. But since the first may initially seem the more natural path for a modus vivendi liberalism grounded in the fact of moral disagreement, it is important to see where it goes wrong.

We can do so by considering Chandran Kukathas's carefully worked out defense of that approach. The role of the state, he says, is "to preserve the order in which [diverse] groups can coexist ... Its purpose is simply to preserve order so that people might live freely together."[22] Kukathas gives three reasons for this emphasis on social order. First, and most obviously, an ordered social world provides a secure environment within which individuals can pursue their goals. Second, appealing to moral ideals as grounds for limiting toleration is likely to undermine social order. "The state should not be concerned about anything except order or peace ... The danger in its attempting to do more is, in part, that it may fall down in its primary role."[23] Social harmony is better promoted by forswearing potentially divisive ideals and concentrating on a goal of obvious value to all. Third, since human reason does not vindicate any single moral value that might be invoked to limit toleration beyond the good of social order, the state can have no justification for constraining behavior beyond those requirements.

Kukathas realizes that on his account the liberal state must permit a range of patently objectionable practices, and in a strong critique Brian Barry has argued that this permissiveness constitutes a virtual *reductio* of Kukathas's argument.[24] For the moment I shall largely bypass their debate, however, because I believe that Kukathas's attempt to rely on the goal of social order to the exclusion of substantive moral ideals is not

---

[22] Kukathas, *The Liberal Archipelago*, 213. Or again: "The task of politics is to work out how ... communities can coexist. The task of political philosophy in these circumstances is to offer an account of the kind of social and political order this involves" (189).

[23] Ibid., 252.

[24] Brian Barry, *Culture and Equality* (Cambridge, MA: Harvard University Press, 2001), 143ff.

just pragmatically dubious, but theoretically problematic in at least three respects. Showing this makes clear why no defense of MVL can avoid moral ideals.

First, the very notion of social order involves not just empirical claims but normative ones as well. No state of affairs announces its own description. Where some see a socially ordered community, for example, others see the forcible imposition of terms masking deep social discord.[25] Just as judging some behavior to be rude presumes a standard of manners, so too does the judgment whether social order is in place reflect one's own distinct critera for such assessments. Second, as I argued in Chapter 5, even if citizens endorsing different moral frameworks agree on what constitutes social order, they may value that goal differently relative to other ideals. In assuming the overriding value of civil order, then, Kukathas is not finding a position outside of the controversies that divide citizens but occupying a position within them.

The most serious flaw with the social order approach, however, is that any such argument must connect social order with certain human goods and in doing so invoke just the sort of contested moral claims whose avoidance motivates that approach in the first place. This becomes clear when we consider Kukathas's response to the objection that his approach, which Ronald Dworkin dubs the "checkerboard" approach, is incompatible with the integrity any legitimate polity requires.

[*Pace* Dworkin,] the checkerboard solution is a principled solution to the problem of disagreement over fundamental questions of morality that might be found in any political society. Although Dworkin believes that "we" need to work out what "we" think, given what "our instincts" condemn, the fact is that we have different instincts; and the problem is what to do when they do thus differ. In these circumstances one obvious, plausible, and not unprincipled solution is to agree to differ, and to allow different standards to prevail in different parts of the country, living under different political authorities. More than this, "integrity" is not a plausible ideal in a society in which there is any significant measure of ethical diversity.[26]

What makes Kukathas's solution principled is its grounding in the idea, defended at great length in an early chapter of his book, that nothing is more important for persons than being free to live in accordance with

[25] Both John Gray and Alasdair MacIntyre, for example, have likened life in contemporary liberal states to the conditions of civil war. See Gray, *Enlightenment's Wake: Politics and Culture at the close of the Modern Age* (New York: Routledge, 1995), 77, and MacIntyre, *After Virtue*, 2nd edn. (Notre Dame, IN: University of Notre Dame Press, 1984), 253.
[26] Kukathas, *The Liberal Archipelago*, 180.

their deepest values. But this, of course, is itself a substantive moral claim, rejected by many. So even if Kukathas is right to defend it, its foundational place within his own argument shows that the good of social order cannot be the chief consideration *all the way down*.[27]

The fact that no appeal to social order can avoid relying on substantive moral claims would be fatal to MVL if it ruled out such claims. But it does not. What distinguishes MVL as I understand it is not its rejection of moral ideals, but instead its commitment to minimal moral universalism grounded in a presumption that the interests of all persons matter equally. By minimal universalism I have in mind a position recently endorsed by such theorists as Bikhu Parekh, Michael Walzer, and Stuart Hampshire, which distinguishes relatively thick moral ideas, embedded in distinct ways of life and views of the good, from thin ideas endorsed by any decent way of life.[28] That liberal democracy is the only legitimate form of government, that capital punishment is cruel, that political institutions should be resolutely neutral regarding religions – these are relatively thick ideas, endorsed by some viewpoints but rejected by others. That rulers ought in some way to be accountable to the ruled, that punishment should be appropriate to the crime, that no person should be forced to worship in a manner they reject – these are thin moral values that any morally decent person must endorse. While people can reasonably differ over the content of thick morality, they cannot plausibly deny the requirements of thin morality. The latter constitute a core set of human rights which the MVL state is committed to protect and which draw the limits of the tolerable. They rule out such evils as slavery and severe or permanent bodily harm, while guaranteeing access to such things as education, basic physical and psychological needs, and security.[29]

---

[27] Kukathas's desire to downplay his own reliance on controversial moral ideals may explain the occurrence of an otherwise puzzling moment in his argument. Immediately after suggesting that the right to exit one's group is the fundamental right in liberalism, he asserts that no one has a fundamental claim upon others to ensure that he can leave a group. This is puzzling because one would think that having a basic right implies duties on others to help secure it and so entails the fundamental claim Kukathas denies. Kukathas appears to defend his position here by mentioning that people disagree over what others are and are not owed. But unless he is suggesting that failure to recognize another's basic right relieves one of the duties that right imposes, the fact that some don't recognize the fundamental right to exit is irrelevant to whether others have a claim on them to be able to leave. See *The Liberal Archipelago*, 96–7.

[28] See Parekh, *Rethinking Multiculturalism*; Michael Walzer, *Thick and Thin: Moral Argument at Home and Abroad* (Notre Dame, IN: Notre Dame University Press, 1994); and Hampshire, *Justice is Conflict* and *Innocence and Experience*. Though Parekh criticizes minimal universalism as not adequately sensitive to the need for cross-cultural dialogue, his own position seems to me more a particular version of minimal universalism than an alternative to it.

[29] For greater detail, see Parekh's account in *Rethinking Multiculturalism*, 131–6.

Minimal universalism immediately invites two important questions. How do we identify the thin content of morality, and why should we attribute greater authority to the thin than the thick? These questions are especially pressing if one thinks morality has a structure in which the thin is somehow foundational, with the thick content derived therefrom, perhaps by a series of logical inferences, or by uncovering allegedly logical preconditions for the thin. On that sort of approach minimal universalism will seem unduly anemic. But we needn't understand minimal universalism this way. Richard Tuck, for example, has argued that the earliest advocates of human rights – Grotius and his seventeenth-century heirs – conceived of rights not as foundational in the way just described, i.e. as such that analysis of them would entail the thick content, but simply as constituting the shared ground (Tuck employs the metaphor of a Venn diagram) that allowed for the creation of a satisfactory common life despite ongoing thick disagreement.[30] Faced with the task of identifying norms that could both underwrite a viable community and be morally acceptable to persons embracing diverse value frameworks, the questions of deriving the thick from the thin or determining their relative priority just didn't arise.

It might seem that this approach renders basic rights hostage to the contingencies of existing citizens' value systems and so fails to capture our sense of their special status and urgency. The first reply to this worry is that it simply does not follow that if minimal rights cannot be employed to yield robust derivations they are therefore any less urgent. Questions of derivation and of urgency are just orthogonal to one another. Nor does the fact that we identify those rights through appeal to existing consensus weaken their force. One might think this if one so rigidly separated the normative and the descriptive as to believe that our notions of human rights must be worked out entirely at the level of philosophical reflection, independent of encounters with diverse ways of life. But it is bizarre to think that our conception of the most urgent moral requirements applying to all persons should be indifferent either to the judgments about such questions that other human beings have reached or to the range of goals they have pursued. Surely consensus across human communities on such

---

[30] "The fact that they were shared in this way did not mean, however, that this common set of moral beliefs was foundational to all the agent's other beliefs, nor that the common beliefs were to be understood as a different *kind* of belief from the others. Rather, it was simply that there were some human needs which were so universal that all societies would have to recognize them in some fashion, and others which were not" (Richard Tuck, "Rights and Pluralism," in *Philosophy in an Age of Pluralism: The Philosophy of Charles Taylor in Question*, ed. James Tully [Cambridge: Cambridge University Press, 1994], 165).

notions provides some evidence that those judgments are in fact correct. This strategy no doubt has its pitfalls – it's not clear, for example, whether Tuck's approach would in the seventeenth century have yielded norms adequately capturing the rights of women – but gross abuses would be kept in check by the insistence on equality of moral status (functioning here, again, as a presupposition of minimal universalism) in conjunction with the ideal of minimal personhood outlined in Chapter 3.

A deeper worry about minimal universalism concerns its compatibility with value pluralism and moral diversity. This worry can be pressed from three directions. First, it might be said that since universal values get concretized in a range of ways (i.e. what constitutes physical injury, humiliating treatment, and so on), minimal universalism in practice must either be impotent or involve an unwarranted imposition of one normative framework over another. Second, some may worry that minimal universalism prohibits the free choices of persons who wish to forgo basic rights out of commitment to a set of ideals: Parekh mentions priests who undergo torture or consent to public degradation for reasons of spiritual growth. Finally, it can be argued that even if different ways of life recognize the value of the elements of minimal universalism, they may still believe that some particular value is outweighed by others that would be threatened by protecting it. What reasons can the MVL state then give for protecting the minimal right over the group's opposition?[31]

In response to the first concern, minimal universalism recognizes both that dialogue across normative frameworks is often needed to determine the meaning of specific practices and that public policy should strive to be flexible enough to register these variations. Granted, no foolproof procedure exists for resolving such matters. But this does not willy-nilly open the gates to relativism. To recognize that values can be instantiated in various ways is not to say that all behavior can reasonably be so described. Just as the wife-beater cannot plausibly claim that battery and abuse are ways of expressing love, so too there are limits on the sorts of practices that can be defended as ways of showing respect, of promoting psychological and physical health, and so on. As for the second objection, minimal universalism does not apply to persons who, like the priests Parekh mentions, welcome evils like torture and public degradation. Its chief concern is with *unwanted* evils, and the principle *volenti non fit injuria* surely removes much of what's morally troubling about such instances.[32]

---

[31] Parekh advances the first and second worries in *Rethinking Multiculturalism*, 135–6. John Gray advances the third in *Two Faces of Liberalism*, 66–7.

[32] Much, not all. See the discussion of false consciousness in Chapter 8 below.

The third objection, i.e. that minimal universalism fails because diverse value schemes will weigh the core universal values differently, is the most challenging. Imagine a group that recognizes education as a good, or sees the value in a young person's free choice of a spouse, but nonetheless believes that securing such goods for all members will undermine other goods especially important within that group's framework – cultural cohesiveness and tradition, for example, or extended family structures bolstered by the practice of arranged marriage. Even if these values are in principle compossible (under a different normative framework), the group may claim that they are not compatible in their particular way of life, which manifests their own expressive liberty. The challenge such groups present is two-fold. First, the pluralist account of choice among non-comparables provides some *prima facie* legitimacy to the claims of such groups. Second, even if a group's claim for noncomparability is flawed, showing this would seem to enmesh MVL in moral argument at a level far thicker than I have allowed.

Though advocates of minimal universalism cannot ignore the force of the challenge here, there are several replies they can offer. To begin with, though some groups may see a conflict between the demands of minimal universalism and their own distinct values, they are not necessarily right.[33] When ruthless despots claim that civil order can be maintained only through secret death squads, for example, the proper reply is not to weigh the goods and harms but to reject the presentation of options. Similarly, claims that educating certain members of a group or abolishing arranged marriages will lead to the destruction of a cherished way of life need to be carefully scrutinized – the more so as they raise concerns about the group's commitment to moral equality and often serve to protect the privileged position of those who advance them.

The sort of conflict just noted – between civil rights and economic growth, say, or education and group traditions – we might call contingent: since the goods in question are logically distinct, we cannot know *a priori* how far protecting one will threaten the other. I just argued that when the claimed threat is specious, the objection to minimal universalism disappears. But conflicts can also be conceptual in nature, as when minimal universalism identifies an interest that some group sees as intrinsically at odds with its norms. For example, some group may believe that God forbids the formal education of girls or certain forms of medical intervention to protect basic health. Claims of conceptual conflict are

---

[33] Parekh points this out in assessing the claim that China's economic development justifies constraints on civil rights (*Rethinking Multiculturalism*, 140).

sometimes mistaken – this may have been the case when Anglican church members objected that the ordination of women could not be reconciled with Anglican values and traditions – but often they are not. Often, too, it is a matter for the group to decide. In these cases, as in those where a group's claims for a contingent conflict are well grounded, the task of reconciling MVL with particular group norms is more difficult.

Nonetheless, we can identify three factors that recommend protecting the core good identified by minimal universalism and disallowing the sort of trade-offs, in the name of pluralism, just discussed. The first is a showing that the right in question connects to other recognized core interests. Much empirical work, for example, draws a connection between levels of education and physical health and longevity.[34] If it turned out that rates of physical abuse are significantly higher in arranged marriages, such a finding would play a similar role. In such cases the cumulative weight of interconnected core goods strengthens the case for overriding a group's objections.

A second consideration is the requirement that the practices allegedly threatened by minimal universalism reflect persons' equal moral status. Since the value pluralism I have defended assumes moral equality, it recognizes noncomparability in the goods a person might choose but does not license denying one person a good because another whose interests count more can thereby gain something of incomparable value. To be sure, it is sometimes difficult to distinguish cases where a good is denied to a person from cases where that person achieves a different, noncomparable good. This challenge is especially urgent in the context of gender equality, the subject of the following chapter. But if (as I argue there) we can articulate reasonably objective criteria with which to assess claims of moral equality, this would further defend minimal universalism against the pluralist worry.

Finally, the case for minimal universalism is bolstered by the built-in demands of any political community with a recognized final authority. Recall that the case for MVL rests largely on the benefits to all citizens of a common political system addressing shared tasks: not just maintaining security, publicizing common rules, and ensuring legal resolution of

---

[34] See Adriana Lleras-Muney, "The Relationship between Education and Adult Mortality in the US," *Review of Economic Studies* 72, no. 1 (January 2005), 189–221; Anne Case, "Health, Income and Economic Development," *Annual World Bank Conference on Development Economics 2001/2002*, ed. B. Pleskovic and N. Stern (Washington DC: World Bank, 2002), 221–41; and John C. Caldwell, "Routes to Low Mortality in Poor Countries," *Population and Development Review* 12 (1986), 171–220.

conflict, but also building the roads, providing affordable electricity, coordinating a money economy, and so on. It is not hard to see how securing the rights specified by minimal universalism would strengthen such a system: mandating education helps yield more gifted persons to occupy various roles within that system, informs citizens of its requirements and expectations, and promotes oversight of governing institutions; meeting basic physical and mental needs increases citizens' productivity and minimizes later health-related expenses that might fall on the state; and so on. Since the assumption behind MVL is that citizens recognize the benefits of an ordered political life, it follows that they have reason to support measures that strengthen it irrespective of other objections they may have. This again undercuts claims for exceptions to minimal universalism.

SUBSIDIARITY V. MODERATE CENTRALISM

The second critical question raised by MVL concerns the general vision of political life the modus vivendi approach recommends. The main issue here concerns the distinction between two such models. On what I shall call the subsidiarity model, political authority is parceled out to smaller locales and jurisdictions in a manner that tolerates departures from the liberal commitments to the harm principle and anti-paternalism. Most subsidiary theorists allow that any such devolution of jurisdictional authority would still be limited by the requirements of minimal universalism. But since neither the maximal zone of Millean liberty nor being free from paternalistic efforts qualifies as a minimal human right, the subsidiarity account of MVL denies that the two central commitments of the liberal state carry universal authority within its borders.[35] The second

---

[35] Versions of subsidiarity have been advanced recently by Kukathas, Galston, and Parekh. Kukathas rejects even the minimal universalism I have defended, acknowledging that his argument "gives a great deal of authority to cultural communities" and grants them "a considerable amount of power over the individuals who constitute their membership" (*The Liberal Archipelago*, 117, 127). Galston, though far less permissive than Kukathas, also endorses the "differentiation" that allows for more local solutions to controversies ("Two Concepts of Liberalism," 530). His endorsement of what he calls "nonchoice societies," which should not be compelled "to recognize the authority of negative liberty over their own constitutive values," also seems to qualify the extent of the harm principle (*Liberal Pluralism*, 54: see also 28, n. 1, which appears to endorse restrictions on those liberties that do not "stand in a significant relation to living our identity"). Parekh defends restrictions on free speech in *Rethinking Multiculturalism*, ch. 10, and though he does not explicitly relate that defense to his general endorsement of subsidiarity, the connection is a natural one. For a brief but helpful overview of the subsidiarity principle, see Robert P. George, "Natural Law and International Order," in *International Society*, ed. David Mapel and Terry Nardin (Princeton: Princeton University Press, 1998), 64ff.

model, which I shall call moderate centralism, demands universal adherence to the defining liberal commitments and forbids any local departures from either.

To see how these approaches differ, consider a community where some citizens wish to prohibit certain modes of behavior or forms of expression that they deem blasphemous, or one whose residents want to install in public schools a curriculum promoting particular values rooted in a widely endorsed normative framework. The subsidiary approach recommends leaving such decisions up to the citizens involved, even if the outcome constrains liberty or constitutes paternalism. Moderate centralism rejects out of hand such outcomes.

At first glance the subsidiarity approach seems the more natural extension of MVL. Tolerating smaller units of decision-making allows for greater diversity in the norms and practices under which individuals lead their lives and, in shrinking the number of citizens who need to agree on potentially divisive issues, seems more likely to promote civil peace. But despite its intuitive appeal, it is open to various objections that collectively make it a less attractive option, given the concerns of MVL, than a moderate centralism firmly committed to the harm principle and anti-paternalism. To show this, I shall first present the drawbacks to the subsidiarity approach and then defend moderate centralism against various prominent objections.

The problems with subsidiarity

The subsidiarity approach has three serious flaws. First, it entrenches citizens' disagreements with one another and so impedes consensus on moral ideals. Though MVL begins in recognition of deep moral diversity among citizens, it does not endorse that diversity as either intrinsically good or preferable to conditions where citizens endorse common values. In more strongly insulating local communities against alien ideals, the subsidiarity approach reduces the degree to which citizens might engage with and respond to alternative frameworks of value. It responds to disputes over values, but does not create conditions conducive to their resolution. Its greater deference to local norms also makes it more likely to foster a dynamic that Ayelet Shachar has called "reactive culturalism," wherein groups have incentive to adopt rigid understandings of their identities in ways that stress their differences from other citizens. One needn't be nostalgic for some lost spirit of *Gemeinschaft* to recognize that citizens can deal with common challenges more efficiently and harmoniously the more they share common goals and values, and even though the MVL state cannot compel that goal, it counts against subsidiarity that it hampers it.[36]

A second problem is that the general concern to protect liberty, which underlies much of the argument for subsidiarity, logically drives its advocates to a universal commitment to liberty along lines captured in the harm principle. Consider, for example, Parekh's discussion of arranged marriage. Parekh argues that the ideal of choosing one's own spouse has only parochial validity, appropriate to societies emphasizing individual choice but without universal authority.[37] He also insists, however, that no one may be coerced into marriage and that states must not allow such marriages. Now if we ask why the state should disallow those marriages, note that Parekh cannot reply that choosing one's own spouse is a core human interest that falls under minimal universalism, for that ideal, he has said, is parochial. His objection to coerced marriages thus ends up invoking a very liberal ideal of individual choice. "If young Asians are happy for their parents to choose or help them choose their spouses, they have chosen to be chosen or co-chosen for, and their choices should be respected."[38] Parekh thinks his view contrasts with the liberal ideal of marriage because he thinks that ideal implies a value at odds with entering into arranged marriages. But it does not. What liberal states protect is marriage between consenting adults (and any number of other acts) on whatever grounds consenting persons find acceptable (romantic love, cultural continuity, religious reasons, etc.). That he is willing to override group norms that deny the importance of a freedom which even Parekh grants is not of universal importance shows that his account implies a strong commitment to personal liberty along lines moderate centralism recommends.

A similar dynamic occurs in Kukathas's argument. Kukathas's strong commitment to subsidiarity leads him to conclude that communities may prohibit homosexuality. This view, he concedes, seems to create a problem for him: after all, he repeatedly stresses the incomparable value of persons' being free to pursue their deepest values, and in such a community homosexuals are prevented from doing just this. To resolve the

---

[36] In *Political Liberalism*, 159ff., Rawls outlines one route whereby the MVL state might move to greater moral consensus. The term "reactive culturalism" comes from Ayelet Shachar, *Multicultural Jurisdictions* (Cambridge: Cambridge University Press, 2001), 35.

[37] "Marriage may be arranged or self-determined, romantic or non-romantic, love-based, duty-based or a matter of convenience … [and] we should be as neutral as possible between these forms" (Parekh, *Rethinking Multiculturalism*, 286).

[38] Ibid., 275.

problem, Kukathas argues that since, on his model, persons are subject only to those authorities to which they acquiesce, homosexuals who would be constrained by such a law can always remove themselves from that community and live freely someplace else. The solution doesn't work, however, for the simple fact that exit from one community likely renders a person not free of any authority but subject to a different one. To put the point in terms of Kukathas's archipelago metaphor, one cannot live at sea but must come ashore somewhere.[39] One may live according to conscience, then, only if there exists (as there may not) an available community that protects that freedom. But this, I suggest, is just to deny a right to live according to conscience. To assert a basic right is not to describe what one may do if the world is a certain way. It is rather to denote a state of affairs that ought to exist, and which should be brought about if it does not. As with Parekh, then, Kukathas's own argument calls for a universal commitment to Millean liberty at odds with his brief for subsidiarity.[40]

I have been speaking as though communities were clearly delineated from one another, exiting one to join another a rather neat affair. But such demarcations are often anything but clear, exit rarely so tidy. This brings us to the third and most serious flaw in the subsidiarity approach. It is a plain fact that in societies where the MVL approach is most appropriate, the coexisting communities generally lack the degree of territorial concentration needed to make subsidiarity coherent and workable. In this respect it is revealing that Kukathas frequently likens liberal society to the international community and suggests the liberal state should allow its constituent groups the same freedom to organize their internal affairs that states allow one another in the international realm. But the analogy is strained, and not just because the Westphalian model it assumes has increasingly come under attack. The larger issue is that inter-state tolerance is greatly facilitated by the fact that citizens in different regimes have little daily intercourse with one another, do not fall under the same governing institutions, are not taxed by the same bodies, do not participate immediately in a common economy – in countless ways are disconnected from one another. The significant level of interaction among citizens of

---

[39] As Kukathas recognizes: "Freedom of exit is fundamental. What is not easily avoided, however, is exit beyond the realm of *any* authority" (*The Liberal Archipelago*, 143). The passage suggests that Kukathas has misspoken here, and that he has written "avoided" where the word he wants is something like "achieved."

[40] Kukathas could escape the problem by permitting anti-homosexual legislation only if there exists some other community where homosexuals can live freely, but I believe he would reject this solution as a constraint on associational freedom.

a single state, however, greatly complicates subsidiarity's commitment to jurisdictional independence.

A good example of this problem is found in Kukathas's discussion of Indian communities in England.[41] There he makes the important acknowledgment that cultural groups who choose to interact with the wider society around them – for example, by owning property, trading with other citizens, and availing themselves of public services – thereby become part of what he calls "the larger legal and political order," and as such become subject to the political norms of the wider society, even to the point that they may challenge their own community's rulings in the name of the wider society's law. Taking as his example a community where coerced marriage is legitimate, Kukathas writes that if the community has "settled in the midst of English society," it cannot demand recognition of those marriages by a wider society that judges such marriages illegitimate. But once granted, this general point cannot be contained. It logically extends to the case of a landlord who refuses to rent to homosexual couples, a storeowner who refuses to hire women, and so on. Even if such persons are members of groups wishing to live under their own norms, their involvement in a common system places them under whatever laws govern that wider political order. If, as MVL posits, liberal principles are what a diverse citizenry is most likely to agree to as governing their interactions, then Kukathas's subsidiarity approach in practice ends up quite close to the moderate centralism I am endorsing.

Some may reply that my final objection, because it points to the contingent fact of territorial integration, does not show the subsidiarity approach *per se* to be mistaken. My objection does not, for instance, apply to conditions where groups are geographically concentrated and have little interaction with one another. This I concede. But it is a weakness in my objection only if one assumes that recommendations about the structure of the MVL state should be independent of the actual conditions obtaining within any political community. That assumption should be rejected, partly for reasons I offer when discussing justification below, and partly for reasons John Gray has advanced: conditions of diversity are themselves diverse, and the political arrangements that promote a morally acceptable social order must be sensitive to particular challenges on the ground.[42] My argument for moderate centralism is aimed at polities

---

[41] Kukathas, *The Liberal Archipelago*, 144.
[42] Gray, *Two Faces of Liberalism*, 126–31. Gray argues that in a state where groups are moved by long-standing ill-will and suspicions, and reside in clearly demarcated geographical regions, modus vivendi reasoning may not recommend the centralist approach I've outlined here and

where citizens endorsing divergent moral frameworks live and work along-side one another and where sufficient diversity exists to prevent any one group from easily imposing its will on the polity as a whole. This is a fair description of many existing states inhabited by the critic I've imagined throughout. Politics is the art of the possible, and political theory shows us which of the possibilities we should work to bring about. But what those are, theory does not determine.[43]

The case for moderate centralism

Having identified various problems in the subsidiarity approach, I want now to bolster the case for moderate centralism by addressing three objections frequently raised against it. The first is that moderate centralism, in refusing to compromise either the harm principle or the prohibition on paternalism, aligns with a rights-based approach inimical to what John Gray calls "the recurrent renegotiation of interests and values [that] is necessary for any sustainable modus vivendi."[44] The absolute character of rights claims means that attendant conflicts become winner-take-all battles, and this ill serves the goal of peaceful coexistence. Rights-based centralism thus fosters not an ordered social world, but "a sort of low-intensity civil war."[45] Gray endorses instead an explicitly "political model, in which these liberties and equalities cannot be made fixed or determinate *by any theory or legalist device*, but are themselves changeable episodes in political conflict and the result of provisional political settlements."[46]

may instead suggest significant devolution of authority on to discrete territories, or even the imposition of terms by outside powers.

[43] The idea that answers to important questions of political morality can vary depending on contingent matters may disturb liberals who favor theoretical purism. But on A. John Simmons's reading, the germ of the idea goes back at least to Locke. According to Simmons, Locke believed that "one is permitted to decline to join oneself to even those morally acceptable arrangements that are essential to the well-being of others, provided only that one's participation in those arrangements is not necessary to their success" (*Justification and Legitimacy: Essays on Rights and Obligations* [New York: Cambridge University Press, 2001], 138). This means that the permissibility of opting out depends in part on how many others want to do the same and how damaging one's opting out will be to the overall arrangement. These questions theory does not answer. Jeffrey Spinner-Halev makes a similar point when discussing modified citizenship status for those who reject the terms of liberal association (*Surviving Diversity: Religion and Democratic Citizenship* [Baltimore: Johns Hopkins University Press, 2000], 105).

[44] Gray, *Two Faces of Liberalism*, 108.

[45] Gray, *Enlightenment's Wake*, 77. Elsewhere he calls this approach "an ideological rationale for social division and cultural warfare" ("Two Liberalisms of Fear," *Hedgehog Review* 2 [Spring 2000], 15).

[46] Gray, *Enlightenment's Wake*, 67 (my emphasis). See also his claim that political reasoning is "essentially circumstantial," and that its goal is the provisional resolution of conflict "in a political settlement that encompasses a compromise among conflicting interests and ideals" (74, 77).

As the underlined phrase makes clear, Gray faults rights-based legalism as both theoretically flawed, because it overlooks pluralist incommensurability, and politically ineffective. But these criticisms, I believe, need to be kept firmly distinct; for even if advocates of rights-based liberalism have been blind to the theory of value pluralism, that approach may nonetheless offer the best chance for civil peace within a deeply divided polity. Indeed, there are two reasons to think that it may be more effective in this respect than the political process Gray endorses.

The first is that rights are more flexible than Gray suggests. As evidence of this point, consider the failed nomination in 1987 of Robert Bork to the US Supreme Court. Bork's defeat reflected several factors, but central was his widely reported denial that the US Constitution recognized a substantial right to privacy. As a matter of legal interpretation, Bork's claim was both plausible and carefully reasoned. But it was deeply at odds with the widespread beliefs, firmly enshrined within the United States' current legal and political culture, that privacy is a central human right and that the Constitution protects such rights. Even a rights-based centralism will thus inevitably reflect changing attitudes about important human interests and how they can be harmed.[47] Rights are more plastic than Gray suggests.

Still, it cannot be denied that once a conception of human interests has been concretized into a set of human rights, it becomes far more difficult for political negotiation to effect change in those areas. But this leads to the second response to Gray's critique: for while he considers this inertia a failing in rights-based centralism, it is better seen as a strength. Among citizens who endorse diverse value frameworks, a state that abjures rights-talk and leaves individual protections subject to political negotiation is more likely to encourage suspicion and competition among citizens, who will then have more both to gain and to lose in political decision-making. The relative fixity of rights helps create unambiguous boundaries for the exercise of political power, precluding the divisiveness that might otherwise ensue. So long as enough citizens find their expressive liberty

---

[47] Stephen Macedo makes a similar point. "It cannot be claimed," he says, "that our Constitution (or any other) managed to 'fix, once and for all, the content of basic rights and liberties.' The contours of every one of our most basic liberties remain a matter of lively disagreement … The Constitution did not so much settle as frame an ongoing debate about the bounds between individual liberty and government power" ("The Politics of Justification," *Political Theory* 18 [May 1990], 287). The inner quotation is from John Rawls, "The Idea of an Overlapping Consesus," *Oxford Journal of Legal Studies* 7 (1987), 1–25. See also the essay by Macedo and Leif Wenar, "The Diversity of Rights in Contemporary Ethical and Political Thought," in *The Nature of Rights at the American Founding and Beyond*, ed. Barry Shain (Charlottesville, VA: University of Virginia Press, 2007), 280–302.

adequately protected and can lead the lives they wish with the freedoms MVL secures (this, recall, is the wager on which MVL hinges), this stability will be valued.

A second objection to moderate centralism is that the more expansive the authority of a central state, the more citizens' deepest identities must be purged of cultural, religious, and moral distinctions, and the more they must instead see themselves as defined by their common status as liberal citizens. Parekh, for example, worries that the conception of the modern state paradigmatic in political theory expects citizens

> to privilege their territorial over their other identities; to consider what they share in common as citizens far more important than what they share with other members of their religious, cultural, and other communities; to define themselves and relate to each other as individuals; to abstract away their religious, cultural, and other views when conducting themselves as citizens ... In short, the state expects all its citizens to subscribe to an identical way of defining themselves and relating to each other and the state.[48]

This demand is both unreasonable and unrealistic: subsidiarity better respects citizens' distinctive identities.

Though Parekh identifies a genuine concern, the level of identification moderate centralism requires on the MVL approach is neither deep nor objectionable. To be sure, it does demand a common identification in some respects: all should see themselves, for example, as persons who do not harm others, who ensure their children are healthy and educated, who obey the laws of their community, and so on.[49] What worries Parekh is the demand that citizens collectively identify in a more profound way, such that they see liberal principles as an extension of their shared deepest values. That demand is indeed unreasonable. But the MVL defense of moderate centralism does not require it. It asks only that they accept those principles as constitutive of a shared political life that is the best compromise they could reasonably hope to bring about. The demand that

---

[48] Parekh, *Rethinking Multiculturalism*, 184. Kukathas similarly objects that the arguments of Ronald Dworkin and the early Rawls demand that citizens' deepest self-understandings be bound up in the principles defining their political community (*The Liberal Archipelago*, 189ff.). See also Charles Larmore's criticism of Rawls's early work for what he calls its expressivist strain, i.e. its suggestion that the "political order must express our personal ideal, in the sense that its highest ideal must mirror or coincide with what are in general our deepest commitments" (*Patterns of Moral Complexity*, 91).

[49] A similar ambiguity arises in Parekh's claim that "liberals insist that all citizens should define themselves in individualist terms" (*Rethinking Multiculturalism*, 184–5). Yes and no: yes, if one wishes to press a claim of assault against another person; no, if one is deciding what's best for one's family or church. We should not think that because the state treats citizens as individual units it therefore demands they see themselves this way all the time (or even most of the time).

through political life they will come to know a good in common greater than they can know alone (to borrow Michael Sandel's phrase) is on MVL put by for another time.

The final objection to moderate centralism raises the greatest fears but is also the hardest to assess. It is that granting a central state power beyond minimal universalism brings further areas of citizens' lives under its authority and so invites a range of intrusive measures likely to undermine their well-being. In its most extreme form, the specter is raised of the plenipotentiary state, which bestows on the elements of civil society (families, cultural groups, churches, commercial enterprises, etc.) whatever rights and privileges they possess.[50] Kukathas cites a former Australian government's policy, grounded explicitly on moral considerations, of removing Aboriginal children from their natural parents and placing them with white families, with inevitably horrible consequences. This is, Kukathas suggests, just a particularly dramatic example of a harm much more likely with a more centralized state than a subsidiarity approach.

Whatever force this objection has rests on the idea that in conceiving of state authority we must choose between (1) an intrusive statism and (2) an approach that recognizes some domains of human interaction as in principle beyond such authority. Neither view is attractive, however, and rejecting one does not entail endorsing the other. Here I shall simply assume that option 1 is unacceptable and that important goods like religious community, family life, and productive commerce are possible only if the state allows citizens significant liberties in these areas. But option 2 – that certain domains are in principle beyond the state's authority – sounds much more plausible. Since its appeal fuels the final objection, I must explain how it misleads.

Its central mistake is to imagine that there are areas of human activity (e.g. child-rearing, religious worship, schooling, married life) in which the intrusion of outside agents is in principle always wrong. There is no such area: we can always imagine cases where interference is warranted. Parents can discipline with brutal beatings, and religious rituals threaten public health; schools can brainwash, and husbands batter wives. If persons have rights under minimal universalism to be free from such harms, intervention to prevent them will be justified. It would, however, be

---

[50] Galston raises the fear of what he calls civic totalism, according to which (1) smaller associations have only those rights conferred on them by the state and (2) "all matters are potentially public matters" (*The Practice of Liberal Pluralism* [New York: Cambridge University Press, 2005], 28). Parekh, too, criticizes the assumption that state authority "extends to all areas of life as most theorists of the state have argued" (*Rethinking Multiculturalism*, 194).

grossly misleading to infer from this point that the state has authority over family life, religious worship, and so on, for that suggests state intervention is always legitimate, and that of course does not follow from the point just made.

Here defenders of subsidiarity may try to defend their position by invoking an important distinction. Even if intervention is justified, they may say, it does not follow that the state may intervene: perhaps only certain agents have that authority. For example, though unsafe drivers are rightly constrained, I do not have authority to pull over such motorists: that is the job of the police. Similarly, even if we grant that intervention in civil society is sometimes legitimate, it may still be true that the state is not an agent that may properly intervene (it should be other family members, other parishioners, etc.).

This reply just repeats the central mistake. At its deepest level morality makes no distinctions among persons. Specific allocations of authority, reflecting particular criteria and concerns, are only ever provisional, and can shift depending on who has the ability to ensure rights protection. Kukathas tries to deny the inescapably provisional nature of authority by claiming that all authority rests ultimately on a subject's acquiescence,[51] but that view is implausible: my authority to interfere with an adult assaulting a child has nothing to do with the acquiescence of either, but derives directly from the moral duty to prevent serious harm to the innocent.

The general concern to limit state authority raised by advocates of subsidiarity is thus a red herring. What really drives such theorists is not the belief that certain domains of human intercourse are in principle beyond the state's authority, but the worry that a state that goes beyond minimal universalism will act in ways it shouldn't. Kukathas is right in suggesting that once one grants that the state may intervene on behalf of thin moral ideals, one cannot argue *in principle* against its imposing thicker ones (though one can, of course, object to the ideals themselves).[52] But neither does a strict attitude of non-involvement ensure the state will not act wrongly. The modern state is a powerful agent, uniquely positioned to protect the core rights identified by minimal universalism. If there

---

[51] Cf. Kukathas's vision of a society in which "all authority rests on the acquiescence of subjects under that authority" (*The Liberal Archipelago*, 5).

[52] Replying to Barry's claim that the state properly intervenes where children's interests are seriously endangered, Kukathas argues: "Once you start you cannot stop … And indeed, it is hard to see where it will stop: for surely it is in the child's interests not to be raised on fatty or sugary foods, or to be allowed to waste precious hours watching television or playing Nintendo games, or to learn his mother tongue if it is a minority language more likely to disadvantage him in his later pursuits?" (*The Liberal Archipelago*, 146).

are cases where someone's urgent interests ought to be protected, then there are cases where by doing nothing the state does the wrong thing. Nothing here ensures the state will act rightly, but no more can this be guaranteed by ruling out such involvement. These are unavoidable risks of political life, not to be escaped by an abstract allocation of authority to different agents. Morality's demands are not discharged at the level of theory.

MVL AND THE IDEAL OF JUSTIFICATION

The final question concerns how MVL stands *vis-à-vis* liberalism's justificatory requirement (JR). Some theorists, it must be said, have raised doubts about the overall importance of philosophical justification in defending the liberal state. Discussing Rawls's connection between the principle of legitimacy and the idea of a well-ordered society, for example, Claudia Mills cautions that "we should not overlook, as Rawls sometimes seems to do, the range of resources for building a shared life: history, culture, the sheer passage of time in one another's company."[53] Mills instead stresses a broadly Humean approach: from birth we find ourselves living under certain rules and institutions, pursuing various goods within available traditions. So long as our society offers prospects of reasonable levels of well-being, and we do not perceive it as characterized by massive injustices, we tend to accept as legitimate our broad political framework. The question whether it satisfies JR simply doesn't arise.

These Humean factors notwithstanding, there are at least two important advantages to a regime's satisfying JR. First, any community is likely to have conflicts over the meaning, implications, and priority of their common rules and procedures. In those cases appeal to principles is justified before all citizens can play an important role, helping channel and constrain what might otherwise be a mere contest of strength.[54] The following two chapters suggest how this process might go in two areas of controversy. Second, regardless of how far ordinary citizens actively concern themselves with public justification, any political theorist who accepts citizens' ultimate sovereignty must be concerned with whether

---

[53] Claudia Mills, " 'Not a Mere Modus Vivendi': The Bases for Allegiance to the Just State," in *The Idea of Political Liberalism*, ed. Victoria Davion and Clark Wolf (Lanham, MD: Rowman & Littlefield, 2000), p. 194.

[54] In *Free Public Reason: Making it Up as We Go* (New York: Oxford University Press, 1996), Fred D'Agostino more than once suggests that if the liberal project of justification is abandoned, the result can be only a politics built around force or fraud.

the liberal state is grounded on reasons citizens would endorse, even if that question doesn't exercise them.[55]

Showing that it satisfies JR would thus strengthen MVL's appeal as a solution to the problem of political life under conditions of diversity. There are, however, several tempting reasons to doubt that MVL satisfies JR. In the rest of this chapter I shall argue that these objections are not decisive and that MVL captures the central insights motivating JR.

The fear of moral compromise

The first objection takes off from the fact that critics who reject the arguments for liberalism considered in Part I believe that political institutions would ideally be shaped by the ends and norms specified by their own value frameworks. But then it seems that if they endorse liberal terms they must betray their deepest values. Advocates of this objection argue that such a compromise, because it sacrifices moral integrity, cannot generate the kind of endorsement demanded by JR.

The general worry here, viz., that compromise on a matter involving important moral values amounts to a betrayal of moral principles, can seem natural.[56] History offers many compromises – the Missouri Compromise in the United States tolerating the expansion of slavery, for example, or Chamberlain's Munich agreement with Hitler – that were morally indefensible. But from the fact that there have been objectionable compromises of moral principles it does not follow that the compromise resulting in MVL is also objectionable. To see why it is not, consider the following specious argument designed to show that one should never compromise one's moral ideals. "Compromising one's moral ideals means agreeing to an outcome different from what one believes should morally come about. But one should never agree to an outcome different from what one believes should morally come about. So one should never compromise one's moral ideals." This argument trades on an ambiguity in the notion of what one thinks should

---

[55] As Thomas Hill notes, it was chiefly this concern for internal coherence, not for the actual stability of existing liberal democracies, that led Rawls in his later work to defend justice as fairness as the object of an overlapping consensus. See Hill's "The Problem of Stability in *Political Liberalism*," in *Respect, Pluralism, and Justice: Kantian Perspectives* (Oxford: Oxford University Press, 2000), 237–59.

[56] Cf. Ayn Rand's suggestion that "when people speak of 'compromise' [on basic principles] what they mean is not a legitimate mutual concession or a trade, but precisely the betrayal of their principles" (quoted in Martin Benjamin, *Splitting the Difference: Compromise and Integrity in Ethics and Politics* [Lawrence, KS: University of Kansas Press, 1990], 4).

come about: that idea can refer either to what is morally ideal, or to the best option given the (often non-ideal) conditions one is in. To be sure, morality demands we do the right thing, and in this sense speci-fies an ideal response in any context. But in a non-ideal world, where some act wrongly and others are prepared to do so, the right response may require endorsing outcomes that are in some respects morally defi-cient – i.e. are not what morality recommends as the ideal outcome.[57] For example, even if a nation's deeply unjust war means that its leaders should be severely punished, concerns that such punishment will only engender greater hostilities might recommend more lenient terms. From the moral point of view this outcome is frustrating, insofar as deserved punishment is not meted out. But if supporting that outcome is what one believes morality requires in this case, then doing so does not com-promise one's moral ideals.

These considerations show how arguments against the idea of a prin-cipled moral compromise in politics can mislead. Simon May, for example, contrasts principled reasons for compromise, where the fact of dis-agreement itself provides a moral reason to compromise ideals identified independently of the disagreement, with pragmatic reasons, which rec-ommend compromise only because the distribution of power makes it impossible to put one's ideals in place. But his argument does not, I think, adequately reflect the degree to which particular judgments, informed by unchanging moral principles, must be sensitive to changeable conditions. He mentions, for example, the belief that one's "initial position [is] mor-ally superior (*setting aside* the relevance of the fact of disagreement)," and refers to the fact of disagreement "as a reason to accept a political posi-tion *otherwise perceived* to be morally inferior."[58] But why should the fact of disagreement be set aside when considering what is in fact morally superior here and now? Why is it relevant to an appropriate solution that a position would be judged morally inferior if there were no disagreement? Moral reasoning involves deciding what to do in a specific context. We should resist the suggestion that when one's response is shaped by oth-ers' failings one is thereby compromising one's moral values. So while the critic may regret that the liberal state is the best solution attainable under

---

[57] Arthur Kuflik makes a related point: "It is important to distinguish: (1) what one judges ought to be done about a matter that happens to be in dispute, leaving aside any consideration of the fact that there *is* a dispute; (2) what one judges ought to be done, *all things considered*" ("Morality and Compromise," in *Compromise in Ethics, Law and Politics: NOMOS 29*, ed. J. R. Pennock and J. W. Chapman [New York: New York University Press, 1979], 51).

[58] Simon Cabulea May, "Principled Compromise and the Abortion Controversy," *Philosophy and Public Affairs* 33, no. 4 (Fall 2005), 318, 319 (my emphasis).

conditions of moral diversity, he may nonetheless believe that supporting it is what he has most reason, morally, to do.

The worry over contingency

I have acknowledged that the critic's agreement to MVL hinges on various contingent factors and that he might, were conditions different, seek to enforce illiberal principles.[59] This gives rise to a second objection against MVL's compatibility with JR. For it seems the critic endorses liberal terms only on instrumental grounds, but does not endorse the principles themselves. As Rawls puts it, the modus vivendi approach does not yield a "consensus in which [liberal principles] *themselves are affirmed*," because citizens do not "support the political conception *for its own sake*, or *on its own merits*."[60] JR, it will be argued, requires such support.

This objection assumes that a salient difference exists between endorsing principles "for their own sake" and endorsing them on modus vivendi grounds. But I am doubtful that this distinction holds up in any way that undermines MVL's consistency with the ideal of justification.[61] Indeed, it shows signs of weakening in Rawls's own work. Both *Political Liberalism* and *The Law of Peoples* portray political justification as a contextual matter and recognize a connection between appropriate political principles and a community's particular traditions. Once we grant this, the distinction between affirming principles in themselves (which would seem a matter indifferent to social context) and endorsing them on other grounds (e.g. because they constitute the best response in a particular social/political context) becomes less firm.

Here the Rawlsian will reply that even if the appropriate principles to govern a society depend on context, this is a fact about the content of the principles, not about the manner in which subjects endorse them, and it is the latter that is key for justification. The Rawlsian can still insist, in other words, that irrespective of their content JR requires that principles be endorsed for their own sake, and in this sense excludes those that, as with MVL, are only provisionally endorsed.

Now it cannot be denied that principles endorsed in themselves, in Rawls's sense, will have for subjects a different kind of authority, and may

---

[59] While agreement on MVL grounds might over time become transformed into unconditional endorsement, along lines sketched by Rawls in *Political Liberalism* (159ff.), the critic I am imagining has not undergone such a shift and continues to regard liberal terms as second best.

[60] Rawls, *Political Liberalism,* 159, 148 (my emphasis).

[61] My argument here is deeply indebted to Claudia Mills's analysis in "Not a Mere Modus Vivendi."

lead to greater political stability, than those endorsed because of contingent factors. But the objection in question concerns neither the kind of authority of such principles nor the relative stability of liberal regimes; it asserts that contingent endorsement fails to meet the ideal of justification. Is that claim well grounded? The strongest support for it lies in the ideas that JR requires agreement on strictly moral grounds and that contingent endorsement is not rooted in such grounds. In the next section I shall argue against construing justification in exclusively moral terms. Here I want to target the idea that contingent endorsement of political principles is somehow incompatible with moral grounds.

The belief in such incompatibility rests on a particular conception of the relationship between morality and power which I shall call the Power-Independence Assumption. PIA assumes that one's endorsement of some policy or principle is morally grounded only if one would not support a different policy or principle under a different balance of power.[62] The general idea seems attractive: if I share our profits equally with you only because I lack the power to take more, my agreement to that split does not reflect moral considerations. If we then accept that on MVL some citizens who endorse liberal terms would not do so if they had the power to enforce alternative arrangements, it follows from PIA that their endorsement does not reflect moral considerations. There are, however, good grounds for rejecting both PIA and its implication that contingent support cannot be grounded in moral reasons.

Consider first a case where one seeks a morally acceptable solution to a potentially deadly conflict between two countries. Appropriate terms for resolving this conflict should surely take into account, along with a moral assessment of the countries' competing claims, the likelihood of those terms being honored. This in turn will require attention to several contingent factors involving existing power relations – the ability of outside parties to enforce those terms and penalize departures from them, the disputants' willingness to fight for the issue (itself often a reflection of their relative strength), the bargaining power of the parties involved, and so on. Such factors do not go into the mix *in addition to* those that

---

[62] Theodore Benditt may be relying on this assumption when he contrasts compromise with bargaining. Compromise, he says, involves "a certain sort of respect" for one's opponent and an unwillingness to use one's superior power to impose a solution. In bargaining, in contrast, one makes full use of one's power to advance one's own interests optimally. Benditt thus omits the possibility that one might use one's superior power to impose a solution not because it advances one's own interests, but because it is best for all concerned, including disputants whose moral status one respects. See his "Compromising Interests and Principles," in *Compromise in Ethics, Law and Politics: NOMOS 29*, ed. J. R Pennock and J. W. Chapman (New York: New York University Press, 1979), 27.

determine the correct terms for resolution. Rather, they partly determine what those terms are. PIA cannot make sense of this.

More intimate cases also debunk PIA. Imagine that your close friend's gambling threatens to squander his family's fortune. Had you the power, you would intercede to protect his interests and those of his family. Lacking it, you can only reason with him and appeal to his better nature, to uncertain effect. Here what you will do depends on your relative power, but either response seems to be grounded in moral concern. Note that one cannot defend PIA here by insisting that it would be wrong to interfere even if you could (because it violates your friend's autonomy, say) and that the right response is therefore independent of relative power, for that observation is irrelevant: PIA addresses not the rightness of one's response, but the question whether it reflects moral concern.

To be clear, I am not denying any difference between endorsing liberal principles in themselves and endorsing them on contingent grounds. My point is that we can grant this distinction without concluding that contingent support lacks moral grounding. Often our moral judgments about what to do, and which principles or policies to endorse, are shaped by contingent factors and our judgment of what higher-order principles suggest we do in those conditions. Modus vivendi endorsement of liberal terms is no different.

Does JR still do any work?

I have argued that the contingent nature of the critic's endorsement of MVL does not disqualify it as reflecting moral considerations. The skeptic might, however, concede the general point about the relation between contingency and morality but still insist that MVL fails to capture the moral ideal at the heart of JR. After all, JR is intended to function as a moral constraint on acceptable political arrangements. But modus vivendi endorsement of liberal terms, it may be thought, reflects only the critic's judgment about how to advance his self-interest under the existing balance of power. His endorsement on modus vivendi grounds thus seems utterly independent of JR as a moral ideal. MVL satisfies JR, then, only on a construal according to which JR does no normative work – that is, only on a construal of JR that eviscerates its role in liberal theory.

This is a powerful objection. Though some might question the sharpness of the distinction it invokes between self-interest and morality, I shall not pursue that line of response: however rough and ready, the distinction seems invaluable in moral debate. A better response to the objection comes in two parts.

First, it is just not true that any critic who agrees to MVL does so only out of self-interest. Most obviously, such a critic will likely be concerned that others who endorse the same value framework also have the freedom to live as it specifies. In this respect the critic is clearly motivated by moral reasons. But more importantly, recall that the critic we are imagining recognizes the equal moral status of all persons, including those who endorse mistaken values. He might believe that his own persuasive efforts, secured by liberal commitments, will bring those others to recognize the correct ends he endorses. And if he thinks this unlikely, because others are intransigently committed to their own ideals, he may conclude that efforts to establish illiberal terms, under existing terms, will be either ineffective or counterproductive. As Simon May notes, political conflict often causes great suffering, especially costly to the most vulnerable. There is no reason why what May calls "the basic humanist commitment" to diminish such suffering cannot be part of the critic's motivation to endorse MVL.[63] Finally, we should not overlook the already mentioned benefits of shared effective political institutions – the regulation of a common economy, collective management of infrastructure, public defense, and so on. The critic will surely recognize these goods as valuable for all citizens, regardless of their ends in life.[64] So long as we assume the critic recognizes the moral status of those with whom he disagrees, these factors suggest he may have some motivation to support the liberal state on recognizably moral grounds.

Advocates of the final objection may find the moral concern just described too thin to capture the ideal of JR. Here the second part of the response comes into play. Central to it is the distinction between, on the one hand, JR as a moral ideal, and on the other, the reasons motivating the endorsement of persons to whom JR applies. The key point is that even if JR as a moral ideal stresses that each citizen should recognize good reasons to endorse the liberal solution to political life, those reasons need not themselves be exclusively moral.

To see the distinction, imagine you are responsible for determining the response to a collective problem faced by a group of people. Accepting

---

[63] May, "Principled Compromise and the Abortion Controversy," 323.
[64] Here I assume that one might believe both that a commitment to certain values is needed to lead the best kind of life possible and that a person can nonetheless achieve genuine goods without such a commitment. My attention to this distinction was spurred by discussions with Sarah Broadie.

JR as a moral constraint, you seek a solution that each can endorse. Imagine too that each has a different first choice as to how to solve the problem, but all have the same second choice. When each makes her case for the first-best option, the others find that option unacceptable. Given your commitment to JR, you rule out each of the first-choice proposals. Because of the urgency of the problem, all recognize that their common second-best option is better than no solution and so agree to that option, which you then enact. In this case your commitment to JR helps you identify a morally acceptable outcome, even if each party is not motivated chiefly by moral considerations. Because it recognizes the place of non-moral reasons in determining which outcomes are justified, we might call this a multivalent account of justification.[65]

This example points up a second distinction important for MVL: between JR as a procedural commitment, and JR as specifying a substantive outcome. For while JR here serves as a constraint on acceptable outcomes, it does not by itself entail any specific one; that can be identified only by considering the actual choices and preferences of the people involved. The same holds for political life. This points to a sharp contrast between MVL and those liberal theorists who seek to derive substantive political principles in a more strongly procedural fashion from such ideals as the reasonable citizen, reciprocity, reasonable pluralism, and the like. While still demanding an attitude of moral concern from its citizens, MVL is more clearly reliant on their actual deliberations.

The question naturally arises: what ensures that the liberal state will result from this approach? The answer is: nothing. I have suggested that under certain conditions persons will conclude they have good reasons (both moral and non-moral) to accept the liberal model, and that in this respect the modus vivendi approach captures much of what we care about in JR. But while the case for the liberal state depends on conditions that are neither universal nor guaranteed, it would be a mistake to think that this concession to contingent circumstances somehow demotes JR. As a criterion of political assessment, JR is not itself contingent.

Best and second-best endorsement

The case of MVL differs from the example above in an obvious respect. In my example the option ultimately selected was no one's first choice.

---

[65] The example, like the challenge facing citizens who must agree to political principles, illuminates two elements of compromise that Martin Benjamin has stressed: "a continuing, cooperative

Many citizens, however, do view the liberal state, unconditionally, as the best political model. Some may think that this difference in the kinds of endorsement among citizens must be either (1) unfair to those who endorse liberalism as a second-best option, or (2) inherently problematic from the standpoint of JR. I shall conclude by showing that neither is the case.

(1) MVL is not unfair to those who support the liberal state as a second-best outcome because the agreement to liberal terms results from a process that does not privilege either some parties over others or some contested value commitments over others (it does not hinge on the liberal ideal of autonomy, value pluralism, etc.). Instead, it models the parties (and their commitments) equally and tries to identify terms of political association that all citizens will find acceptable under common conditions. So even if some of the parties endorse liberal terms with more enthusiasm than others, the case for the liberal state is not driven from the outset by assumptions in its favor. In this respect no one has grounds for complaint.

This shows the way past what might seem a damaging *reductio* to my claim that MVL captures the justificatory ideal. Consider institutionalized slavery: we don't want to say slavery satisfies JR, but it may have been true that many slaves, faced with the option between accepting slavery and suicidal resistance, correctly judged that accepting their condition was what they had most reason to do. If the ideal of justification required only that one accept an outcome one has most reason to accept, then JR would indeed become nugatory, as the slavery example implies. But JR operates with several assumptions in place that ward off that *reductio*. To begin with, any outcome must be consistent with the requirements of minimal univeralism. Second, JR assumes that the parties who must agree on terms for common life accept that the interests of others matter equally. Third, JR rules out outcomes brought about by threat (here, the threat of would-be slaveowners). Lastly, JR requires that anyone affected by political principles in question can affirm the social world thereby created, in the sense of believing that within it one and those one cares about can lead fulfilling lives. In all these respects slavery, and other similarly objectionable arrangements, will not satisfy JR.

(2) Nor is the difference between best and second-best endorsement problematic from the standpoint of JR. It might be so if we assume what

relationship, and an impending nondeferrable decision affecting [all] parties" (*Splitting the Difference*, 30).

I will call a binary account of justification, on which political principles, institutions, and so on are either fully justified (in the manner of unconditional endorsement) or not justified at all. If we see justification of political arrangements instead as scalar, adjudging political terms as more or less justified, then we will conclude that cases of second-best endorsement can satisfy JR to a substantial degree. Factors on such a scale would include (a) the degree to which citizens believe they can lead fulfilling lives under their governing principles, institutions, laws, and so on; (b) the intensity with which they desire or agitate for change in those principles, etc.; (c) their affective attitude towards, and pride in, their overall political community; and (d) the authority they unreflectively attribute to important decisions made in accordance with their fundamental political principles. A reckoning of such factors (in no way exhaustive) will be scalar in two senses: within each factor, and in rating the strength of one factor relative to another.

Is rejecting a binary account in favor of a scalar one simply an *ad hoc* move to preserve MVL's compatibility with JR? No, for several reasons. To begin with, it seems reasonable to preserve conceptual space for principles falling between those we see as ideal and those we find unacceptable – i.e. those that are not ideal but which we have some good grounds to accept. In denying such space the binary account saddles political justification with a burden we do not impose on justification in other contexts. That burden becomes even more dubious on the assumption of value pluralism, which suggests that value judgments are less precise and more likely to be marked by reasonable disagreement. Seeing political principles as more or less justified better captures the spirit of pluralism.

A further reason for the scalar account is that the liberal ideal of justification already contains scalar elements. In an earlier chapter I noted that while JR cannot require the assent of every rational person, it must nonetheless succeed in persuading sizeable numbers of them. This I captured in the (admittedly vague) idea of an argument that tends to win assent when faced with reasoners appropriately situated. But the notions of tending to win assent and of appropriate situatedness can be interpreted with different degrees of robustness, and this in turn suggests that the question whether justification is met will depend in part on how one understands those scalar features.

Indeed, as Fred D'Agostino has shown, liberal theory reflects diverse conceptions of justification that differ in how they weight various elements. There are differences, he notes, not just in the desiderata behind JR (theorists want justified principles to motivate people, to be independent of particular social histories, to be relatively determinate), but also in terms of how the process of justification is construed (some stress dialogue while others are monological; some stress actual consent, others hypothetical; some appeal to volitional capacities, others to cognitive ones; and so on). Some accounts do better in some respects, others do better in others. This should not, D'Agostino stresses, be seen as a failure in theorizing justification, as though some ideal account might give us everything we want. Different approaches simply have different payoffs in terms of costs and benefits, and this again argues for seeing justification as a matter of more or less, rather than either-or.[66]

A final reason for liberals to adopt the account of justification advanced here derives from the principle that "ought" implies "can." If liberals are correct that political principles ought to satisfy JR, there must exist some that can do so. Part I argued that in the face of deep diversity the case for the liberal state cannot satisfy the more robust ideal of justification dominant in liberal theory. We must then either conclude that such polities cannot meet the ideal of justification or adopt the scalar, multivalent account I am defending. This is an instance not of corrupting a concept to let us say something we shouldn't, but of interpreting it so that it can apply to the domain in which it is meant to do normative work.

This last point strengthens the case for MVL against a lingering worry that has no doubt occurred to the reader. I have allowed that the critic who endorses liberalism on modus vivendi grounds would under certain conditions support illiberal principles. But then it appears the critic is himself unreasonable, since he would impose on others terms they would reject, thus violating JR. And if the critic is unreasonable, his objections to the liberal state, chronicled in Part I, are of no account. Now I have already given the general response to this argument: the critic may believe that the principles he recommends are accessible to all who reason properly about such matters and may simply think others are unable to do so now – not because of any intrinsic failing, but because they lack the appropriate conditions, training, models of moral deliberation, and so forth. Indeed, his belief that it contributes to a state of affairs that impedes citizens from reasoning properly about supremely important values may be part of his opposition to the liberal state. This general response interprets the notion

---

[66] "There is good reason to believe that there are multiple independent desiderata associated with the ideal of public justification and to believe that, in many cases, satisfaction of one, say, moralistic desideratum means, *ipso facto*, inadequate performance with respect to other, particularly realistic, desiderata" (D'Agostino, *Free Public Reason*, 89).

of justification differently from that of many contemporary liberals. But we can now see better why this is defensible.

For there is, I think, no uniquely correct answer to the question how robustly to interpret the idea of justifiability. The inescapably imprecise terms through which the idea is advanced – references to principles that all "can reasonably be expected to endorse … in light of their common human reason," that are "accessible in some sense to common human understanding," or that could "in principle command the assent of all persons" – exemplify the inescapably imprecise and contested nature of the idea itself.[67] Faced with that challenge, one sound approach is to adopt a conception of justification that both captures its general appeal and accommodates, as far as possible, other important values one endorses. This is one way to understand the critic. He believes that if justification requires respecting grossly deficient and remediable judgments about value, and according them full weight in political argument, it becomes a far less attractive ideal. In a similar vein A. John Simmons has criticized liberal theorists who define the reasonable citizen as one committed above all else to arriving at political principles consonant with other citizens' existing value frameworks even if this involves excluding what one takes to be the best reasons *simpliciter*.[68] To Simmons's criticism we can add that even the liberal theorist he refers to, like the critic I have imagined, imposes conditions on the sort of citizen owed justification: they simply differ in the stringency of those conditions, reflecting the balance they seek to strike between the ideal of justification and other important values. If, as I have tried to suggest, the critic's construal of the ideal of justification represents one reasonable attempt to capture the range of values to which political theory should be responsive, then the charge that he is unreasonable seems itself unacceptably dogmatic.

Some might say that this defense of the critic, along with the overall account I have advanced, reflects a failure of pluralist nerve. If not all goods are combinable, then some may have to drop out; justification may be one such casualty. But we should accept that outcome, I think, only

---

[67] Rawls, *Political Liberalism*, 137; Greenawalt, *Private Consciences and Public Reasons*, 27; Robert Talisse, "Liberalism, Pluralism, and Political Justification," *Harvard Review of Philosophy* 13 (2005), 58.

[68] See Simmons, *Justification and Legitimacy*, 143–4. As Stephen Macedo notes in contrasting wide accessibility with what one takes to be the best reasons *simpliciter*, the standard of reasonableness must be at least partly determined by considerations "*from within* our comprehensive view, and not only from a public perspective" ("The Politics of Justification," *Political Theory* 18 [May 1990], 291).

when there is no way to reconcile the various ideals we value highly. The account I have advanced here aims to show how diverse citizens might agree to liberal terms on modus vivendi grounds without compromising the basic insight behind JR. That account, I realize, may not give liberals all they want. But I have tried to show that it gives them enough, and in any case, all they can reasonably demand.

CHAPTER 8

The challenge of gender equality

WOMEN AND CULTURAL GROUPS

By and large the critic I have been imagining does not generate *de novo* the normative framework he endorses, but comes to it through a process of responding to and often reshaping various formative influences around him. Especially influential here are those intergenerational communities that strive to sustain and transmit their distinct identity-conferring norms. Such groups define themselves by a common normative framework and set of practices they see as properly structuring a person's world in a range of important contexts: how the young should be educated, standards of appropriate behavior and dress, relations between the sexes, family life, recreation, religious worship, and so on. These cultural groups, with their obvious potential to shape deeply the inner lives of liberal citizens, present a serious challenge to the liberal state: for while they may produce citizens who object to liberal commitments, the importance of expressive liberty means liberal states must tolerate those efforts to some substantial degree.

In this and the following chapter I consider the implications of MVL with respect to such groups, concentrating on the areas of gender equality and compulsory education. Not only are these areas of intrinsic interest and practical urgency, but discussion of them can as well help clarify the nature of the minimal universalism to which MVL is committed. And since some may worry that minimal universalism is too thin to defend important human interests, it makes sense to concentrate on those individuals historically most vulnerable to abuse – women and children. As we shall see, an adequate response to the worry over gender equality will involve claims about mandatory education. Some of what I say here, then, will involve a promissory note, cashed out in the next chapter.

The central objection concerning gender equality is that the very thin moral commitments of the MVL state require it to adopt a policy of strong tolerance towards illiberal groups in a way that unacceptably endangers the welfare of females within them. Though the general concern here extends to all vulnerable members (including children and minority dissenters), the fate of women is taken to present an especially acute problem, given the widely held view, starkly expressed by Susan Okin, that "discrimination against and control of the freedom of females are practiced, to a greater or lesser extent, by virtually all cultures, past and present."[1] On this view, strong tolerance of the norms of such groups, in the manner MVL seems to recommend, translates to privileging men's interests over women's. But this, it is said, is incompatible with the idea (to which MVL is also committed) that the interests of all persons matter equally. The objection thus points to a fatal instability at the heart of the MVL approach: while the MVL state promises to allow groups to lead lives consistent with their own norms and practices, in practice its commitment to moral equality demands a far greater degree of intrusion into such groups and draws much narrower boundaries to acceptable norms involving gender and sexual roles.

That the norms of cultural groups can disadvantage women is distressingly easy to establish. Ayelet Shachar has discussed how the canons of family law embraced by certain Jewish and Islamic sects are biased against women's interests, and Martha Nussbaum has offered a similar account chronicling threats women face as a result of cultural norms and practices in such areas as family law, education, employment, property rights, and bodily integrity.[2] In highlighting the risks to women presented by such groups, critics like Okin, Shachar, and Nussbaum draw attention to a concern that no liberal theory committed to moral equality can ignore. Nonetheless, to assess what that worry implies for the MVL state, we need to distinguish two questions. The first concerns the legal realm: should liberal states in some instances excuse cultural groups from laws that demand adherence to gender neutrality, or grant legal force to a group's rules even when these are gender-structured? The second focuses on the non-legal realm: how far may liberal states go to combat the tacit

---

[1] Susan Okin, "Is Multiculturalism Bad for Women?," in *Is Multiculturalism Bad for Women?*, ed. Joshua Cohen, Matthew Howard, and Martha Nussbaum (Princeton, NJ: Princeton University Press, 1999), 21 (cited hereafter as *MBFW*). Okin was the most persistent feminist critic of accommodating cultural groups who departed from liberal ideals, raising a number of objections in a series of important essays. Her untimely death deprived political theory of one of its most absorbing talents, and multiculturalism of perhaps its most powerful opponent.

[2] Ayelet Shachar, *Multicultural Jurisdictions: Cultural Differences and Women's Rights* (New York: Cambridge University Press, 2001), 57–61, 81–3, and *passim*. Martha Nussbaum, *Sex and Social Justice* (New York: Oxford University Press, 1999), chs. 1–5, esp. ch. 3.

understandings and social norms of such groups when these depart from distinctive liberal ideals of gender neutrality?

As a way into the first question, we can begin with Ayelet Shachar's *Multicultural Jurisdictions*, the most substantial attempt yet to reconcile feminist concerns with some legal accommodation for the practices of illiberal groups. Shachar begins by noting that various rules and norms apply in distinct domains, serving a range of functions: in the family realm, for example, different rules demarcate membership and govern the distribution of benefits and burdens. Rejecting the idea "that binding legal norms must originate in a single source of authority,"[3] she argues for dividing between the state and cultural groups primary authority over different sub-areas within any one domain. So while a group member could choose which set of norms (i.e. group- or state-sanctioned) to live by in any particular sub-area, she would also be guaranteed various "moments of reversal," in Shachar's phrase, when she could place herself under the terms of the alternative authority. Because it structures this competition for allegiance, Shachar claims that her model captures the importance of group affiliation while simultaneously improving the bargaining position of women within heretofore sexist practices: if those groups do not improve their treatment of female members, women will opt out and the practices fall into desuetude. In addition, since Shachar's model allows group members to opt out of practices at various points, it does not force them, as other models do, to choose irrevocably and often tragically between their citizenship and their group membership.

Though I cannot do justice here to the richness of Shachar's account, I am doubtful that her model of multi-sourced authority can achieve the reconciliation she seeks. The central problem concerns the contrast between her own joint governance approach and what she sees as the competing conception of authority dominant among political theorists. The latter, she says, accords the state "absolute and unilateral control over all norms and regulations that affect its territory and citizenry."[4] Now this claim can take two readings, a strong one and a weak one. The problem is that neither helps her case.

[3] Shachar, *Multicultural Jurisdictions*, 131. See also 15: "In today's day and age, no single authority can expect to be the sole source of legal norms and institutions affecting its members."
[4] Ibid., 131, n. 25.

On the strong reading, the claim is one she is right to reject but few theorists hold. If, for example, she has in mind a quasi-Hobbesian view, according to which the state in principle cannot exceed its rightful authority, she is imagining a view with few serious defenders. Since at least Locke's time there has been broad agreement that state authority has a bounded purview, and while debates have raged over the extent of that purview, that is a question quite different from whether such purview is unlimited. If we then opt for the weak reading of Shachar's claim, such that "absolute and unilateral control" means only that the state always retains a fundamental right to interfere in any domain when reasons are weighty enough (a right that in principle extends even to family practices and religious worship), then the dominant account of authority is not just reasonable in itself (as the previous chapter argued), but something Shachar's own approach requires. This can be seen in at least two instances.

The first is her discussion of the approach she calls contingent accommodation, in which the state grants groups rights to govern themselves by distinct rules so long as they meet certain moral criteria. Shachar rejects this approach because it requires "a complex regulatory regime" and invites, given its unavoidable reliance on "broad and vague" standards, "bias and discrimination" against such groups.[5] But her own position requires that group members achieve adequate levels of education, skills, and emotional independence so that they have real options to exit their group. Given her worry that some groups will fail to ensure these, she cannot avoid granting the state authority to make such assessments through a regulatory process, however complex, in which bias and discrimination are always a risk. The second instance involves her assertion that "'opting out' [of the norms governing any sub-area] is justified only when the relevant power-holder has failed to provide [meaningful] remedies to the plight of the individual."[6] The question, of course, is: who determines whether meaningful remedy has been provided? If the individual, then opting out is justified whenever one desires: but then the group's norms are not binding. If the group is judge, the vulnerable remain unprotected. Having no judge leaves the issue unresolved. The state must then be the judge, claiming again the unique authority Shachar wants to avoid.[7]

---

[5] Ibid., 110.   [6] Ibid., 123.

[7] At one point Shachar asserts that the state and cultural groups "operate in an institutional environment where each authority's powers are constrained" (121). But it is unclear how this relationship of mutual constraint is to be understood.

The failure of joint governance may lead some to conclude that when faced with groups who want to govern themselves by rules reflecting distinct gender practices, the liberal state must choose between two options: accommodate such groups, or override them on grounds of gender neutrality. On the accommodation approach, for example, the state might permit sex discrimination in certain contexts, or recognize as legally binding terms of marriage that favor men relative to women. On the overriding approach the state would disallow such arrangements and permit only those that satisfied a norm of gender neutrality.

In considering this choice, we must not forget that the MVL state values nothing more highly than protecting individuals' expressive liberty. Citizens may enact that liberty by aligning themselves with groups that are in various ways illiberal and entering into relationships marked by attitudes to gender that seem retrograde or demeaning. Tolerating such choices does not constitute endorsement of them, however much liberalism's facile critics have sought to elide the distinction. Taking the distinction seriously, in turn, not only shows why liberal states have good reasons both to tolerate members of illiberal groups and to recognize the legal authority of group norms when these are endorsed by its members, but also lets us see how the choice between the apparently mutually exclusive options presented above – accommodating and overriding – was misleading. Under MVL there is only one norm that prevails: the value of people's freedom to lead their lives as they choose under ideals they embrace. So while their being freely endorsed does not render such norms liberal, that fact does remove the grounds on which the liberal state can object.

To see what this entails, consider two topics prominent in recent discussions. Shachar expresses concern that the Jewish *get* and the distribution of property after divorce under Jewish law favor men and so violate gender equality. On my account the MVL state would allow persons to enter marriage under such terms, and give those agreements legal recognition, for the same reason the liberal state now enforces prenuptial agreements: it respects the choices men and women make about how to order their marriages, a domain often seen by both parties as involving especially important religious requirements.[8] Similar reasoning rules out objections to polygamy and polygyny grounded in the

---

[8] Where such decisions affect the critical interests of children (for example, in the allocation of property after divorce), the state may have grounds to interfere – in this case, because the children are affected by choices they did not or were not competent to make.

idea that permitting such relationships is inherently disadvantageous for women: such objections impugn the judgment of those persons, men and women, who endorse such marriages as their preferred model of family life. To those who charge that polygamy can be chosen only by women who are either unaware of other options or lacking the basic resources for free choice, the proper response is not to outlaw polygamy but to remedy those obstacles. In the end, I suspect pragmatic objections are decisive in ruling out marriage to more than one spouse: in the modern state the administrative complexities of sorting out such issues as responsibility for children, property ownership and inheritance, insurance coverage, and so on are simply enormous. My point here is simply that judgments about the intrinsic moral acceptability of such marriages cannot be the basis for the MVL state's attitude towards them.[9]

The second topic involves equal opportunity in employment. Consider the case of *Ohio Civil Rights Commission* v. *Dayton Christian Schools* (DCS), involving a school that terminated the contract of a pregnant teacher because its religious beliefs prohibited mothers of young children working outside the home. Though some have seen this as a straight-forward case of objectionable sex discrimination (since a male teacher would not have been fired under the same conditions), the issue is more complicated. The liberal state cannot deny religious groups the freedom to determine how to fill positions that are relevant to their religious mission, even if this involves making distinctions that would be invidious in other contexts: Catholics can refuse to hire women as priests; Christians can reject a Muslim as a Sunday school teacher. So long as the requirements for such positions are publicly communicated and plausibly relevant, respect for religious freedom provides a reason to tolerate departures from otherwise binding liberal norms of equal treatment. Few would deny that the teacher in question could properly have been fired had she rejected important aspects of the school's faith – Jesus' divinity, for example. On the same grounds, we cannot deny the school's right to terminate her contract for acting in a manner contrary to its basic commitments about how children should be raised.

This defense of DCS may appear problematic in two ways. First, it seems to grant to men opportunities that are denied women. But as just

---

[9] Joseph Carens and Melissa Williams have argued that polygamy should be tolerated if both women and men may have several spouses, but Brian Barry has noted the logistical night-mare such a policy would create. See Carens and Williams, "Muslim Minorities in Liberal Democracies: The Politics of Misrecognition," in *Secularism and its Critics*, ed. Rajeev Bhargava (Delhi: Oxford University Press, 1998), 137–73, and Barry, *Culture and Equality*, 369, n. 96.

indicated, this is already the case in various contexts (e.g. religion). In the DCS case the reasons for tolerating discrimination are weighty, the reasons for intervening less so, assuming there exist opportunities to teach in schools not committed to the beliefs of DCS. This last qualification is important, because if only fathers but not mothers could serve as teachers in area schools, the equal freedom of women would be seriously compromised. So long as sufficient teaching opportunities exist, however, the ideal of equal freedom is satisfied. To deny this, to believe that equal freedom entails the right to teach at a parochial school even while opposing important aspects of that school's creed, is just to deny a right to parochial education.

The second objection to my defense of DCS is that it seems to protect any institution that establishes its own criteria for relevant distinctions, so long as these are publicly announced and sincerely held. This implies that a restaurant, for example, may refuse to serve women or blacks so long as its owner believes that only white men should dine in public. This I grant would be a *reductio* of my argument. But the implication is blocked if we keep in mind two salient factors that distinguish cases like DCS from that of the imagined restaurateur.

The first is that running a business for commercial gain, such as a restaurant where one sells food to unknown customers, is an intrinsically public venture where criteria of select membership have no place, and it is the office of the MVL state to establish a single set of rules facilitating interactions in common public space. In the Jim Crow era in the USA, restaurants that served only whites were not soliciting white *members*: they were simply not serving blacks. The DCS case, in contrast, involved a private organization whose members consciously united around shared religious beliefs, and so presents an instance where the freedoms of association and religious expression figure centrally. The other factor blocking the troubling implications of the DCS case concerns the obvious importance of religious freedom and relative triviality of the desire to profit through restaurateuring. This may be only a contingent fact about the sorts of issues for which persons have been willing to fight and to die: it's not logically impossible that one might think one's meaning hinges on being free to operate segregated restaurants for profit. But to insist that we devise a political morality that would apply to beings quite different from any we've known would fatally derail the enterprise of political philosophy. Along with the zealous restaurateur, must we also consider persons with no objection to physical pain or humiliation? At some point political theory must be responsive to the interests of persons as they are, and to what they show they care about.

The approach I am defending will, however, be much less tolerant when adults appeal to distinct gender norms to defend practices involving children. The facts that minors are not fully competent decision-makers, and that accommodation affects the welfare of someone other than the person requesting it, make it appropriate to hold such claims to a higher threshold. Given the ideal of equal freedom, an obvious additional concern will be the degree to which the practice has consequences that are either irreversible or extremely costly to undo should the minor later come to reject that group's norms. The request to practice clitoridectomy on girls demonstrates the basic idea here. Assuming the procedure severely compromises a woman's capacity for sexual pleasure,[10] those who undergo it will be unable to pursue a life in which such pleasure figures as an important good. Because it irreversibly constrains another person's freedom without her mature consent, liberal states have good reason to forbid it.

Advocates of extreme tolerance may object that the idea of reversibility is insufficiently precise as a ground for political decisions and threatens to rule out a range of canonical liberal freedoms. For example, someone who undergoes first communion within a strongly Catholic upbringing may be so deeply affected that subsequent departures from the faith are for him inconceivable: isn't this a case of irreversible shaping as well? The response is that this objection misconstrues the ideal of reversibility relevant to the liberal state, because it overlooks important differences in the way options are and remain narrowed in the two cases. Clitoridectomy closes off an option irrespective of a woman's later values and preferences; even if she comes to value a life where sexual pleasure is important, for her it cannot be a goal. The rite of communion, in contrast, does not exclude options this way: if one comes to reject Catholicism, having undergone communion will not rule out options inconsistent with Catholic doctrine. The potential conflict between values and options that marks the clitoridectomy case thus cannot arise.

Recognizing that practices at odds with gender neutrality face a higher threshold of tolerance when they involve minors does not, however, imply

[10] For doubts about this assumption, see Richard A. Shweder, "'What About Female Genital Mutilation?' and Why Cultural Understanding Matters," in *Why do Men Barbecue? Recipes for Cultural Psychology* (Cambridge, MA: Harvard University Press, 2003), 168–216. For an even more radical argument questioning the connection between sexuality and fixed physiological response, see Sander Gilman, "'Barbaric' Rituals?," in *MBFW*, 53–8.

that they should not be tolerated. After all, a major way in which persons live out their commitment to normative frameworks is through choices they make for their children and family life generally. An approach that sought to accommodate only adults' departure from the norms of gender neutrality while ensuring that minors remain subject to them is thus not just impracticable but incoherent. Accepting this does not imply that one views children as mere chattels of their parents. It reflects instead the inevitable result of protecting expressive liberty under conditions of real diversity. Liberals should not expect tolerance to be costless.

THE WORRY OVER SOCIALIZATION

The argument thus far invites an obvious objection. It is that allowing individuals to place themselves under norms that depart from gender neutrality ignores the degree to which socialization in cultural groups compromises the equality of female members and so undermines conditions of genuinely free choice. Indeed, Okin claims that the control of women occurs chiefly not through the medium of public law, but "in the private sphere by the authority of either actual or symbolic fathers, often acting through, or with the complicity of, the older women of the culture."[11] On this view, tolerating the choices of men and women simply papers over the enduring problem, preserving a system of formal equality and substantive injustice.

One might reply to this worry by taking a very hard line, insisting that liberal states never have grounds to interfere with extra-legal socialization, but that position is hard to defend. The MVL state protects all citizens' equal freedom because it recognizes their moral equality. Now human beings, history shows, are malleable. In particular, they can form conceptions of themselves as morally inferior and so fail to develop a proper sense

---

[11] Susan Okin, "Feminism and Multiculturalism: Some Tensions," *Ethics* 108, no. 4 (July 1998), 679. Creating a world in which "no assumptions would be made about male and female roles," Okin says elsewhere, "requires major changes in a multitude of institutions and social settings outside the home, as well as within it" (*Justice, Gender, and the Family* [New York: Basic Books, 1989], 171, 172). Shachar and Nussbaum also discuss the problem of extra-legal pressures, but Okin's account is especially clear in both its presentation of the problem and its sympathy for state intervention to address it. Nussbaum stresses that the "distinction between social pressure and physical force should also remain salient, both morally and legally" (*Sex and Social Justice*, 123), and it is hard to imagine her endorsing Okin's suggestion that liberal states consider discriminating against the Catholic Church (Okin, "Justice and Gender: An Unfinished Debate," *Fordham Law Review* 72 [April 2004], 1537–67). Shachar seems similarly compelled to accord less weight to social pressure than does Okin, given the greater value Shachar sees in group membership.

of their moral status.[12] Imagine, then, a family or group that succeeds in encouraging its members to believe, in Okin's words, that "women are not human beings of equal worth but rather subordinates whose primary (if not only) function is to serve men sexually and domestically."[13] Such a group runs afoul of the requirements of moral equality to which the MVL state is committed and as such can claim no protection against that state.

But if the hard-line reply to the worry over socialization does not succeed, does it follow that any group that seeks to instill norms at odds with gender neutrality is a legitimate target of state intervention? It would follow if all groups that reject gender neutrality also communicated that the well-being of females matters less than that of males. But not all such groups do this, I want to argue now, and that fact seriously complicates the case for state intervention in socialization among illiberal groups.

To see why, consider Okin's gloss on feminism: "By *feminism* I mean the belief that women should not be disadvantaged by their sex, that they should be recognized as having human dignity equal to that of men, and that they should have the opportunity to live as fulfilling and as freely chosen lives as men can."[14] From this starting point gender neutrality does not follow: that a group endorses gender distinctions does not imply that it distinctly disadvantages women, constrains only their freedom, or fails to respect their equal dignity. To think it does is to ignore the distinction between gender differentiation and gender subordination. Okin appears willing to dismiss that distinction, and in criticizing an argument advanced by Joseph Raz expresses strong skepticism that gender differentiation might operate in non-oppressive ways.[15] If Okin is right, the commitment to moral equality requires gender neutrality. But there are, I think, two good reasons to doubt that gender differentiation is always objectionable to an extent justifying state action. The first is that many women who claim to see themselves as having moral worth equal to men's embrace various forms of gender differentiation. The other is that such differentiation has figured prominently in virtually all cultures and religions known to human history. If liberalism requires alignment with an ideal of gender neutrality not just in the juridical domain but at the level of socialization as well, it stands against the beliefs and traditions

---

[12] For a dramatic account of this process, see Elinor Burkett's "God Created Me to Be a Slave," *New York Times Magazine*, 12 October 1997, 56–60.
[13] Okin, "Is Multiculturalism Bad for Women?," 18.   [14] Ibid., 10.
[15] Raz raises the possibility that a group might endorse gender differentiation in non-oppressive ways in "Multiculturalism: A Liberal Perspective," in *Ethics in the Public Domain*, 170–91. Okin's critique appears in "Mistresses of Their Own Destiny: Group Rights, Gender, and Realistic Rights of Exit," *Ethics* 112 (January 2002), 205–30.

through which a great number of citizens, men and women, understand the meaning in their lives.[16]

It therefore merits effort to see whether the distinction between differentiation and subordination stands up. Let us say that the sexes are differentiated within a normative framework when it articulates distinct conceptions of what's involved in the flourishing of each, or of the important virtues each should develop, or of the sorts of activities appropriate to each, and so on. A framework endorses subordination, in contrast, when it systematically recommends that one sex uncritically defer to the other's decisions, or favors the well-being of one sex over another, or distributes burdens and benefits to the disadvantage of one sex, and so on.

What conditions, then, support the judgment that differentiation exists as opposed to subordination? I suggest the following five criteria.

1. The argument for differentiated roles does not grossly misrepresent the abilities of either sex: a set of practices built around the belief that, for example, women "lack the intellectual ability and discerning judgment" needed for various careers, to cite a statement by one Muslim cleric, violates this criterion.[17]

2. Goods made available to one sex are not achieved at the other's expense: communities where young girls are routinely married off to older men violate this criterion.

3. The well-being of one sex is not substantially lower than that of another. This criterion will sometimes be controversial, sometimes not. It is not controversial when one of the sexes is disproportionately deprived of a basic human good – when, for example, women's lifespans are radically shorter than men's, or they are denied basic education.[18] Where more precise judgments of the good are at stake – for example, in debates over the merits of domestic versus professional life – controversy is more likely.

4. The differentiated roles reflect some degree of mutual negotiation among both sexes, in a manner allowing for what Uma Narayan calls

---

[16] Revealing here are Okin's debates with Azizah Al-Hibri, Bonnie Honig, and Martha Nussbaum on the degree to which major religious traditions are sexist at their core (see their essays in *MBFW*: Al-Hibri, "Is Western Patriarchal Feminism Good for Third World/Minority Women?," 41–6; Honig, "My Culture Made Me Do It," 35–40; and Nussbaum, "A Plea for Difficulty," 105–14). One would have thought that for liberals such debates are best left to adherents to work out among themselves, rather than being resolved by the state.

[17] The statement, which Nussbaum quotes in *Sex and Social Justice*, 94, is cited in Akram Mirhosseini, "After the Revolution: Violations of Women's Human Rights in Iran," in *Women's Rights, Human Rights*, ed. Julie Peters and Andrea Wolper (New York: Routledge, 1995), 75.

[18] See Amartya Sen, "More than One Hundred Million Women are Missing," *New York Review of Books* 37, no. 20 (1990), 61–6.

the "*normative contestations and re-descriptions* of the ways particular institutions and practices adversely affect groups of people."[19]
5. Allegiance to the group's norms is secured through the consent of members, all of whom have the option to exit.

This list is not exhaustive, and each criterion merits greater elaboration. But it seeks to balance two attractive yet potentially competing ideas. The first is that groups who instill the belief that women's interests are less important than men's commit a serious wrong that legitimates intervention by the MVL state. The second is the importance of respecting the choices made by women and men, individually and collectively, to lead their lives in accordance with their deepest values – choices that model relations between the sexes in a range of ways.[20] In stressing the need for women to choose from an assumption of gender neutrality, Okin delegitimizes one choice (i.e. for non-androgynous cultures) that many women wish to make. This would be unobjectionable if such cultures served only as a mechanism for male privilege, but pitched at the level of generality that characterizes Okin's argument, that criticism does not adequately engage the attitudes of female members who reject gender neutrality, who do not feel victimized, and who would object to being told that their preferences are corrupted.[21]

To be clear, I'm not arguing that gender differentiation is not problematic. My point is that it is not obviously problematic to the degree needed for its presence alone to sanction intervention by the MVL state. Any robust defense of freedom will recognize that people may use their liberty in any number of morally objectionable ways.[22] The wrongness of an action, especially one that manifests expressive liberty, is thus not by itself sufficient grounds for intervention: what must also be shown is that the harm involved is severe enough to outweigh the infringement

---

[19] Uma Narayan, *Dislocating Cultures: Identities, Traditions, and Third-World Feminism* (New York: Routledge, 1997), 34.

[20] For example, Al-Hibri portrays her own participation within Islam's "established etiquette of difference" as freely chosen and so non-objectionable ("Is Western Patriarchal Feminism Good for Third World/Minority Women?," 46).

[21] Both Al-Hibri and Honig fault Okin's depiction of "patriarchal" cultures as too monolithic and not sufficiently sensitive to cultural complexity and tension. Even Shachar, strongly sympathetic to the worry that multicultural accommodation may threaten women's welfare, criticizes Okin for portraying women in minority cultures as "victims without agency" (Shachar, *Multicultural Jurisdictions*, 66). For a recent influential account that Islam is far more friendly to women's interests than many have assumed, see Leila Ahmed, *Women and Gender in Islam: Historical Roots of a Modern Debate* (New Haven: Yale University Press, 1992).

[22] For an argument that a right to freedom entails a right to act wrongly, see Jeremy Waldron, "A Right to do Wrong?," *Ethics* 92 (October 1981), 21–39.

on liberty that such intervention requires. Thus far I've tried to show that gender differentiation *per se* is not so obviously objectionable. Let me now indicate four serious costs with such intervention.

The first is that the measures needed to combat such socialization significantly depart from canonical liberal positions.[23] To see the problem, consider the factors that shape socialization: the comments and behavior of one's parents; the lessons conveyed by one's religious heritage; the influence of one's peers; and the images and stories encountered in the available culture. It's not at all clear that liberal states can reshape these processes,[24] but even if they could, the sort of intervention required would involve constraints on a range of liberties (to religious worship, child-rearing, and expression) long viewed as central by liberals.

A second worry is that such measures require the state to act on contested norms and judgments in just the way MVL seeks to avoid. Sanctioning gender neutrality as the attitude citizens should adopt will strike many not as a criterion reflecting minimal universalism but as the imposition of one parochial normative framework over others.[25] Such measures will both engender resentment among a range of citizens and encourage more active petitioning on behalf of other contested ideals – precisely the situation MVL seeks to avoid.[26]

A third cost to liberal intervention reflects a dynamic Uma Narayan identifies in India's battle against British imperialism.[27] Insisting that cultural groups conform to alien norms often triggers a defensive reaction, wherein leaders of such groups ascribe undue emphasis to distinctive practices and norms and portray them as more rigid and less open to negotiation than they have been. Not only does this dynamic make it more likely that women who endorse gender neutrality will be seen as traitors to their group, but it also interrupts the ongoing process whereby norms about gender get reinterpreted and reshaped by those who endorse them.

The final problem with such intervention involves the importance to human beings of normative frameworks generally and the cost that may

---

[23] Feminists have long debated whether the liberal tradition can adequately respond to their concerns. For a recent statement of deep incompatibility, see Tracy Higgins, "Why Feminists Can't (or Shouldn't) Be Liberals," *Fordham Law Review* 72 (April 2004), 1629–41.

[24] Discussing the case of a young girl who thinks respecting her parents requires marrying whomever they choose, Kukathas opines: "It is hard to see what the state can do to prevent such things from happening, or what punishments it can mete out to alter people's thinking" ("Is Feminism Bad for Multiculturalism?," *Public Affairs Quarterly* 15, no. 2 [April 2001], 95).

[25] As Robert Post notes in "Between Norms and Choices," *MBFW*, 65–8.

[26]. Cf. Kukathas's reply to Barry in *The Liberal Archipelago*, 146.

[27] Narayan, *Dislocating Cultures*, 17ff. Shachar calls this phenomenon "reactive culturalism."

result from state efforts to alter them in the direction of gender neutrality. In concentrating on the way such frameworks disadvantage women, Okin downplays the degree to which they provide the conditions, for both men and women, for the exercise of freedom liberals celebrate. Charles Taylor has consistently stressed this point, noting that evaluative frameworks "provide the background, explicit or implicit, for our moral judgments, intuitions, or reactions," and that persons identify with those values to such a degree that the demand to abandon them can appear a great evil – in some cases, as a threat to the self. Such frameworks simultaneously create some options and close off or discourage others, and they can do the first only by also doing the second.[28] Given the way these frameworks connect to the good of expressive liberty, the threshold justifying the MVL state's interference with them must be very high. The objections I've raised suggest that this burden is not met simply by showing that a group endorses gender differentiation.

THE CRITERIA FOR DIFFERENTIATION: TWO WORRIES

My attempt to distinguish subordination from differentiation invites two lines of critique. The first quarrels with various individual criteria, while the second argues that my position is self-refuting, because no group can satisfy the criteria without in effect endorsing liberal norms of gender neutrality. In the next section I discuss the self-refutation worry. Here I'll discuss the first line of critique, beginning with objections that focus on the idea of exit and then turning to the worry that consent is vitiated by false consciousness.

The relevance of exit

Some may deny that exit is relevant to the moral assessment of a group's practices. The moral character of a set of practices is one thing, one might think, its members' ability to leave quite another. Leslie Green,

[28] Charles Taylor, *Sources of the Self* (Cambridge, MA: Harvard University Press, 1989), 26. Catherine Cookson notes the relevance of Taylor's work here in *Regulating Religion: The Courts and the Free Exercise Clause* (New York: Oxford University Press, 2001), 99–108. Cf. Bikhu Parekh's observation that every culture "both opens up and closes options, both stabilizes and circumscribes the moral and social world, creates the conditions of choice but also demands conformity. The two functions are inseparable and dialectically related" (Parekh, *Rethinking Multiculturalism*, 156). Jeffrey Spinner-Halev captures the same idea in the phrase "enabling constraints" (*Surviving Diversity: Religion and Democratic Citizenship* [Baltimore, MD: Johns Hopkins University Press, 2000], 61).

for example, has argued that "if a certain social structure is unjust, it cannot become just merely by being avoidable," and Shachar expresses a similar concern, noting that spousal battery is not justified by the fact that a wife has the option to leave her marriage.[29] Such critics are right in pointing out that the opportunity to exit does not alone vindicate any and all institutions and practices. That fact does not detract from the relevance of exit in determining whether state intervention is acceptable, however, because the exit option functions not as a sufficient condition legitimating any set of practices, norms, and so on, but only as one that is necessary for tolerating a group's norms and that strengthens such a case.

Consider again the objections. Physical assault of a spouse plainly violates the MVL state's commitment to protect its citizens from bodily harm, and so should not be tolerated even if spouses can leave. Nor does Green's distinction between justice and exit undermine exit's relevance to moral assessment. To see why, compare an unjust regime that does not allow its members to exit with a similar regime that does. Surely we judge the second as, *ceteris paribus*, less morally objectionable than the first. This judgment shows that we believe either (1) that the exit option makes the second less unjust, or (2) that justice is not the only concern relevant to the moral assessment of a community. Accepting (1) allows that exit reduces injustice, *pace* Green, and so weakens the claim for intervening in illiberal groups. Accepting (2) allows that exit is relevant to claims against intervention, captured now not via a judgment of relative justice but through an overall moral assessment. Either way, then, exit remains relevant to the claim against intervention.

Seeing the exit option not as sufficient grounds against state intervention but only as a necessary condition strengthening the case against it also mitigates the worry that stressing the value of exit fails properly to register the connection between identity and group membership. Daniel Weinstock has argued that the model of exit, with its image of a person comparing the costs and benefits of leaving the group, is out of place in cases where group membership is, in Weinstock's phrase, "identity-conferring." When group membership goes so deep inside a person that there's no way she can imagine herself outside the group, the idea of *her*

---

[29] Leslie Green, "Internal Minorities and Their Rights," in *The Rights of Minority Cultures*, ed. Will Kymlicka (New York: Oxford University Press, 1995), 266; Shachar, *Multicultural Jurisdictions*, 42. So as not to misrepresent Shachar's position, I should add that she endorses the exit option as critical to the "transformative accommodation" strategy she defends. The problem of domestic abuse may be more closely related to the danger of false consciousness, which I take up in the next section.

exiting makes no sense. Exit then cannot be a helpful criterion in assessing the acceptability of a group's norms and practices.[30]

I agree with Weinstock that identities can be deeply bound up in the normative commitments that define groups – indeed, my reference in the first paragraph of this chapter to identity-conferring groups borrowed his phrase. But this point does not defeat the relevance of exit, for three reasons. First, the cases that most concern Weinstock are those where members receive what he calls "harsh treatment" at the hands of their group. Though this phrase is not elaborated, to the extent that harsh treatment violates other criteria on my account it counts in favor of intervention, and does so conclusively when it violates minimal universalism. Second, an exit option exists only when a group's members have adequate knowledge of the world beyond their group and possess skills that will allow them to participate in some of its roles. When members continue to see their group as identity-conferring under those conditions, that identification is less worrisome, insofar as identity-formation is not a wholly passive process but involves as well a person's response to and endorsement of the ideals that partially constitute her identity. So even if a person believes that leaving the group is tantamount to the death of the self, we are not confronted only with freedom's constraint: being in that condition itself reflects some exercise of agency, albeit one marked by varying degrees of self-consciousness. The third consideration mitigating Weinstock's worry is that exit is often not best understood through the model of a conscious accounting of costs and benefits. What is more likely is that prior to such an accounting members find themselves, through greater awareness of alternatives and/or their own growing dissatisfaction, uncertain about how far they identify with their group's norms. Where that uncertainty has already arisen with the urgency that would lead one to self-conscious accounting, it is much less likely that group-conferred identity will be so encompassing that a person simply cannot conceive of herself outside the group. Where such accounting occurs, in other words, worries over its appropriateness are already mitigated.

Consent and false consciousness

A second objection targets the relevance of members' consent to norms of gender differentiation. On this objection, stressing consent overlooks

---

[30] Daniel Weinstock, "Beyond Exit Rights: Reframing the Debate," in *Minorities within Minorities: Equality, Rights and Diversity*, ed. Avigail Eisenberg and Jeffrey Spinner-Halev (Cambridge: Cambridge University Press, 2005), 227–46.

the possibility that false consciousness may generate a set of preferences that are not good for women to hold because they do not in fact advance their interests.[31] (I shall use "preferences" to refer to such things as desires, goals, guiding values, sense of virtues appropriate to oneself, and the like.) However much women might endorse gender differentiation, it will be said, where that endorsement reflects false consciousness it cannot render such practices legitimate – if anything, it makes them even more troubling. The charge of false consciousness thus makes two connected objections to taking women's preferences as a factor against state intervention: their content is objectionable, in the sense that pursuing them will not advance women's well-being; and their genesis is corrupted, such that they have little relevance to justifying social arrangements.

The possibility of false consciousness must be granted. It is surely conceivable that some slaves believed they were better off under slavery than they would have been as free men and women, just as spouses in abusive relationships can wrongly think they are best served by remaining in them. When such beliefs result from the drive to reconcile oneself to miserable or deeply unjust conditions (perhaps because one cannot imagine their ever changing),[32] or from a closely managed process of socialization designed to inculcate beliefs in a way that precludes rational deliberation, the problem of false consciousness arises. Though some might downplay the worry, arguing that "freedom is a matter not of what preferences [people] have but of whether they may act in accordance with them," this

---

[31] On adaptive preferences generally, see Jon Elster, *Sour Grapes: Studies in the Subversion of Rationality* (New York: Cambridge University Press, 1983). Martha Nussbaum offers an extended discussion of how the problem affects women in ch. 2 of *Women and Human Development: The Capabilities Approach* (New York: Cambridge University Press, 2000). Though Nussbaum speaks chiefly of adaptive preferences, I stress the idea of false consciousness, in part because of arguments Harriet Baber makes in her paper "Adaptive Preference," presented March 28, 2004, at the APA Mini-Conference on Global Justice in Pasadena, CA. Baber argues convincingly that what Nussbaum calls adaptive preferences are not as troubling as Nussbaum imagines, because in the cases Nussbaum cites, the person in question would opt for a better option (i.e. one more conducive to her well-being) were it available. The problem thus lies not with the preferences, says Baber, but with the option set: "Making the best of a raw deal when no other alternatives are available is not the same as preferring it," she insists. I stress the idea of false consciousness, then, because the cases that really worry critics like Nussbaum and Okin are those where a woman's conception of her proper role and abilities is so distorted that she would neither choose the better option were it available nor advocate for its availability. Baber's critique of Nussbaum's use of adaptive preferences does not directly address this deeper worry, though in private communication she has expressed doubts that the problem of false consciousness is as widespread as Nussbaum and Okin suggest.

[32] Cass Sunstein suggests that false consciousness can result from "dissonance-reducing strategies," whereby victims "lower their own self-esteem to accommodate both the fact of victimization and the belief that the world is essentially just" (*Free Markets and Social Justice* [New York: Oxford University Press, 1997], 27).

reply misses the point.[33] Freedom matters because it allows a person to pursue ideals she believes central to a good or worthwhile life. Where these ideals are mistaken as a result of a process reflecting another's will, the value of freedom comes into question. The danger in attending to false consciousness, of course, is that it may lead one to disrespect others' agency and to substitute one's own judgment of life's meaning and value for theirs. The challenge is thus to balance concern over false consciousness with the choices of women to embrace the gendered roles their group norms specify.

To tackle the problem, note first that the possibility of false consciousness implies that persons can be understood apart from their preferences. Were we constituted entirely by our mental states, there would be nothing to which these could be false. (They might be inconsistent, but critics of false consciousness want to target even consistent sets.) The worry over false consciousness thus assumes that each person possesses some sort of built-in nature, immune to ideologically driven socialization processes, that might not be best advanced by the preferences they come to have.[34] One might construe that built-in nature in a radically individualist fashion, but critics of false consciousness generally stress interests and capacities common across persons. It follows, then, that the narrower one's conception of human nature, the more likely one will see a set of preferences as indicative of false consciousness. The broader one's conception of human nature, the less likely one will be to see preferences that way.

Now while accounts of human nature are notoriously controversial, ranging from heavily social-constructivist accounts at one extreme to the view that enculturation is a mere veneer on some fundamental unchanging substrate at the other, the most compelling accounts fall in the middle, recognizing that human beings are born with a finite range of in-built tendencies and potentials which cultures channel in distinctive ways. Bikhu Parekh offers an exemplary account of this sort, stressing

---

[33] Kukathas, *The Liberal Archipelago*, 109.

[34] Recognizing that her argument would be undermined if people's desires "were really adaptive through and through," Nussbaum asserts that "the human personality has a structure that is at least to some extent independent of culture, powerfully though culture shapes it at every stage … Desires for food, for mobility, for security, for health, and for the use of reason – these seem to be relatively permanent features of our makeup as humans" (*Women and Human Development*, 155). Her justly famous listing of capabilities constitutes one such account of human nature. But given the importance she ascribes to that account, it's not clear why in a roughly contemporary essay she suggests that the liberalism she defends does not depend on "the proposition that men and women have an equal metaphysical nature, or any other theory of human nature" ("A Plea for Difficulty," 109). I may, however, simply not understand what Nussbaum means here by a theory of human nature, metaphysical or otherwise.

the plurality of ideals, excellences, and goals available to human beings and the impossibility of any one person or group achieving them all. For Parekh, this plurality, conjoined with the existence of distinct cultures that shape how persons develop and come to see themselves, means that along with those commonalities we share with other human beings, each of us comes to possess in part a nature deeply shaped by our cultural context. "To be human," he writes, "is to belong both to a common species and to a distinct culture, and one only because of the other."[35]

Cultures thus shape who we are – in large part by their collective endorsement of certain goals, character traits, and so on as especially admirable and action-guiding, their judgment of others as corrupt, misguided, and worthless. Since cultures differ on these judgments, it follows that the nature of individual selves will differ as well: some may come to possess a nature whose expression hinges on self-creation through the exercise of critical autonomy, others may develop selves whose deepest expression drives them to seek harmony with nature, while the fulfillment of still others may be bound up with the goals of sustaining group solidarity and maintaining cultural traditions.[36] So long as these diverse aims involve goods that persons plausibly see as fulfilling their natures, their endorsement of them is not a case of false consciousness. Even if it is true counterfactually that such persons would have come to endorse different preferences if raised under different circumstances, that just means they would have had different preferences if they had become different persons. That hardly seems a criticism of the preferences they do have. The capaciousness of Parekh's account of human nature suggests that the threshold for a judgment of false consciousness should be very high indeed, and that apparent consent for plausible goods should be taken, absent powerful evidence to the contrary, as legitimating.

Against this defense of the consent criterion, those concerned about false consciousness might offer two objections. First, they might insist that the roles many such groups recommend for women – which often involve domestic and child-rearing tasks – do not in fact offer genuine fulfillment, because the goods they make available are less valuable than

---

[35] "Cultures are not superstructures built upon identical and unchanging foundations, or manifestations of a common human essence, but unique human creations that reconstitute and give different meaning and orientation to those properties that all human beings share in common, add new ones of their own, and give rise to different kinds of human beings ... As members of a cultural community, human beings *acquire* certain tendencies and dispositions, in some cases as deep and powerful as those they are deemed to possess by nature" (Parekh, *Rethinking Multiculturalism*, 124).

[36] Ibid., 339.

others they might pursue. This claim, however, faces at least three serious problems. It is highly dubious in itself; it is likely to be rejected by many of the apparently reflective and thoughtful citizens in whose name it is invoked; and it takes up a substantive position on controversial value claims in the manner MVL seeks to avoid.

The second objection is less easily dispatched. It is that much of the gender differentiation within such groups, to which women appear to consent, extends to norms about who makes important decisions at both the collective and individual level, with women being encouraged to defer to men. The justification of such norms most often proceeds via arguments stressing men's superiority as decision-makers, their God-given place as head of the family, their intrinsic ability to lead, and so on. But such claims, it will be said, violate the ideal of moral equality: no one with a proper sense of her equal moral status would so consent. When a group's gender norms take this form (as, critics suggest, they overwhelmingly do), it thus becomes a reasonable target for intervention by the MVL state.

This is a challenging objection. It is, however, controversial in key respects. To begin with, it is not always obvious to what degree women are excluded from the process of decision-making in important areas. Members of such groups (many of them female) have recently offered arguments to show that women exert greater agency, both public and private, than outsiders often infer, and this point is especially relevant given the value of groups' changing as a result of their own internal momentum rather than through outsiders' influence.[37] Note as well that those who advance the objection sometimes note that women do exercise special authority over the domestic sphere, especially with reference to childrearing. If such objections are meant to show that women's agency is somehow less significant, they assume that matters of collective or public deliberation are intrinsically more important than domestic ones. If we measure importance by the clear impact one's decision has on the lives of others, that assumption appears problematic.

Even if these replies fail, so that we accept that women have on balance a diminished decision-making role in some cultural groups, the second objection would be open to two further criticisms. One concerns

[37] For examples of this genre in different religious contexts, see Ahmed, *Women and Gender in Islam*; Amina Wadud, *Qu'ran and Woman: Reading the Sacred Text from a Woman's Perspective*, 2nd edn. (New York: Oxford University Press, 1999); Blu Greenberg, *On Women and Judaism: A View from Tradition* (Philadelphia, PA: Jewish Publication Society of America, 1981); and Kumkum Sangari and Sudesh Vaid, eds., *Recasting Women: Essays in Indian Colonial History*, (New Brunswick, NJ: Rutgers University Press, 1990).

its assumption that judgments about a person's relative ability to occupy leadership roles inevitably entail judgments about a person's relative moral status. Given the obvious ways in which people differ in this respect, such an assumption would challenge the dominant view of moral equality: that view attributes equality of moral status to all who meet some threshold of rationality, above which differences in other respects are morally irrelevant. On that view, the claim that men are on the whole naturally better suited to leadership is not obviously incompatible with the ideal of moral equality.

The other weakness in the second objection involves its account of the source of our moral status. One influential line of thought holds that it is our capacity for reason that confers on us our special status as ends in ourselves. Among the many competitors to that account (some of which stress our affective capacities over or alongside our rationality), there are various influential strands of thought which hold that our moral status and dignity derive from our relationship to God and our special place in a sacred order of creation. On many such views, that relationship is not just compatible with but closely connected to the idea that God has assigned to the sexes distinct roles in social reproduction, and gender differentiation is seen not as violating the ideal of moral equality but as representing how God intends us to live out that ideal.

The important question here, I think, is not which account of moral equality political philosophers endorse, but whether the MVL state should reject the latter as a reasonable construal of moral equality. It should not. The issue of what ultimately grounds our moral equality is the subject of deep controversy, dividing liberal citizens and moral philosophers alike. The MVL state may no more impose on all citizens any one answer to that question than it may impose any one normative framework specifying how to lead a life. Even when some answers, in either context, seem from the philosophical standpoint not fully adequate, their long history of persuasiveness, along with the built-in deference to citizens' rationality that marks liberalism, provides strong *prima facie* reasons for the MVL state to accept such frameworks as reasonable ways of capturing moral equality.

ACCEPTABLE DIFFERENTIATION AND *DE FACTO* LIBERALIZATION

The second general critique against my suggestion of acceptable gender differentiation argues that groups cannot meet the criteria listed earlier without becoming de facto liberal groups. My position is thus self-refuting if meant to articulate conditions for tolerating illiberal groups. This point is especially likely to be pressed against my emphases on the exit option and the importance of mutual negotiation. I shall discuss these in turn.

The conditions of meaningful exit

The worry over exit is nicely illustrated in an exchange between Chandran Kukathas and Will Kymlicka.[38] Kymlicka charges that despite Kukathas's avowals of extreme tolerance for illiberal group norms, Kukathas must in practice allow much of the sort of intervention he seeks to exclude. The reason is that the measures needed to protect the substantive basic right of exit that Kukathas stresses – measures like general literacy, formal education, familiarity with the outside world, perhaps even some degree of psychological resilience against the social pressure of one's group – will likely involve overriding illiberal groups' norms.[39] Kymlicka's general point may seem to hold against my emphasis on exit as well. Women have a real chance to exit their group only if they are presented with the range of roles in wider society they might take up, have developed the skills that will allow them to assume positions there, and possess sufficient psychological independence so that leaving is a live option. But putting such measures in place, some will say, requires that cultural groups liberalize their norms and practices in a manner that largely rules out any strong gender differentiation. It is thus impossible for illiberal groups to satisfy a substantive exit option while maintaining the strongly gendered norms that structure differentiation.

Now it must be said that Kukathas's account of exit, with its strong emphasis on freedom of association, invites just this sort of objection. Freedom of association suggests a model of persons consciously reflecting on the groups with which they will affiliate. But alongside that picture, we can discern in Kukathas a subtly different account, one that downplays the model of voluntary association and stresses instead acquiescence to communal practices and norms. Here Kukathas moves away from seeing groups as the result of choices and emphasizes instead the way such

[38] Chandran Kukathas, "Are There Any Cultural Rights?," *Political Theory* 20, no. 1 (February 1992), 105–39, and Will Kymlicka, "The Rights of Minority Cultures: Reply to Kukathas," *Political Theory* 20, no. 1 (February 1992), 140–6 .

[39] "What is crucially important here, however, is the extent to which the individual does enjoy a *substantial* freedom to leave … The freedom of the individual to dissociate from a community is a freedom with considerable substantive bite" (Kukathas, "Are There Any Cultural Rights?," 133).

groups "shape individual commitments and give meaning to individual lives – lives for which individual choice or autonomy may be quite valueless." On this second account, the key question in assessing a group's acceptability is not whether its way of life results from members having chosen it from a range of options but, more modestly, "whether the individuals taking part in it are prepared to acquiesce in it."[40]

It is important to see here why moving from a model emphasizing voluntary association to one stressing acquiescence does not abandon the liberal ideal of expressive liberty. The two models differ not in how they value such liberty, but in how they construe it. To see this, we can distinguish three groups: (1) those in which membership is compelled; (2) those resulting from a conscious act of choice; (3) those where membership neither is compelled nor originates in a conscious act of choice. While all liberals reject (1), MVL recognizes (3) as a legitimate expression of liberty and on that ground defends an account of exit that does not require the liberalization that would make cultural groups more like voluntary associations. On this account, then, there is no reason to think that the expressive liberty that liberals cherish requires overriding norms of gender differentiation so as to maximize the range of choices available to group members.

There are, I believe, two good reasons for construing voluntary group membership through the model of acquiescence (3) rather than conscious choice (2). First, choice is not the sole good, and amplifying choice can undermine other important values. For example, we might expand children's religious choices by insisting that they closely observe a range of diverse religious practices, but this would violate an important freedom of parents and potentially dilute religious worship. Or again, making divorce easier might increase the options of those who are married but would at some point undermine the commitment that contributes to the value of marriage. Suggesting that group membership be understood strictly on the model of free choice also has costs. Not only does it challenge the interests many have in passing on their cultural heritage and risk making one's involvement in such traditions shallower and less authentic, but emphasizing choice can also (as Chapter 3 argued) undermine faith in the existence of norms independent of our will and so advance a creeping subjectivism about values.

The other reason for endorsing the model of acquiescence is that it is more accurate as an account of human agency. In discussing the value

---

[40] Ibid., 122, 124. The index to *The Liberal Archipelago* lists fourteen entries for "acquiescence."

of groups, Michael Walzer criticizes as an example of "bad utopianism" the ideal of "a world where all associations are voluntary, a social union composed entirely of freely constituted social unions."[41] That ideal misleads in two ways. Not only do the existing associations within which we chart our lives not reflect our own decisions; in addition, the liberal citizen who sees her flourishing as bound up in a life of self-conscious choice – who celebrates critical reflection, individuality, independence, and the like – is herself the result of a specific socialization process aimed at developing just such dispositions. Even liberal heroes do not create themselves, but instead reflect the influence of a distinct cultural context.

The virtues in the model of acquiescence recommend construing the exit option in relatively modest terms. Instead of requiring sympathetic engagement with a wide variety of normative frameworks, the state may demand only that citizens be informed about a range of alternatives outside their group. Instead of seeking to immunize individuals against social pressure from family and group members, the state should tolerate such pressure as an expression of liberty and concentrate instead on clear cases of coercion. Instead of enforcing an ideal of gender neutrality, the state should insist only that women develop a sense of their equal moral status, one that would as well encourage them to exit from arrangements where their interests are sacrificed to men's. One needn't have read Aristotle to see that some lack of precision is unavoidable here, that there is no escaping the need for judgment in determining how much awareness and what sorts of skills exit requires. But there are numerous contexts where such judgments are similarly unavoidable (tests of clear and present danger, compelling state interests, undue burdens, etc.) yet there exists consensus sufficient for broad continuity in public decisions.[42] The modest account of exit is imprecise, but not unworkable.

There remains one final objection against the modest account, grounded in the ideal of equality. In groups where men have greater control over

---

[41] Michael Walzer, "On Involuntary Association," in *Freedom of Association*, ed. Amy Gutmann (Princeton: Princeton University Press, 1998), 64.

[42] Catherine Cookson argues that courts have by and large demonstrated their ability to make such judgments without succumbing to arbitrariness. Of the US experience, she writes, "All courts regularly 'do the impossible' in the course of a day's work: determine the best interests of a child in a custody case, assess what dollar amount to place on an individual's pain and suffering, balance risk against utility in a products liability case, determine fault in a negligence case and intent in a criminal case, and so on" (Cookson, *Regulating Religion*, 106). See also Stephen Macedo, *Diversity and Distrust: Civic Education in a Multicultural Society* (Cambridge, MA: Harvard University Press, 2000), 195ff.

income or are more likely to possess skills valued in the wider society, exit will be easier for men. Now morality demands that basic rights be distributed equally to all persons. If the right to exit is a basic right, it too should be distributed equally to all persons. But then it follows that the state may take steps to ensure that men and women are equally able to exit their groups, and this may again involve significant intervention into groups whose strongly gendered norms and practices make exit easier for men.[43]

Now as a reminder that an exit option must be real and not merely notional, this objection is salutary. But it is a mistake to think that the ideal of equality requires equalizing ease of exit across gender lines, for two reasons. The first involves the economic cost of exit. So long as differences of wealth exist, exit from any group (including the liberal polity) will be easier for some than for others. Ensuring substantive equality to exit would then require equalizing wealth across all citizens. If we allow that the right to exit does not require such extraordinary measures, we will construe it as requiring only that the state ensure that all citizens have an adequate ability to exit – in the same way, for example, that a commitment to provide health care for all is a commitment to provide it to all at an adequate level, even if some citizens can purchase a higher level.[44] Adapting a point Harry Frankfurt has made, we might say the main concern is not that men and women face equal costs if they choose to leave, but that the costs be low enough for all so that each has a genuine opportunity to exit if they wish.[45]

The MVL state thus has no obligation substantively to equalize ease of exit. Are such measures permissible? No, because of the second reason against equalization: since groups differ both on the terms that define membership and the degree to which they discourage defection, any

---

[43] The general objection here is pressed by Okin in "Mistresses of Their Own Destiny," 205–30.

[44] Where a group's property relations are such that exit involves renouncing all accumulated wealth (as with the Hutterites in Canada), some provision may have to be made to ensure that the exiter has the resources to lead a decent life outside the group. Ideally, cultural groups would set aside funds for their members who wish to exit, but this seems unduly hopeful. More likely the liberal state will have to take steps – perhaps by providing startup payouts to those who leave such communities, putting constraints on acceptable property arrangements within such groups, or requiring that groups make such funds available. The economic aspects of exit are noted by both Spinner-Halev (*Surviving Diversity*, 77 ff.) and Shachar, who quotes Carole Rose's observation that "the propertyless or entitlement-less person has no alternative game to play" (Rose, "Women and Property: Gaining and Losing Ground," *Virginia Law Review* 78 [1992], 453, quoted in Shachar, *Multicultural Jurisdictions*, 67, n. 21).

[45] "What is important from the point of view of morality is not that everyone should have *the same* but that each should have *enough*" (Harry Frankfurt, "Equality as a Moral Ideal," *Ethics* 98 [1987], 21).

policy aimed at equalizing exit would require unequal interference with the norms of such groups in a manner hard to square with MVL's commitment to equal freedom. Some groups are relatively tolerant of exit; others present it as a kind of social death and discourage all contact with those who leave. Such cases of ostracism may be not only painful to those who exit but morally objectionable as well. But the office of the liberal state is not to compel persons to act like angels. It is to ensure them the space within which they can make a range of decisions about how their lives shall go, including bad choices that affect not just themselves but others as well. The result of that protection, admittedly, is that exiting one's group may be easier for some citizens than for others, but so long as it is available to all, this is an outcome liberals must live with.

Norms and negotiation

A second way of showing that my account of acceptable differentiation is self-refuting targets my acknowledgment that some degree of mutual negotiation between men and women strengthens a claim for differentiation as opposed to subordination. The thought behind that criterion is that greater input from women on such questions makes their relation to governing norms more consensual, mitigating the concern that gender differentiation amounts to subordination. Such negotiation takes on added importance once we recognize that the norms and practices of various groups are neither fixed nor self-interpreting and that members are bound to disagree on such questions as the relative priority of shared values, the specific practices demanded by mutually endorsed norms, and so on.[46] It might seem that ensuring women a genuine voice in this process requires that various measures be in place: women must occupy positions of power within bodies entrusted with interpreting their traditions, be exposed to a range of views about how to view their own tradition and other groups', and be encouraged both to express opposition to prevailing interpretations of norms and to explore roles different from those women have traditionally occupied in their community. But any group meeting these criteria, some will argue, will already have

---

[46] Rejecting what she calls "reductionist sociologies of culture," Seyla Benhabib asserts that "cultures are not homogeneous wholes; they are constituted through the narratives and symbolizations of their members, who articulate these in the course of partaking of complex social and significative practices" (*The Claims of Culture* [Princeton: Princeton University Press, 2003], 61). Steven Lukes echoes Benhabib's worry in *Liberals and Cannibals*, 19, 34.

left behind illiberal gender norms. The conditions of mutual negotiation that defang the worry over gender subordination, and so strengthen the claims of illiberal groups against state intervention, can thus be met only by groups that have already liberalized their gender practices along lines feminist critics champion.

Faced with this objection to my account, one possible response is to argue that the concern over mutual negotiation can be accommodated without requiring substantive changes to the norms of cultural groups. This is the general route Jeff Spinner-Halev takes when he insists, in response to Okin's criticism, that a group's laws "be established by democratically accountable representatives, not just the traditional male leaders." Anticipating the objection that such a requirement amounts to substantial intervention into such a community's norms, Spinner-Halev insists that his proposal is not "a reform of the community's laws; nor does it entail the state demanding that the community change its laws … the state will allow the community to decide upon its personal laws, but the state will not then choose who does the deciding as it currently has. The community itself will decide who establishes its rules."[47] In this way, group autonomy and the demands of democratic negotiation are reconciled.

Spinner-Halev's solution, however, tries to have the cake and eat it too. It assumes a distinction – between a community's substantive identity and norms, and its procedures for determining these – that cannot stand up in just the areas where it needs to do most work, i.e. in groups where the meaning and priority of norms are settled in ways that fall short of internal democracy. The case of the Catholic Church shows the general problem. A demand that the church rearrange its governance structure to make its major officials "democratically accountable" (however we understand that phrase here) would be tantamount to demanding major revisions in the nature of that organization. To think that the demand extends only to how the church goes about establishing its defining rules, and touches not the constitution and character of the church itself, is to misunderstand that community and its belief that some persons have special authority in determining the progress and shape of their community. The same point can be shown from the other way round, as it were, if we consider a democratic state. Within certain constraints the laws of such a state should reflect the collective will of its members. But that

---

[47] Jeffrey Spinner-Halev, "Feminism, Multiculturalism, Oppression, and the State," *Ethics* 112 (October 2001), 108–9.

laws should be democratically decided is not itself a position validated by democratic procedure, and any departure from that commitment would significantly change the nature of the community. So whether we are considering a process where a group moves towards democracy or away from it, we should not imagine that its procedures for determining defining rules can be easily distinguished from its substantive character. That character is largely a function of its practices and norms, the latter understood to include what we might call meta-norms indicating both how the meaning and relative priority of substantive norms are to be understood and the authority by which conflicts over such matters are to be resolved. Tolerating only robustly democratic meta-norms significantly constrains expressive liberty.

The case against such a stringent standard is strengthened by two further considerations. First, even where groups fall short of internal democracy there may still be mechanisms in place allowing members to express their views about group norms and to influence them. In arguing for the equal moral standing in international society of what he calls "consultation hierarchies," Rawls stresses that what is critical for their legitimacy is that the voices of all members be heard, in a manner appropriate to "the religious and philosophical values of the society as expressed in its idea of the common good."[48] This approach is not unproblematic: voices can be heard without being given any weight, just as ideas of the common good can fail to register moral equality (think of caste systems, for example). But what drives Rawls here is a commitment to self-rule understood in terms of persons' living under norms they endorse as an expression of their own values. So while self-rule is not democracy – desiring to live under non-democratic institutions does not make them democratic – the two are not unrelated, and abandoning the stringent demand that groups align themselves with internal democracy offers a better way of reconciling the ideal of self-rule with the value of expressive liberty.

The second reason for relaxing that demand is that there exist various ways of promoting democratic input that do not directly mandate change in the meta-norms of the groups in question. Ensuring an exit option is one such measure, insofar as it increases the leverage of disaffected group members and so makes their voices more powerful. Here again, however, we should note reasons against always making

[48] John Rawls, *The Law of Peoples: with "The Idea of Public Reason Revisited"* (Cambridge, MA: Harvard University Press, 1999), 72.

exit easier: since easier exit makes it more likely that persons who support democratic meta-norms will depart rather than lobby for internal reform, mutual negotiation may be strengthened by making exit available but not too easy.[49] Another factor promoting mutual negotiation is women's levels of education. The more women possess powerful skills of analysis, expression, reflection, and so on, the more likely they are both to ask intelligent questions about their traditions and to reject inadequate answers. The current explosion of scholarly interest on women's roles within Islam exemplifies this dynamic.[50] While it has various sources, one central factor has been the rise of a generation of highly educated Islamic women exploring just these issues. True, the levels of education involved here go beyond what the MVL state can require either on grounds of exit or through the guarantee of education as a basic good. But as I argue in the following chapter, the level of education the MVL state may reasonably demand of all citizens is substantial, and cultural groups cannot shield girls from that requirement by appealing to their own norms.

The provision of that education, in conjunction with the inevitably liberalizing effects of living in a liberal state governed by laws that are gender neutral, should increase the number of women who can speak with authority and influence on their group's norms, further weakening the need for the MVL state to intervene in groups with heavily gendered norms. So while it may be true (if we set aside the worry over reactive culturalism mentioned above) that various groups will find it easier to pass on distinctive gendered norms under the MVL approach than under a more robustly interventionist liberal state, that is not to say they'll find it easy to do so. That fact, coupled with the recognition that such norms are endorsed by many of the men and women subject to them, suggests that so long as various criteria are met, the choices of liberal citizens for

---

[49] The point Alan Patten makes with reference to democratic deliberation applies as well to exit generally: "Theories of secession that make 'exit' too easy leave insufficient incentive for 'voice'. Members of a territorially concentrated minority will be less inclined to 'invest themselves in the practice of principled debate and deliberation' if they believe that they could secede easily instead ... Encouraging principled democratic participation in the face of persistent majority/minority conflicts requires striking a balance between too much exit and too little" ("Democratic Secession from a Multinational State," *Ethics* 112 [April 2002], 586). The phrase Patten quotes comes from Allen Buchanan, whose account of secession Patten discusses.

[50] For examples of the trend towards internal critique with respect to Islam, engaging with but not limited to its relation to feminism, see Omid Safi, ed., *Progressive Muslims: On Justice, Gender, and Pluralism* (Oxford: Oneworld, 2003), and Amina Wadud, *Inside the Gender Jihad: Women's Reform in Islam* (Oxford: Oneworld, 2006).

gendered social norms should largely be respected. Various groups, however, seeking to immunize their norms against precisely the dynamic just described, may try to block the compulsory education that liberal states have long insisted on. Whether such objections deserve a hearing, and the general structure of that education in the MVL state, are the subjects of the next chapter.

CHAPTER 9

Compulsory education in the MVL state

ROBUST LIBERAL EDUCATION

Debates over education in liberal states reflect both practical and conceptual challenges. At the practical level, education represents both a substantial cost to parents (through tax-funded schools) and a far-reaching intrusion into their children's lives. Disagreement among parents over the nature of that education is thus bound to create controversy among liberal citizens. But these debates also point to serious and revealing tensions at the heart of liberalism. For example, liberal states distinguish between adults, who have equal claims to extensive freedom, and children, who are not fully capable of exercising freedom responsibly. But children learn those skills within families, themselves important areas for the expression of freedom. How then to balance family privacy with the legitimate concern over children's development? Or consider that education seems to require consensus on which achievements, skills, and ideas are especially worthwhile. The liberal state, however, is in part defined by its not taking sides in such debates. Or again, consider the place of patriotism within liberal education. While some regard schooling as a unique opportunity to instill patriotism and cognate attitudes, others argue that the ideal of moral equality rules out any attempt to instill moral partiality.

A major challenge in entering such debates is to say something correct that goes beyond mere bromide. That children are not the chattels of their parents, that parents rightly have some say over their children's values, that liberal states function better if citizens display certain virtues – no one denies these truisms: getting beyond them is the hard part. To gain traction, I shall in this chapter concentrate on the question of what sort of education the MVL state may demand of its citizens, and I shall focus on one especially prominent answer advanced by various theorists: the liberal state should ensure that all children within its borders receive what

I shall call a robust liberal education (RLE).[1] Now as I present it RLE is admittedly an ideal type, and I shall not try to show that existing curricula correspond to its various elements (though I think many do). Rather, I am concerned with a general view about the purpose of education that is both familiar and influential in current debates, one often invoked to defend particular positions in recurrent controversies. This guiding conception stresses the overriding value of educating children to view more favorably and with greater sympathy a diversity of ways of life, normative frameworks, belief systems, and so on, in the hopes that such exposure will lead them to be both less critical in their judgments of alternative ideals and more reflective towards their own. While RLE does not assume that it is good for children to leave behind the ways of life and ideals in which they have grown up, it does assume that a central task of education is to motivate children self-consciously to consider alternatives to them presented as favorably as possible – to create what Harry Brighouse describes as a state of discontinuity between the norms at home and those confronted in school.[2]

In contrast to RLE's advocates stand those who believe liberal states should be less stringent in the sort of education they demand, and, in particular, should be more tolerant of educations that do not stress children's sympathetic encounter with alien norms. One especially important instance of this more modest approach, which I shall call directed education, takes the view that education should be designed with an eye to the child's endorsing some particular normative framework with its attendant values, goals, and so on.[3] I shall return to directed education at several

---

[1] Note that I am asking neither about the ideal education for a human being, nor whether the MVL state should support educational programs that some citizens favor. Both raise interesting issues, but my concern throughout has been how liberal states can answer the objections of the critic, and in this context that means citizens who object to educational demands that liberal states might impose. Such objections can take a number of forms – parents can ask that children opt out of certain aspects of public school curricula, that they be educated in private schools with substantial leeway to set their own educational agenda, that taxes that would otherwise pay for public schools be redirected to schools of their own choice, and so on. What I say will be relevant to those more specific issues, but I shall not explore them directly here. Note finally that I shall not defend the general principle that all persons should be educated to some degree and will simply assume that some degree of education counts among the basic goods specified by minimal univeralism.

[2] Harry Brighouse, "Channel One, the Anti-Commercial Principle, and the Discontinuous Ethos," in *Philosophy of Education: An Anthology*, ed. Randall Curren (Malden, MA: Blackwell, 2007), 208–20.

[3] By directed education I have in mind something similar to what Shelley Burtt calls "comprehensive education," which seeks "to fit the child with the worldview, personal commitments, and moral understandings that his parents and the faith community he inhabits believe to be necessary to live a good life" ("Comprehensive Educations and the Liberal Understanding of

places in my discussion, not only because it sharply opposes the central thrust of RLE but also because many liberal citizens who object to RLE do so because they fear it threatens their attempts to provide their child with directed education.

Whatever form the modest alternatives to RLE take, however, it is critical that they not be straw men. To see why, consider two accounts of child-rearing that have figured in recent philosophical argument. According to Richard Arneson and Ian Shapiro, the Amish provide their children with "an acculturation program expressly designed to limit critical thinking, to get children to accept things on faith without submitting them to reasoned reflection." The goal of the Amish, on their reading, is "to manage consciousness" in a manner excluding "abstract and rational modes of thought." In a similar vein, Kenneth Maddock describes Australian Aboriginal children being raised to see their social world not as the result of human choices but as something like an ontological given. Children are taught that "an order having been laid down, all that remains to do is to conform to it," presumably in a manner that does not invite the participants to give a rational accounting of it.[4]

The overall accuracy of these accounts may be a fair question, but it is not my concern. My point is that neither account describes a competing model of education to RLE, because neither describes a model of education. Education as such, and directed education *a fortiori*, involves acquiring to some substantial degree the following skills and knowledge:

• Skills of interpreting the products of the human world (including contributions in the arts and sciences), understanding relatively complex utterances, and communicating one's thoughts both orally and in writing.
• Skills of abstract reasoning, critical thought, and numerical literacy.
• Knowledge of the diversity of the natural world and of major views governing scientific thinking in those areas of knowledge (e.g. the solar system, atomic theory, flora and fauna, etc.).
• Knowledge of major events in human history (e.g. the rise and fall of various civilizations, exploration of the globe, world-shaping wars and conflict, etc.).

Autonomy," in *Citizenship and Education in Liberal-Democratic Societies*, ed. Walter Feinberg and Kevin McDonough [New York: Oxford University Press, 2003], 179).
[4] Richard Arneson and Ian Shapiro, "Democratic Autonomy and Religious Freedom," in *Political Order: NOMOS 38*, ed. Ian Shapiro and Russell Hardin (New York: New York University Press, 1996), 393–4. The quotations about "managing consciousness" and excluding abstract modes of thought come from Donald Kraybill, *The Riddle of Amish Culture* (Baltimore: Johns

- Knowledge of the various forms human communities have taken across time and space, and of the ways human beings have shaped these.

This list is hardly exhaustive, and it has none of the specificity needed to assess whether a proposed course of study meets the criterion of education as a basic good. I advance it here in broadest outline only to indicate the logical space between child-rearing that aims at mindless indoctrination on the one hand, and RLE, with its emphasis on sympathetic exposure to alien frameworks of value, on the other. The modest accounts of education I shall discuss, and directed education in particular, occupy that middle ground.

In this chapter I defend such modest alternatives and argue that RLE is unreasonably demanding. Forceful arguments for RLE have been advanced in recent years by a range of theorists, and I cannot hope to engage with all of them.[5] Fortunately, despite the nuances separating those accounts, we can identify three powerful and recurrent arguments for RLE. The first, which connects to the idea of minimal autonomy mentioned in Chapter 3, claims that RLE is needed to ensure that each citizen is genuinely self-governing. The second appeals to the idea of equal opportunity. The third stresses RLE's centrality in engendering especially important civic virtues. These arguments I assess below. Before doing so, though, I must explain the overall approach that informs my assessment.

COMPETING INTERESTS, COMPETING CLAIMS

Any approach to compulsory education must consider possible benefits and harms to relevant parties. I shall accept the widespread view that

Hopkins University Press, 1989). Kenneth Maddock, *The Australian Aborigines: A Portrait of Their Society* (Ringwood: Penguin, 1972), 193–4, quoted in Kukathas, "Are There Any Cultural Rights?," 120.

[5] Important defenses of RLE are found in Eamonn Callan, *Creating Citizens* (New York: Clarendon Press, 1997); Meira Levinson, *The Demands of Liberal Education* (New York: Oxford University Press, 1999); Bruce Ackerman, *Social Justice in the Liberal State* (New Haven: Yale University Press, 1980); Amy Gutmann, *Democratic Education* (esp. the Epilogue), and "Civic Education and Social Diversity," *Ethics* 105 (April 1995), 557–79; Arneson and Shapiro, "Democratic Autonomy and Religious Freedom"; and Harry Brighouse, *School Choice and Social Justice* (New York: Oxford University Press, 2000). Brighouse might object to being grouped as a defender of RLE as I have described it, for in distinguishing his view from Gutmann's he insists that on his approach children "are not taught sympathetically to address views about the good other than their own; [they are taught] only about such views, and how to engage them seriously" (*School Choice and Social Justice*, 80). But he also recommends presenting children with alternative views of the good "in a way that reflects the reality of the lives lived according to these commitments. Exposure to moral views would be done best by allowing proponents of views to address children

these parties are children, parents, and the state.[6] To be sure, it will often be the case that an education benefiting (or harming) one of these parties will also be good (or bad) for another. But there is no guarantee that such interests will either align or be seen to align. The crucial question, then, is how to adjudicate among these diverse interests and claims. How much weight to give the interests of the state I discuss below, where I consider the argument for RLE grounded in the civic virtues. Since most attention in debates over education revolves around the relation between children's interests and parents' interests, however, it is critical that I make clear at the outset how I construe that relationship.

That parents have some right to steer their child's education is denied by almost no one. Disagreement arises over the scope of that right (how far does it extend?), its content (what does it include?), and its grounding (why do parents have that right?).[7] Since answers to the scope and content questions hinge on understanding how the right is grounded, I focus on the latter question here. In addressing that question, many assume that any such grounding must proceed through an account that is either child-centered or parent-centered, and then, concluding that any version of the latter will fail to register the child's equal moral status, quickly endorse the former. This approach is not wrong so much as it is simplistic. While the ideal of moral equality does suggest that a child's interests must be central, there are two ways of taking that idea that should be resisted. First, some take child-centeredness to mean that the nature and content of the proper education for a child is determined only by facts about the child itself, without regard to parents' (often controversial) beliefs about what ends the child should adopt, what shape its character should take, what dispositions it should develop, and so on. Second, some believe that on a child-centered view parents' desires about the structure of their child's education have no intrinsic weight. I want to argue against both conceptions.

---

in the controlled environment of the classroom" (75). Since such proponents appear with the school's support and would naturally present their own position as sympathetically as possible, this recommendation brings his proposal quite close to the Gutmann position he rejects.

[6] William Galston, for example, asserts: "There are … three parties to the educational transaction: children, their parents, and the state" (*Liberal Purposes*, 254). Even if we assume that "the state" encompasses the welfare of fellow citizens, this tripartite transactional distinction omits a possible fourth party with relevant interests: persons outside one's own political community. Including the interests of such persons would raise a host of complicating issues, however: the limits of partiality, the scope of universalism, the moral significance of community membership, and so on. For this reason I shall bypass the important question how far education in the MVL state should aim to instill moral cosmopolitanism.

[7] Here I am influenced by Brighouse's account in *School Choice and Social Justice*, ch. 1.

The independent status of the child

The idea that the proper education of a child depends not at all on its parents' values and ideals can seem a natural consequence of the idea that children are independent persons of equal moral status. But the inference does not follow. To see why, imagine you are raising a child in a community whose members greatly value certain traits of character and skills – reliability and punctuality, say, along with an ability to understand the poetry of its culture. Since your child wants to be liked and respected, you advance its interests by educating it to become proficient in these areas. Here the child's education is shaped by others' conceptions of the sort of person it should become, but this seems neither objectionable in itself nor a violation of its equal moral status: you advance its interests by ensuring that it develops appropriate skills and knowledge, though what these are is a function of others' beliefs, values, and so on. Now if this be granted, there is no reason in principle to think that allowing parents' values and goals to shape their child's education in itself compromises moral equality. We need to distinguish, that is, between (1) a child's education being structured to advance the interests of others, and (2) its being structured in a way that reflects another's controversial conception of her interests. Moral equality rules out the first, but says nothing about the second. And there are, I think, several reasons to permit the second.

The first involves the value of a child's goals and values aligning in important ways with its parents'. Here I am thinking not solely of the ideal of intimacy some theorists have stressed,[8] but of related feelings like the child's beliefs that it can rely on its parents for guidance at critical moments, that its parents understand and care about its circumstances and needs, that they support its values and choices, and so on. By and large these things are aided by the child's general value framework not diverging too radically from its parents' (though it needn't mirror theirs in every respect). Children also benefit from developing values and ideals that hang together as a coherent whole and define them as persons of moral integrity. If they undergo an education that promotes values at odds with those of their parents, one of two things must happen. Either that education will have little effect on them (in which case it's wasted effort),[9] or children will feel torn between the values taught at home and

---

[8] See Ferdinand Schoeman, "Rights of Children, Rights of Parents, and the Moral Basis of the Family," *Ethics* 91 (October 1980), 6–19.

[9] As even a strong advocate of RLE like Amy Gutmann acknowledges, "studies seem to show that public education has not been very effective in producing intended educational effects in cases

those taught at the school. Forcing such choices might be justified if either parents' norms are sufficiently objectionable or the goods RLE advances are sufficiently valuable. But on the MVL approach it will be difficult to establish either claim. Regarding the former, I am assuming objections to RLE from parents whose norms satisfy minimal moral universalism. As for the latter, since the MVL state is defined by its agnosticism on the value of different ways of life, it cannot claim that the values likely to be enhanced by RLE (for example, celebrating diversity, legislating one's own values, choosing in conditions of maximal choice) are sufficiently great to offset competing goods. Even if some advocates of RLE are not troubled by an education that promotes "cross-cutting memberships and complex identities, [in which] the fragmentation and multiplicity of our social lives means [*sic*] that our identities will also be fragmented, and our associations with others always partial and provisional," this is too controversial an ideal with which the MVL state might justify a program of compulsory education.[10]

The values of intimacy-related goods and moral integrity constitute strong *prima facie* reasons, consistent with recognizing the child's equal status, for letting its education be significantly shaped by its parents' desires that it develop values associated with particular normative frameworks. A further reason for that view is that beyond various biological needs, a person's well-being is closely connected to her important goals, themselves often rooted in distinct value frameworks. It thus gets it backward to defend a child's need to be exposed to a wide range of value frameworks by appealing to its interests: the latter can be specified, in any substantial way, only by reference to some such framework or other. Advocates of RLE might try to deny this by identifying interests at a less precise, more formal level – a person's interest in having self-respect, developing talents, experiencing emotional closeness, etc. But these, I have argued, will be compatible with any education rooted in a moral framework consistent with the basic commitments of MVL, and so they cannot be the ground for demanding RLE.

I suspect some resist the position of strong parental authority outlined here because the goods in question benefit not just the child but parents as well: parents, too, value intimate, supportive relations with their children;

where a supportive home environment is lacking" ("Children, Paternalism, and Education: A Liberal Argument," *Philosophy and Public Affairs* 9 [1980], 356).
[10] Macedo, *Diversity and Distrust*, 251. Macedo quickly adds that "within limits we should allow havens outside the mainstream for those with peculiar needs." I am arguing for securing those havens and ensuring the mainstream remains within its banks.

parents, too, hope their children acquire moral integrity of a sort that does not depart too far from their own value frameworks. This alignment of interests can make the case for parental authority look weaker than it really is, for it can suggest that parents' authority over a child's education is grounded chiefly in the parents' interests – their claim to religious liberty, say, or their right to treat their children as extensions of themselves.[11] I've argued that one shouldn't see the issue this way, and that structuring a child's education in response to parents' conceptions of its interests does not abandon a focus on the child's interests. Where defenders of strong parental authority differ from advocates of RLE is not in believing that such authority is not bound by children's interests, but in doubting that RLE really advances those interests in the manner needed to outweigh parental objections. The case for strong parental authority is further strengthened, however, by recognizing that the child's interests are not the only relevant consideration here. Parents' interests, too, have an intrinsic weight in such considerations, as I shall argue now.

The claims of parents

No one denies that parental authority over a child, in any domain, is strongly bound by an obligation to protect its interests. That claim, however, does not imply that in making decisions for children, parents' interests have no legitimate weight, for one can grant such weight while still seeing children's interests as central. Critics of strong parental authority sometimes overlook this, as shown in the widespread criticism that met Charles Fried's account of strong parental authority. Fried's argument appealed to the idea of children as in some sense extensions of their parents, thereby implying that parents have the same kind of right to make decisions about their children's education as they have to make decisions about their own lives. For this Fried was roundly criticized on grounds of ignoring the independent moral status of children. But Fried's own account acknowledges parents' obligation "to care for and educate the child in the child's best interests," and after suggesting the view of children as extensions of their parents, he immediately adds, "But of course

---

[11] For example, Arneson and Shapiro suggest that in claiming to speak for the child, some parents "regard the child as a mere empty vessel for their own religious convictions" and "use their children ... for [their] own benefit" ("Democratic Autonomy and Religious Freedom," 384, 380). Amy Gutmann casts the claim for religious freedom in a similarly unflattering light, referring to "the idea that parents have a right on the basis of their religious freedom to prevent their children from thinking for themselves about their own lives" ("Civic Education and Social Diversity," 575).

this is only an analogy."[12] His account does not simply subordinate the child's interests.

Still, Fried's analogy is helpful in directing attention to important interests that advocates of child-centered education sometimes overlook. For even if we take children's interests as central, we should not conclude that the proper exercise of parental authority means always choosing in a way that benefits a child optimally. Parenthood is not servitude, and children's interests do not always come first. Though summer school at Andover may benefit my child's intellectual growth more than the local alternative, I may be right to put those resources instead towards a pilgrimage to Troy that has been my life-long desire – right not just in the sense that it is a decision liberal states must permit, but right all things considered (the local school may be pretty good, Troy may soon be sold to Disney, etc.). So long as parents attend to the needs of their child above some robust threshold level, morality on occasion not just permits but may even demand that parents' interests take priority over a good to the child.

Now I suggested earlier that opponents of RLE who wish to pass on particular frameworks of value as parents seek not to advance their own interests but to transmit to their children the virtues, goals, and so forth that allow for a flourishing life and which they see RLE as threatening. But though their aim is not some good to themselves, it nonetheless reflects an interest that is enormously important. Though sometimes cast in terms of religious liberty, the interest involved takes a broader description: helping one's child become a person of moral integrity committed to values that rightly order a human life. Accounts of parental authority that deny the intrinsic weight of this interest are, I believe, misdirected from the outset. A passage from Amy Gutmann exemplifies the problem: "If we ask why parents and not other institutions of the democratic state ought to have [the right of paternalistic agency over children], the only answer we are likely to defend is that, among available agents, parents can best serve the interests of children."[13] But surely part of the answer to Gutmann's question is that raising children is for many persons a source of unmatched fulfillment, joy, and meaning, and it can be these things only if they have significant freedom in how they do this. Acknowledging this neither expunges nor displaces the emphasis on the child's interests: the latter can be the central consideration without being

---

[12] Charles Fried, *Right and Wrong* (Cambridge, MA: Harvard University Press, 1978), 152.

[13] Gutmann, "Children, Paternalism, and Education," 344. A similar one-sidedness mars Arneson and Shapiro's argument for RLE (see n. 4 above), which asks what sort of education a neutral guardian, concerned only with the welfare of a child, would choose for it. Such guardians by definition lack the engaged relationship with the child the importance of which I have stressed.

the only one. When we add the instrinsic weight of parental interests to
the realization that a person's interests can take a range of forms, corresponding to the different normative frameworks he or she might endorse,
the case for robust parental authority over a child's education appears
very strong indeed.

OVERRIDING STRONG PARENTAL AUTHORITY

Advocates of RLE offer three general arguments to override the presumption of strong parental authority. The first, which appeals to the idea of
minimal autonomy mentioned in Chapter 3, runs thus. The capacity to
reflect critically on ourselves and our ends, and to govern ourselves accordingly, distinguishes us as persons and confers on us special moral status.
Such self-rule is, however, an achievement, not a biological given: we can
imagine individuals so indoctrinated that they can conceive no significant goals beyond those that others have implanted, or utterly lacking the
self-respect needed to see choosing their own ends as an appropriate task.
The various elements of civil society (e.g. the family, religious groups, the
marketplace, the media) cannot be counted on to cultivate and protect
the capacity for self-rule in all citizens. RLE, with its emphasis on encouraging children's sympathetic engagement with a range of lifestyles, ideals,
and norms, thus stands as a vital guarantor of self-rule – "the antidote to
ethical servility," in Eamonn Callan's phrase.[14] Anyone who values the
minimal autonomy connected to personhood thus has strong reason to
endorse RLE.

Meira Levinson has advanced a powerful version of this argument that
is especially apt here, because it targets a minimal conception of autonomy that denies the supremacy of the liberal ideal in terms broadly similar to those I endorsed earlier.[15] Her target is Gerald Dworkin's idea that
autonomy centrally involves monitoring one's lower-order desires in light
of higher-order desires. In his account Dworkin intentionally eschews
substantive requirements on these higher-order desires, saying little about
either their content or their relative revisability, because he wants to allow
both that autonomy is compatible with a wide range of commitments
and that those commitments may be constitutive of the self in such a way
that an agent does not them as revisable. In this way Dworkin aims to
articulate a non-trivial account of autonomy that is compatible with deep
diversity and so does not imply the superiority of the liberal ideal.

[14] Callan, *Creating Citizens*, 154.   [15] Levinson, *The Demands of Liberal Education*, ch. 1.

Levinson objects that any such structural account will fail to capture the idea of self-rule at the heart of autonomy.[16] To make her point she imagines two men, Harry and Abner, each of whom monitors his lower-order desires through the higher-order desire to do whatever his mother tells him. Each does so, however, for different reasons: Harry is psychologically dependent on his mother, while Abner judges that such obedience will help him achieve his goals.[17] On Dworkin's structural account the two appear equally autonomous, but this seems the wrong conclusion, Levinson says, for two reasons. First, Harry's life seems to be shaped by another's will, whereas Abner's obedience simply reflects his own judgment of how best to get what he wants. Second, Harry's obedience seems unconditional (Levinson describes him as following his mother's commands "regardless of the consequences"), whereas Abner's depends on his continuing judgment that such a policy will get him what he wants. In this way Harry seems more conclusively to have forfeited agency.

Now Harry's situation is no doubt troubling. But, for the example to bolster the argument for RLE, Levinson must further establish both that cases like Harry fall short of self-rule to a degree that warrants state intervention and that RLE should be part of such intervention. For several reasons, I do not believe she shows this.

To begin with, we might ask how a self-abnegating personality like Harry might have developed. The likeliest possibility, of course, is that Harry's childhood and home life were marked by deeply unhealthy psychodynamics. Levinson describes him as "enslaving himself" to the "absolute control" of his mother. Given that etiology, it is hard to see how RLE's emphasis on sympathetic engagement with alien frameworks of value will be very effective in battling Harry's pathological lack of self-respect. Consider, then, an alternative account of the sort of dependency Harry displays, according to which his submission reflects the norms of a particular cultural group. How might such a group justify this demand?

There are two main possibilities. First, the group might insist that the well-being of those in authority has greater intrinsic weight than others'. Because such cases violate the minimal norm of moral equality, the MVL state should impose an education that aims to counter such teachings. For reasons already given, however, there is no reason to think this entails RLE. The second possibility is that the group believes that certain

---

[16] Levinson also objects that the structural account cannot ground a range of traditional liberal freedoms, but that concern seems to me secondary to the argument I concentrate on, since it is that argument that explains the importance of those freedoms in the first place.

[17] Levinson, *The Demands of Liberal Education*, 26.

members (usually occupying clear roles) have special insight into important but difficult issues (often these will be moral issues, but they needn't
be). Part of being Catholic, for example, involves treating papal decrees as
having a special moral authority, and similarly authoritative agents figure
prominently in other religious groups.[18] Adherents of such faiths see them
not just as consistent with the equal moral worth of human beings but,
often, as explaining that fact. For the state to override citizens' judgments
in this case, in the manner needed to mandate RLE, would require a
clear showing that their faiths either involve a profound moral wrong or
violate moral equality. In most instances this standard of proof will simply not be met.

The other feature of Harry's case that troubles Levinson is the apparent
unconditionality of his obedience. But here again her objection ultimately
implies a position too controversial to be a basis for policy in the MVL
state. As an alternative to what she sees as the unconditional forfeiture of
the self, Levinson endorses a robust model of self-rule that both requires
a "plurality of constitutive desires and values" and excludes what Stanley
Benn, whom Levinson approvingly cites, calls absolute commitments. To
quote Benn:

An absolute commitment ... involves the distancing of oneself thereafter from
the considerations that initially led to it. For if the commitment is to be absolute, the question whether there really were, and still are, good enough reasons
for making it is not to be reopened. Though the rule is genetically one's own ...
both the rule and the prescriptions proceeding from it now confront one from
the outside: the rule is now as much an alienation of the self as is the brute exter-
nality of a stone idol that one might carve to venerate.[19]

This passage, however, presents too simplistic a dichotomy: either one
regards one's fundamental commitments as always provisional, or one
puts oneself once and for all beyond the pull of reasons. A third option is
that one undertakes a commitment, on the basis of good reasons, which
then assumes such centrality in one's life that one cannot imagine living without it – think of marriage, vocation, or religious faith. In such
cases persons have not put themselves beyond the reach of reason, and
often enough they find themselves re-examining their commitments in
a way they would not have thought possible earlier. But often, too, they

---

[18] The four Sankaracharyas who head monastic lineages are especially influential for some Hindus,
for example, just as in Shiite Islam the pronouncements of the Ayatollah carry special authority.
Thanks to Eliza Kent and Mahdi Tourage for communications on this subject.

[19] Stanley Benn, *A Theory of Freedom* (Cambridge: Cambridge University Press, 1988), 228, quoted
in Levinson, *The Demands of Liberal Education*, 29.

will both describe their commitments as unrevisable and not consciously review them, and the legitimacy of this perspective must not be denied in any reasonable account of self-determination. Indeed, since it is not logically possible for all our values to rest on more fundamental values, our agency always involves higher-order desires that are in some sense unconditional.[20] We should thus reject the idea that genuine self-rule requires either that one frequently review one's fundamental commitments or that one be able to imagine living without them.

A final reason favoring a conception of self-rule that allows unconditional commitments has to do with the challenge of distinguishing cases where a person *does not* revise her commitment from cases where she *cannot* do so. After all, part of self-rule involves determining for oneself how much weight to assign reasons for action. This discretion is not limitless, but commitment to the value of self-rule means that one should have evidence of a gross failure of rationality before concluding that another lacks the ability to revise her commitments and does not simply give reasons a weight different from one's own. My worry, then, is that in seeing cases of absolute commitment as failures of self-rule, Levinson is not so much unpacking what she calls a "minimal conception of autonomy" as defending a particularly modern and ruggedly individualist conception of it. That conception is not unattractive, but as grounds for policy in the MVL state it is too narrow.

My argument, however, is open to a serious objection Eamonn Callan has pressed. Like Levinson, Callan wants to stake out a conception of self-rule midway between a "primitive level of agency" and being "a virtuoso of self-rule."[21] Taking off from Thomas Hill's discussion of servility, Callan suggests that the concern over servility can arise not only when one sees one's own welfare as less important than another's, but also when an education is structured to lead the child to values and ends rooted in a particular normative framework. Callan's worry is that directed education, because it aims to have children endorse ends determined by someone else, advances a state of servility at odds with the ideal of moral equality. RLE best protects against this fear.

Callan's objection is crucial in part because it undermines the distinction, which I just invoked in criticizing Levinson's argument, between subordination to another person and commitment to a categorical set

---

[20] Cf. Arneson and Shapiro's allowance that "being prejudiced or having one's mind made up on some valuation is necessary for autonomy, not an obstacle that precludes it" ("Democratic Autonomy and Religious Freedom," 391).

[21] Callan, *Creating Citizens*, 152.

of norms that recognize others' special authority. In stressing the *process* through which normative frameworks are acquired, as opposed to their *content*, it promises as well to avoid Levinson's problematic commitment to the self's fundamental plurality. Nonetheless, I believe Callan overstates the conflict between directed education and the modest idea of self-rule he sets out to defend. A more charitable reading of directed education can accommodate his worries, thereby weakening his case for compulsory RLE.

On Callan's framing of the issue, the critical issue is whether directed education consigns a person to a "primitive level of agency" short of authentic self-rule. Callan thinks it does because he believes that parents who promote directed education have "substantially the same aim" as parents who want their child to defer to their wishes in the manner characterizing servility: in both cases they seek "permanent control of [the] child's conduct," directed education achieving this by instilling "settled affective dispositions" that will powerfully dispose the child to resist alternative ways of life and ideals.[22] To assess this objection, we thus need to ask two questions: what is the nature of the permanent control Callan has in mind here, and why is it objectionable?

To begin with, note that if "permanent control" over children's conduct involves seeking permanently to shape their subsequent conduct, this is hardly objectionable in itself. I hope the values I'm teaching my children will lead them always to stand up against abuses of power, to work hard to develop their talents, to oppose inhumane treatment in all its forms, and so on, and one way I do this is by inducing in my children "settled affective dispositions" against a range of corresponding vices. Though Callan worries that directed education may "pre-empt serious thought ... about the alternatives to [a parent's] judgment,"[23] not only are such efforts often permissible; they are to some degree what parenting is. It would be odd twice over to criticize me here for seeking to control them – odd to see what I'm doing as a form of control, odder still to criticize it.

Where the charge of seeking permanent control is objectionable, it involves one of two worries: that the child will be motivated to advance its parents' interests and not its own, or that such control somehow violates self-rule. The first worry has little relevance to the debate here. If it results from parents' attempts to instill frameworks built on the moral

---

[22] Ibid., 153. A page later Callan puts his worry in terms of "ongoing compliance with another's will."
[23] Ibid., 154.

subordination of some to others, the MVL state should not, for reasons already given, accommodate those efforts. Alternatively, if the first worry simply reflects a concern over grossly self-centered parents, there is no reason either to associate this especially with directed education or to think RLE will be any better at combating it.

The second worry, i.e. that directing children towards a specific normative framework threatens self-rule, is more worrisome. But defenders of directed education have three good replies. First, some of the virtues parents reasonably seek to inculcate – including, we should note, virtues conducive to self-rule – will in their eyes be rooted in particular normative frameworks. For example, many see the prohibition on torture and our duties to aid the less fortunate, along with the importance of developing our talents and avoiding corrupting pleasures, as bound up in a view of human beings as instances of the divine. Notwithstanding Richard Rorty's breezy characterization of secular liberals as "freeloading atheists," living off the moral capital built up by religious communities, many citizens insist that important virtues can be both grounded and broadly motivating only if rooted in some specific metaphysical framework. If they are right, directed education may be vital in inculcating important virtues.

A second reply on behalf of directed education is that the skills and knowledge developed in any genuine education – skills of critical thinking, logical reasoning, and interpretative sensitivity; and knowledge of the belief systems and moral frameworks of other human beings over time, and of the basic laws and history of one's own community – carry a built-in critical potential not entirely controllable by the educator.[24] This potential is amplified by the fact that most normative frameworks of any real influence are marked by internal contestation over how to read canonical texts and figures, understand traditional practices, and honor characteristic values. Here again we need to avoid positing a straw man: directed education aims to raise not robotic acolytes simply going through motions, but mindful practitioners who will see the reasons behind their commitments and practices. It thus necessarily involves conveying to children the reasons for some practices and beliefs and against alternatives, and so promotes some degree of reflectiveness, even if it be

---

[24] Michael Billig has suggested that we understand thinking as "a form of internal dialogue, modeled on outward dialogue" (*Arguing and Thinking: A Rhetorical Approach to Social Psychology* [Cambridge: Cambridge University Press, 1996], 1). If so, then any education that promotes thinking will establish a conversation partly beyond the reach of anyone outside the student, including the teacher.

less radical than RLE's advocates would like.²⁵ Nor is it easy, in liberal societies, to shield children from others who endorse norms at odds with those parents seek to instill. Factors like the growing diversity of the workplace, the proliferation of media, and the increasing presence of the internet make it ever more difficult to raise children without such exposure. Under these conditions some degree of reflectiveness towards one's own commitments is inevitable.

A final reason favoring directed education is that self-rule does not require choosing from a limitless field, but is consistent with some ways of life simply not being live options. Partly this is because space in the social world is finite (I cannot live as a samurai). But it is also, in part, because we develop a character before our reflective consciousness is fully formed, and that character necessarily rules out some pursuits. Now if substantial self-rule is compatible with some options never really being available, the key issue becomes how far directed education constrains the range of significant options. If we take a narrow perspective of religious faith, for example (to concentrate on one common foundation of directed education), we may think there is *some one thing* that it is to lead a Catholic life, a Jewish life, a Muslim life, and so on. But we should resist that way of thinking. Not only is it blind to the internal complexity of such religions, but it ignores the fact that they leave a range of important choices to the discretion of their followers. What their careers shall be, whom they shall marry, how they shall recreate, who their friends shall be, what aesthetic pursuits they shall engage with – in countless respects they allow for a substantial exercise of self-rule beyond mere primitive agency. This is not to say that we cannot imagine frameworks that specify how a person should act in all such areas: some groups have claimed such control over their members, and the MVL state's concern for minimal autonomy rightly justifies interference with them, at least where they seek to oversee the maturation of children. But these are grounds for interfering not with directed education *per se*, but only with those versions that aim at something like the death of the self. There is, however, no intrinsic conflict between minimal autonomy and directed education.

RLE AND EQUAL OPPORTUNITY

The second and third arguments for overriding parental authority and mandating RLE hinge on the concern for justice. This concern can lead

---

²⁵ Shelley Burtt stresses the importance of internal contestation in "Comprehensive Educations and the Liberal Understanding of Autonomy."

in two main directions. RLE can be defended either as critical in producing citizens who will be motivated by the virtue of justice, or as itself a constituent element in any just social arrangement. In the next section I consider the motivational argument. Here I concentrate on RLE as a necessary part of a just social order.

The strongest version of this argument connects RLE with the ideal of equality of opportunity, a requirement of justice that few today deny. That ideal specifies that all citizens should have an equal chance to lead good lives and that differences in the quality of their lives should, as far as possible, reflect choices they have made rather than circumstances over which they had no control. From that relatively thin starting point, we get the following argument for RLE.[26]

Assume what Harry Brighouse calls "constitution pluralism," i.e. that persons have innately differing temperaments, characters, proclivities, and the like. Imagine a homosexual boy whose parents endorse a normative framework deeply hostile to homosexuality and educate him around that framework's ideals. If we accept that intimate romantic relationships are an important good, we have to conclude that such a boy "has far less opportunity to live well … than others growing up in his community."[27] Not only is he likely to be especially inhibited in his pursuit of romantic love, but even if he does act on such feelings he may feel compelled to practice a deception that will deny him many of the goods that characterize loving relationships (e.g. confirmation by family and friends of the value of his relationship, ease and security in public spaces with his beloved, the availability of models for overcoming inevitable challenges). He is also more likely to develop a diminished sense of self-worth, perhaps even feelings of self-loathing. In all these ways he faces obstacles to a good life that result not from choices he has made but from circumstances beyond his control. This violates equal opportunity. RLE, in contrast, because it exposes students to a range of ways of life more likely to be commensurate with their individual constitutions, significantly bolsters equal opportunity. The threat to equal opportunity arising in the area of sexual orientation, the argument concludes, also arises in any case where particular normative frameworks constrain the range of acceptable options more narrowly than the range of possible personality types. RLE better protects that ideal.

---

[26] The specific argument I discuss is advanced by Brighouse, *School Choice and Social Justice*. Arneson and Shapiro make the same general case in "Democratic Autonomy and Religious Freedom."

[27] Brighouse, *School Choice and Social Justice*, 73.

Some opponents of RLE may object that the argument begs the question in assuming that an intimate relationship with the object of one's love is an important human good. Not so, they may say: only intimacy with a person of the opposite sex makes a life go better. But this objection is weak. The argument from equal opportunity need not assume the controversial view in question. Since the liberal state is committed to protecting expressive liberty, it requires only the claim that some non-trivial number of people appear to value such intimacy and pursue it in mutually consenting relationships. The MVL state's commitment to protect those pursuits implies nothing about their objective value.

The argument is, however, open to a deeper worry, concerning the very notion of equal opportunity. We might think that idea indicts any world where some have less opportunity to lead a good life than others as a result of circumstances beyond their control. But a moment's reflection shows this interpretation is too strong – indeed, mandating RLE would violate it. The reason is that one way constitution pluralism manifests itself is in the degree to which people are naturally disposed to the character types associated with RLE.[28] While some will experience RLE as fulfilling and expansive, to others it may produce a distressing anxiety and leave them feeling unmoored. The latter then have less of an opportunity to lead fulfilling lives than the former, as a result of circumstances beyond their control. We should not, then, deem a social structure acceptable only when all within it have equal opportunities to lead good lives: on constitution pluralism there will be no such structure.

Still, there may be reasons to favor some arrangements over others. If we are comparing educational approaches, the one that provides people with the widest number of options (as RLE does) seems a better choice, *ceteris paribus*, for reasons captured by what we might call the "lose nothing by liberalizing" argument. For the result of RLE will be that children either stick to their old ways, in which case they're no worse off, or reject them for goals that RLE made them aware of, in which case they're better off (at least by their own lights, which is all the MVL state cares about). So even if RLE may be discomfiting for some, and parents may lament their children striking out to lead different lives, such costs are outweighed by the overall contribution RLE makes to individual well-being.[29]

---

[28] For the argument that RLE is inevitably character-forming, see Eamonn Callan, "Liberal Legitimacy, Justice, and Civic Education," *Ethics* 111 (October 2000), 141–55.

[29] Andrew Mason advances an argument broadly similar to this in *Community, Solidarity, and Belonging*, 75–7.

Though this is a powerful argument, its success ultimately hinges on three questions that are difficult to resolve conclusively. (1) Is the diversity within liberal states inevitably and adequately communicated to all citizens even without RLE? (2) Will a more modest model of education that includes clear communication of the strong legal protections for personal liberty stimulate children sufficiently to consider alternative ways of life? (3) Does RLE, despite its claim to be presenting a range of lifestyles for students, implicitly champion a single form of life? I want to argue now that an affirmative answer to each question is plausible and that this fact significantly weakens the equal opportunity argument.

First, in modern liberal societies it is difficult to remain ignorant of the diversity of goals and options other citizens pursue. That there exists a gay and lesbian community campaigning for equal rights, that many persons either have no faith in God or endorse radically different theologies, that contraception is widely available and widely used, that many people believe humans descended from apes – few liberal citizens are ignorant of such things. Granted, many parents seek to ensure that their children develop a mindset that will predispose them to reject many of those options, and this may somewhat compromise equal opportunity. Were that the only value at stake, concern over parents' influence might be conclusive. But equal opportunity is not the only relevant value. Family privacy and intimacy, intergenerational continuity, the child's moral integrity, and parents' desire to express their own moral commitments – these factors have a cumulative weight that counts against a single-minded commitment to equal opportunity.[30] What's important, then, is not that all children have equal opportunity in all respects (assuming for the moment the coherence of that idea), but that they have a sufficiently robust set of opportunities from which to choose. The inevitable exposure to diversity in liberal societies may well satisfy that level.

This reply is strengthened by considering question (2), which asks about the connection between education and awareness of diversity. Recall that along with exposure to works of art and literature, the modest alternative to RLE insists that students learn about the various ways communities around the world have lived, the ideals they have endorsed, their spiritual beliefs, and so on, as well as about some of the conflicts – over the state's

---

[30] In an influential paper James Fishkin has argued that a trilemma exists among the goods of equal opportunity, rewarding merit, and family autonomy: any firm commitment to two of these compromises the third. The proper response, he suggests, is not to deny entirely the claims of any one of them, but to strike an appropriate balance. See Fishkin, "Liberty vs. Equal Opportunity," *Social Philosophy and Policy* 5 (1978), 32–48.

relationship to religion, say, or worries over discrimination – especially prominent within their own political community. In addition, the modest model communicates to all students their guaranteed equal freedom and protection under the laws. When children so educated nonetheless choose to abide by the norms they were raised in, this will reflect their own assessment of the alternatives. So long as that is reasonably informed, the liberal state cannot demand more.

I cannot deny, however, the limits of the view I am defending. To return to Brighouse's example, merely being informed that the state protects one's right to homosexual relationships, absent a more imaginatively compelling depiction of such a choice, may leave gays and lesbians facing problems that would be lessened under RLE. Or again, RLE may increase the chance that some women will depart from gendered norms and pursue options more suited to their character and abilities. It is, however, no fatal objection that a political arrangement permits some harms that would be better controlled under different arrangements, and this point has special relevance to liberal states committed to protecting individual choice. Where one's choices demonstrably and seriously harm others (theft, assault, physical coercion, and so on), liberty is properly constrained. But the cases we are considering here do not rise to that level: they involve parents trying to pass on to their children ideals that, while perhaps mistaken, are not harmful in this way (e.g. that God intends sexual intimacy to occur between men and women, that women are especially well-suited to be caregivers for young children). To permit expressive liberty concerning such ideals is *pro tanto* to permit parents to shape their children in various ways. The MVL state cannot protect one and exclude the other.[31]

The final question, (3), raises the deepest worry to the argument from equal opportunity. Does RLE really present students with a range of ways of life, or simply variations on a single view of the good? Eamonn Callan captures with unmatched brio one version of the latter worry:

What exposure to diversity really amounts to is very often something like this. We instill a consumer hermeneutic that offers a ready interpretation of anything that comes its way, from religions to art to forms of family life and sexual expression … The social world that engulfs the child insistently says that objects of

---

[31] For this reason I am dubious of Arneson and Shapiro's claim that they are criticizing only the child-rearing practices of the Amish, not Amish culture generally ("Democratic Autonomy and Religious Freedom," 374). Given the importance to any cultural group of passing on distinctive values and norms to successive generations, child-rearing practices will almost always figure centrally in a culture's self-conception.

consumption alone are fit objects of desire, or at least the only key to all that is desirable ... The ease with which just about anything can be "read" according to the code of consumption creates an appearance of diversity that disguises the leveling uniformity beneath ... The consumer hermeneutic makes more or less unimaginable the value of lives that track ends other than consumption.[32]

This worry returns on RLE's defenders the criticism they level against directed education: RLE stands accused of "so thoroughly immersing [students] in a total ... world with its own language, symbols, and world view" that other ways of life become only notional.[33] The fear here is that RLE, in presenting differing values and ideals as so many objects to be tried on until the child finds some that fit, portrays the pursuit of the good life as something like a shopping trip, wherein the desires of the self, understood as what Iris Murdoch called "the brave naked will," rule with unquestioned supremacy to the exclusion of ways of life structured around humility, piety, communal service, and so on.

This objection is usually met with two replies. The first is that while it describes the way some schools implement RLE, the proper response is not to abandon RLE but to revise those schools.[34] To RLE's critics this is cold comfort. They are concerned with the influence on their children of existing schools. To be told these are a flawed embodiment of RLE, that better schools will someday follow, hardly addresses their concerns. The second, better reply is that the objection misconstrues RLE. The sympathetic presentation of alternative ways of life, advanced in the spirit of the discontinuity ethos, neither endorses the supremacy of individual choice nor suggests that all options are to be decided by personal taste alone.

This second reply hinges on some subtle distinctions: between a school's presenting alternatives in the most attractive way and endorsing them as

---

[32] Callan, "Autonomy, Child-Rearing, and Good Lives," 135. (Callan does not, of course, regard this objection as fatal to RLE.) Michael Walzer raises his own version of the worry, imagining "a cohort of adolescent individuals-in-the-making swept by waves of fashionable and earnest eccentricity." Would they, he asks, be "any more differentiated, any more individualized, than the children of committed Jews or Catholics, say, or strongly identified Bulgarians or Koreans? Would they, indeed, be any more tolerant of someone in their peer group who chose not to do the done thing, not to create himself by himself, and who announced to scandalized friends, 'I am just going to copy the life plan of my parents'?" Invoking Harold Rosenberg's phrase, Walzer sums them up as "a herd of independent minds" ("On Involuntary Association," 71).

[33] The accusation, made by Donald Kraybill against Amish education, is quoted by Arneson and Shapiro, "Democratic Autonomy and Religious Freedom," 370.

[34] Cf. Arneson and Shapiro: "The correct inference from the observation that there is a gap between the obligatory norms we profess and the degree to which we fulfill these norms is that we should narrow the gap by doing more to fulfill the norms" (ibid., 378).

worthwhile, for example; or between students learning that they must select for themselves the norms to structure their lives and their believing that such norms have no authority without their endorsement.[35] The problem is that even if these distinctions hold up, the critic might wonder whether students can draw them clearly and consistently. Moreover, the anxiety driving those who worry about the insidious message of schools committed to RLE extends not only (perhaps not even chiefly) to curricular issues, but to a dominant culture that, they fear, will be forcefully and near irresistibly conveyed both by their teachers and by the attitudes, beliefs, and behavior of other students. Strictly speaking, this last concern over the influence of other students does not criticize RLE in theory, since it does not *per se* demand attendance at public schools characterized by substantial diversity. But to the degree that putting RLE into practice will have some such consequences (as some advocates suggest), the worry over student culture constitutes a further cost to RLE, and makes it even more doubtful that the ideal of equal opportunity is sufficient to override parental objections.

RLE AND THE CIVIC VIRTUES

The final argument for RLE stresses its inimitable role in cultivating civic virtues. This argument reflects a trend in recent liberal thought that challenges Kant's notorious claim that the problem of political association can be solved "even by a race of devils, so long as they are intelligent," and argues instead that liberal regimes depend on citizens' possessing certain skills and dispositions whose acquisition is not inevitable.[36] Such skills include the capacity for critical deliberation, the ability to occupy different perspectives, and the knowledge required to understand important issues of the day. The dispositions include a concern for the public good, a desire to participate in collective political decisions (through voting, attending to public debate, etc.), and a willingness to tolerate different ways of life. Such skills and dispositions I shall refer to collectively as the civic virtues. The general claim behind the argument, then, is that a citizenry lacking such virtues invites a host of problems – capricious and

---

[35] Cf. Richard Dagger's assertion that persons should "choose the principles by which they live" (*Civic Virtues: Rights, Citizenship, and Republican Liberalism* [New York: Oxford University Press, 1997], 38).

[36] Along with Dagger's *Civic Virtues*, important works here include Steven Macedo, *Liberal Virtues: Citizenship, Virtue, and Community in Liberal Constitutionalism* (New York: Oxford University Press, 1990), and Peter Berkowitz, *Virtue and the Making of Modern Liberalism* (Princeton: Princeton University Press, 1999).

ill-informed government, diminished law-abidingness, decreased concern with overall justice, and so on – and that RLE serves as an important prophylactic against such woes.

The structure of the argument is clear enough in outline, but to assess it we need to be sharper about its central claim. Is it (1) that the overall quality of life in liberal regimes will be improved if more citizens possess the civic virtues? Or (2) that liberal regimes can sustain themselves only if citizens possess those virtues? Or (3) that ensuring some important level of justice or rights protection depends on citizens' possessing such virtues? These are claims of varying urgency and persuasiveness. The first seems not strong enough to ground a requirement of RLE, since there are a number of measures that might improve the quality of life in liberal regimes (require various citizens to undergo cosmetic surgery or psychotherapy, for example) but which the state should not compel. While claim (2) seems more promising, its problem is that if conditions arose where the fears it invokes were well-grounded, the length of time required for RLE to work makes it unlikely to have much effect. And in any case, the claim of dependence (2) asserts is very hard to assess. Kant may have erred in downplaying the civic virtues' importance, but it is at least plausible that the so-called consumer model of citizenship, which understands liberal institutions largely as a device for achieving stable equilibrium among competing self-interests, might alone be enough to sustain liberal states.[37]

Claim (3), in contrast, offers real promise for grounding the civic virtues. The argument is this: When large numbers of citizens are indifferent to the public good and the welfare of other citizens, they are unlikely either to enact policies or to elect politicians who will ensure justice is done. Even if they were so moved, to the extent they are uninformed about basic issues, ignorant of basic axioms of governance, or unable to think through proposals, they cannot be expected to make choices that will advance justice. Nor does the problem lie only with voters: justice is also threatened when judges, civil servants, and those who enforce laws are not moved by the civic virtues. Indeed, the general worry extends beyond the passage and enforcement of laws, for many of the basic requirements of justice (e.g. non-discrimination in housing, equal opportunity in hiring, security in public spaces) are a function of private decisions over which the state has only uncertain control.

---

[37] For discussion of the consumer model see Dagger, *Civic Virtues*, 104ff.

RLE seems naturally to connect to the civic virtues so understood. Many of them – e.g. concern for the welfare of other citizens, awareness and understanding of public matters, vigilance over public institutions and officers – do not arise inevitably and may be especially hard to generate in MVL states, which cannot encourage solidarity by appealing to a shared normative framework. RLE, with its stress on understanding and being sympathetic to alien ways of life, makes it more likely that citizens will see things from a perspective wider than their own group's and be concerned with the just treatment of others who are different. In championing self-scrutiny and critical reflection of inherited norms, RLE also increases the chances that citizens will come to possess the skills of rational deliberation needed to both identify correct policies and oversee their enforcement. In these ways requiring RLE significantly improves the prospects for justice in the liberal state.

This argument hinges on three claims: (1) that the civic virtues are vital to liberal justice; (2) that RLE is critical to engendering those virtues; (3) that these two factors outweigh parental objections to RLE. I shall discuss these in turn, concentrating on four virtues: the capacity for critical deliberation; a desire for civic engagement that sustains justice; tolerance of others' ways of life; and mutual respect. While not an exhaustive list, these four are widely seen as especially important and as bearing especially close connection with RLE. To focus on them is thus to consider the civic virtues argument in something like its strongest form.

Before proceeding, one caveat. Though most advocates of the civic virtues argument assume that all children within the state's borders qualify as citizens who will eventually hold all attendant rights and responsibilities, that assumption has been challenged. Some have argued that states may treat inhabitants as citizens only after they have clearly signaled their willingness to join the political community; others have raised the prospect of partial citizenship, where persons have fewer claims on the state, and fewer duties to it, than full-fledged citizens.[38] I shall not engage with these important worries and shall simply accept the assumption from which the civic virtues argument proceeds. Were that assumption problematic in the way these critics suggest, the argument would be significantly weakened. But as I shall argue, it faces significant problems as it stands.

---

[38] For an example of the former, see A. John Simmons, "Justification and Legitimacy," in his *Justification and Legitimacy*, 122–57. For the idea of partial citizenship, see Jeffrey Spinner-Halev, *The Boundaries of Citizenship* (Baltimore: Johns Hopkins University Press, 1994), 97–9.

The need for the civic virtues

The main problem facing claim (1) is not that it is false, but that the sense in which it is true does not make the case for RLE. Consider first the virtue of critical deliberation. Though citizens of the MVL state must be able to identify and respond to central challenges facing their community, the move from this general point to RLE is complicated in at least two ways. First, even if citizens possess ultimate political power, it does not follow that they must have the skills and aptitudes appropriate to those making law and policy. The distinction between elector and elected reflects not merely pragmatic necessities, but also the importance of such things as political judgment, experience, and expertise. This point should lead us to be less stringent in the demands of deliberation, critical rationality, and so on that can reasonably be imposed on citizens. The other factor complicating the case for critical deliberation is that there exists no clearly defined set of urgent challenges over which citizens should rationally deliberate. The identification of such challenges largely reflects one's normative frameworks, and this point significantly complicates the case for RLE insofar as those frameworks often entail distinct strategies for thinking through such challenges correctly – e.g. appeal to church teachings, canonical texts, etc. The interconnectedness of critical deliberation, common challenges, and competing comprehensive frameworks raises real questions about whether there might be an unbiased account of critical deliberation and common challenges sufficiently robust to make the case for RLE.

Nor can anyone deny the importance of the second virtue, i.e. civic engagement that works to bring about and maintain justice. Not only does the massive power of modern states entail a duty to see it directed in appropriate ways, but many relevant issues are of such scope that the state is the only plausible agent for oversight (e.g. just war, the protection of basic rights, environmental concerns).[39] Nonetheless, with respect to the civic virtues argument we need to distinguish three ideas: being motivated to do what justice requires; being motivated by a sense of justice compatible with MVL's basic commitments; and being motivated by a particular account of justice. The last is too strong: demanding that all citizens endorse only a single account of justice (rooted in Kant, Islam, the

---

[39] For these reasons I think Brighouse is wrong to reject Gutmann's claim that all citizens need to be able to engage responsibly in political life (see Brighouse, *School Choice and Social Justice*, 68). Either significant injustice exists (in which case efforts to offset it are obligatory), or it may soon do so (and so one must be prepared).

Torah, etc.) is incompatible with MVL's tolerance for normative diversity. The real issue is between the first two options. To resolve it, we need to determine whether citizens will be motivated to do what justice requires in the absence of RLE, whether RLE makes it much more likely that citizens will act for the sake of justice, and whether the latter is sufficiently superior to the former, from the standpoint of the civic virtues, to justify RLE. These questions I discuss in the following section.

What about the final two virtues, tolerance and mutual respect? The value of tolerance, seen here as a commitment not to interfere in other citizens' ways of life, is relatively clear-cut. The exigencies of common life mean that liberal citizens are bound to have frequent contact with one another, and citizens unwilling to tolerate others' modes of life threaten both the secure public space MVL is built on protecting and others' expressive liberty. But if we grant tolerance as an important virtue, does that also make the case for mutual respect? Amy Gutmann has argued that it does, that the considerations of fairness and equality in which tolerance is rooted drive one to the ideal of mutual respect. After all, storeowners or landlords may be willing to tolerate other citizens' pursuing their strange ways of life but still refuse to hire them or rent them property. Gutmann thus concludes that liberal justice requires that citizens also develop mutual respect, i.e. "reciprocal positive regard" for those who pursue different ways of life consistent with the freedom and equality of all.[40] Mutual respect is also, she suggests, central to any process of political deliberation that genuinely respects "opposing political perspectives," insofar as the latter "are often associated with different ways of life."[41]

Though Gutmann is right that justice requires more than not interfering with others' pursuits, and extends to respecting them as persons with interests of their own, this point need not drive us to mutual respect as she construes it, i.e. as entailing respect for others' ways of life, ideals, and goals. Indeed, there are two good reasons to endorse an alternative account that sharply distinguishes, *contra* Gutmann, respect for citizens as loci of intrinsic moral concern from respect for their views of the good.[42] First, not all ideas of the good merit respect: we properly disdain the view of the good life centered on the boundless consumption of luxury objects, for example, or the relentless pursuit of sexual encounters with no emotional attachment. If respecting persons requires respecting

---

[40] Gutmann, "Civic Education and Social Diversity," 561.   [41] Ibid., 572, 578.
[42] Cf. Rawls's claim, in his reply to Thomas Nagel, that justice as fairness seeks to be fair to persons, not to their conceptions of the good (Rawls's "Fairness to Goodness").

their views of the good, persons who endorse such views do not deserve equal respect. This, however, is hard to square with the commitment to moral equality. Second, not distinguishing the two threatens citizens' expressive liberty. The reason is that many of the normative frameworks citizens endorse entail negative judgments about others' ways of life. But if so, to demand that citizens have positive regard for others' views of the good is to demand that they betray their own commitments.

That last demand might be reasonable if respecting others' equal moral status hinged on it. But it does not. One can respect others for reasons independent of one's judgment about their views of the good: they are embodied souls, children of God, sentient beings, and so on. Even when respect on such grounds leads one to conclude that others should be free to pursue their view of the good, that conclusion is not itself a sign of respect for that view. This more modest account of respect may not, I realize, yield Gutmann's desideratum of citizens' being more inclined to see value in proposals reflecting alien views of the good. But this is a failing only if such views make those proposals more persuasive, and MVL begins from the idea that citizens have not been given good grounds to believe this last claim.

RLE and promotion of the civic virtues

Turning to claim (2), even if we accept that citizens should possess the virtues of deliberative rationality, civic engagement to achieve justice, tolerance, and respect, RLE does not follow. To show this I will first take up the virtues individually, then conclude with a general point about the effort to inculcate civic virtues through RLE in conditions of diversity.

Consider first the connection between RLE and the skills of critical deliberation required of liberal citizens. If the only competitors to RLE are the models of Amish or Australian Aboriginal indoctrination, then RLE wins by default. But there is no reason to think skills of critical assessment, reflection, analysis, and the like can arise only if students sympathetically engage with diversity in the way RLE requires. Defenders of directed education, for example, believe that moral reflection should occur within a context structured by deliberative procedures, norms, and values that are rooted in a particular normative framework and are presented not as lacking any rational foundation but as distinct repositories of wisdom and accounts of what rationality involves. This approach does not abjure critical reasoning, but simply construes it differently from RLE.

Advocates of RLE might here reply that directed education does not promote genuine open-mindedness, in which all commitments are in principle open to revision and the individual is called upon, in Meira Levinson's revealing phrase, to "determine her own values."[43] Though not entirely without presuppositions (it assumes the value of logical consistency, rules of inference, and so on), RLE's much thinner account of deliberation, free of the substantive content that marks directed education, means that it fosters a more robust capacity for critical deliberation of the sort appropriate to liberal regimes and so is preferable.

This reply would be troubling if RLE's radically thin account of deliberation were compelling. But it is problematic in three respects. A first worry relates to the concern over the child's moral integrity noted earlier. Few will deny that the emphasis on individual freedom in liberal societies has coincided with an increased skepticism about the objectivity of values independent of human will or desire. To the degree that children come of age within a social context that encourages its members to see values in these ways, directed education offers helpful ballast the other way. RLE's radically thin account, in contrast, in encouraging the importance of critical deliberation cut off from substantive values, can accentuate a dilettantism about values that already plagues liberal society.

Second, the connection between RLE and important liberal norms (that all persons have equal moral status, for example, or that rights should not be sacrificed for gains in utility) is uncertain. Though some believe that the idea of rational deliberation logically presupposes basic liberal norms, this is a minority view with a sizeable number of critics. It may, then, be important in citizens' moral development that substantive norms be embraced in a manner that renders them independent of the potentially corrosive power of RLE's radically thin conception of critical rationality. This will be especially true if, as mentioned above, those norms are themselves rooted in frameworks that connect critical deliberation with substantive values incompatible with the radically thin conception.

The final problem with the radically thin account of critical deliberation concerns its connection to an overly controversial conception of the self. Consider the well-worn objection that liberalism untenably privileges the unencumbered self. The liberal reply is that while liberalism is consistent with such a picture of the self, it does not require it. Given the justificatory requirement, this is the right sort of reply to make, since many liberal citizens see themselves as defined by their commitment to various

---

[43] Levinson, *The Demands of Liberal Education*, 48.

ends and ideals. The more the liberal state stresses that critical deliberation and moral reflection require distancing oneself from the substantive
values of any particular framework, however, the more it implies that
moral deliberation requires the sort of unencumbered self that invited
the original criticism. A better response is not to override directed education in the name of RLE, but to provide oversight ensuring that students
become sufficiently reflective within those traditions and frameworks.

Consider next the relation between RLE and tolerance. That the two
are connected is naturally tempting (surely a better understanding of
why others have chosen different ways of life will render one less critical
of them), and some empirical studies do suggest a correlation between
schooling and tolerance.[44] Setting aside the familiar worries such studies
face (e.g. how we measure tolerance, how we distinguish it from opposition to others' values, how we separate the influence of schools from that
of families, and so on), bear in mind that the argument must show not
just that schooling increases tolerance, but that schooling in the model of
RLE does so far more than other models. The evidence for this, however,
is not conclusive.[45] Nor should we easily accept the armchair reasoning.
While learning about others who endorse alien frameworks may sometimes render people more positively disposed to them, it can also have
the opposite effect (e.g. here's why Jews don't think Jesus is the Messiah,
here's why Hindus regarded some people as untouchable).[46]

Even if the evidence did show that RLE promotes tolerance especially
well, a further question would have to be answered. The civic virtues
argument is largely driven by the fear of intolerance between groups. But
various groups who oppose RLE out of concern that their own members
might defect also adopt a broadly "live and let live" attitude towards non-
members; intolerance as such, in other words, is not always a civic vice from
the standpoint of the polity as a whole. What is most likely is that groups
who oppose RLE will differ in their degree of intolerance towards other
citizens. Where that is virulent (where, for example, a group champions

---

[44] Gutmann, in "Civic Education and Social Diversity," 567, n. 17, cites a variety of studies showing
that formal schooling significantly increases tolerance.

[45] Stephen Gilles notes: "A wealth of evidence shows that children educated in non-public schools
are *more* tolerant and engaged in civics than their public school counterparts" (*Education Next* 1,
no. 1 [Spring 2001], www.hoover.org/publications/ednext). See also Jay P. Greene, "The Surprising
Consensus on School Choice," *The Public Interest* 144 (Summer 2001, www.thepublicinterest.com),
chronicling studies that cite the effectiveness of Catholic schools in promoting civic virtues
generally.

[46] Nor is it obvious that RLE will increase tolerance in two especially prominent areas – gender and
race. Intolerance in these cases typically reflects not uninformed judgments about others' ways of
life, but views about intrinsic inferiority that have little to do with their chosen goals.

harm towards some class of citizens), the case for RLE gains force. But this counsels a more casuistic approach, not the blanket imposition of RLE on all citizens.

Turning to the final virtue, citizens' motivation to achieve justice in the MVL state, I believe the case for RLE is again inconclusive at best. My view partly relies on a claim about the relationship between justice and equal respect that I shall defend shortly. But it also relies on the thought that important goods that the MVL state makes possible – the preservation of social stability and the guarantee of equal freedom under conditions of pluralism – also provide citizens with reasons to see that others are treated justly.

To see why, note first that the belief that one has been treated unjustly leads to resentment, disaffection, and, potentially, opposition to the demands of a common scheme of cooperation. Citizens who value the MVL state as providing acceptable conditions for expressive liberty thus have some reason to ensure that others do not feel they are being treated unjustly and so to honor their claims to justice. Further motivation comes from the fact that the claims advanced by some citizens often parallel those raised by others committed to quite different views of the good, giving members of different groups a common incentive to see that others are treated fairly. (For example, an American Indian's claim to use peyote may have implications for similar demands from Orthodox Jews or Christian Scientists.) Nor, finally, should we overlook the Madisonian point that continuing and robust diversity benefits citizens insofar as it helps guard against any single group becoming dominant and threatening the agreement to liberal terms. Granted, this point applies most acutely to groups whose numbers make their own political dominance unlikely, but here what Rawls has called the fact of pluralism (viz., that freedom generates deep diversity) works as a stabilizing force, securing the plurality whose value Madison stressed.[47]

RLE's defenders may offer the Kantian objection that these considerations show only that under MVL citizens may be motivated to act

---

[47] In *The Federalist* no. 10 (1787), James Madison famously asserts: "The smaller the society, the fewer probably will be the distinct parties and interests composing it; the fewer the distinct parties and interests, the more frequently will a majority be found of the same party; and the smaller the number of individuals composing a majority, and the smaller the compass within which they are placed, the more easily will they concert and execute their plans of oppression. Extend the sphere, and you take in a greater variety of parties and interests; you make it less probable that a majority of the whole will have a common motive to invade the rights of other citizens; or if such a common motive exists, it will be more difficult for all who feel it to discover their own strength, and to act in unison with each other" (in *The Federalist Papers*, ed. Clinton Rossiter [New York: Penguin, 1961], 83).

in conformity with justice, not that they will act for the sake of justice. RLE, they may insist, is invaluable in promoting the latter. Opponents of RLE who are skeptical of our ability to be consistently motivated by duty itself may find this no criticism at all, and may instead see the alignment of self-interest with the requirements of justice as a powerful asset in the case for MVL. They may also note that the civic virtues argument is concerned chiefly with virtues that shape the state of the polity through citizens' behavior, not with their internal characters *per se*. But the Kantian objection can also be met with a more positive reply.

Recall that MVL tolerates only educational approaches that recognize the moral equality of all persons. Since being motivated by justice is in large part being motivated to see that others' interests are counted fairly (i.e. equally), any acceptable alternative to RLE will also advance the virtue of justice. It may be that the virtue so engendered will neither extend as widely nor operate as robustly as in the ideally virtuous citizen imagined by advocates of RLE. But in liberal states the pursuit of the ideal outcome is always bound by constraints reflecting the need to respect individuals' freedom (no loyalty drugs in the water, etc.). Between RLE and more modest alternatives, then, the question is not which promotes the maximal concern for justice, but whether only RLE instills such concern above the threshold the MVL state can reasonably demand. There is no reason to think that students educated along different lines must fall below that threshold.

Having explored the connection between RLE and specific virtues, I conclude with a general worry about the costs of any attempt to instill civic virtues over citizens' opposition. Even when successful, such a program is bound to engender resentment and alienation in parents, to that degree undercutting the civic virtues.[48] But there are also, I think, good reasons to doubt the success of such efforts. Children's views of the good are likely not to depart too deeply from those of their parents. Since children (like all of us) tend to develop affection for what advances the good of themselves and those they care about, and to oppose what threatens these, they are likely to share their parents' resentment to the imposition of RLE. In addition, RLE may increase parents' efforts to offset its

---

[48] Galston worries that such educational efforts will "produce dissent, resistance and withdrawal" (*Liberal Pluralism*, 106). The surge in homeschooling in the USA over the last two decades, fueled in part by the perception that public schools were increasingly championing moral values at odds with those embraced by parents, is one such effect. According to Rob Reich, by conservative estimates homeschooling in the United States increased from about 10,000 in 1970, to 60,000 in 1983, and to 1.3 million in 1998 ("Testing the Boundaries of Parental Authority over Education," in *Moral and Political Education: NOMOS 43*, ed. Stephen Macedo and Yael Tamir [New York: New York University Press, 2002], 277–8).

influence, thereby furthering the dynamic of reactive culturalism discussed in Chapter 8. Finally, mandating RLE by appealing to the civic virtues implicitly suggests that the duties of citizenship bear no relationship to one's deep normative frameworks. Consider Sanford Levinson's observation that Catholic candidates for political office in the USA have by and large "been forced to proclaim the practical meaninglessness" of their religious beliefs.[49] While some may see this as a welcome development, it can hardly be expected to increase civic engagement from the large number of citizens whose thinking about basic issues of rights, justice, equality, and so on is deeply shaped by religious ideals – in ways, we should note, that often advance liberal ideals. For all these reasons, it may be self-defeating for the state to solicit attitudes of engagement and support by imposing a model of schooling that parents strongly oppose.

Some may object that my general worry here should be discounted because it implies that strong opposition *as such* can be a legitimate reason against some policy, thereby legitimating a kind of political blackmail. My reply is that the dynamic in question – the legitimation of opposition as such – is not in itself objectionable. For example, if we are close friends, your strong opposition to something I'm about to do, even if it does not reflect good reasons, provides me with some reason against doing what I had planned; the mere fact that you care strongly lends your concern weight. And while the MVL state is not built on the model of friendship, a structurally similar relationship obtains. Being grounded in a commitment to protect equally its citizens' expressive liberty (so long as expressions of that liberty honor basic commitments of minimal universalism), the MVL state must in practice treat as equally important whatever goals citizens pursue in their lives. Those goals merit that treatment, we might say, simply because citizens care about them. This conclusion may trouble some liberals, because it concedes that liberal states will often have no grounds on which to distinguish value claims from preference claims. The collapse of that distinction, however, is a bullet liberals must bite, given their commitment to equal freedom.

Other goods

Even if the preceding objections fail, and RLE advances important civic virtues, producing virtuous citizens is neither the only nor the most

[49] Sanford Levinson, "The Confrontation of Religious Faith and Civil Religion: Catholics Becoming Justices," *DePaul Law Review* 39 (1990), 1049 (quoted by Macedo in *Diversity and Distrust*, 136).

important goal of liberal states. Its priority must, as claim (3) recognizes, be weighed against other liberal commitments. I have already mentioned particular goods (family intimacy, developing an integrated moral personality, parental support) that might be threatened by RLE. I want to argue now, more broadly, that the overall thrust of the civic virtues argument is fundamentally at odds with the liberal state in a way that counts strongly against RLE.

The tension arises because the central good the MVL state provides is a secure social space that protects citizens' expressive liberty. When the liberal state constrains their freedoms in areas they care about deeply, it must thus appeal to some good whose value outweighs the loss of freedom. In imposing RLE against unwilling parents, the MVL state constrains their freedoms by appealing to the civic virtues' role in sustaining liberal states. But this is incoherent: how can the state reasonably demand that citizens give up a vital freedom on the grounds that doing so is critical to sustaining a form of political association predicated on the protection of their vital freedoms?

Advocates of RLE will reply that liberal states often quite rightly deny freedoms regardless of how citizens view such measures. The legitimacy of prohibitions on assault, murder, and theft, for example, does not depend on citizens' seeing them as reasonable. Perhaps, then, the great importance of instilling civic virtues similarly overrides objections to RLE. There are, however, two important differences between the cases. First, both the urgency of the interests involved and the threat to them are much more pronounced in cases like theft, assault, and murder than is the decline in the life of the polity associated with citizens' low levels of civic virtue. Second, the connection between RLE and the civic virtues is much less direct and clear than is the connection between, say, physical security and laws prohibiting assault. Indeed, one often finds high levels of civic engagement precisely among citizens whose own educations followed a model quite different from RLE and whose parents strongly opposed it.

This last observation invites the final defense from the civic virtues argument. It may be that citizens who have not received RLE and whose parents opposed it also tend overwhelmingly to endorse positions at odds with MVL (on issues like the limits of free expression, church/state separation, and laws regarding sexual mores), and that RLE does much better at producing citizens who endorse liberal views. In this way RLE may seem to bolster citizens' support for the liberal state. Note that this reply significantly shifts the argument: the claim now is not that RLE promotes a range of virtues that motivate citizens responsibly to discharge the duties of citizenship, but that it helps produce citizens who endorse the dominant ideals of their political community. This way of defending RLE I shall call the alignment strategy. It suffers from two serious failings.

The first, raised with special acuity by Harry Brighouse, concerns the ideal of legitimacy embodied in the justificatory requirement. A regime meets that ideal, Brighouse notes, only if citizens endorse it through the free exercise of reason. But state-run efforts designed to secure endorsement of that regime (including education programs) undermine the possibility of free consent. "By conditioning consent without encouraging reflection, the state seeks consent while giving it the wrong kind of character, thus undermining its own capacity for legitimacy." This worry takes on greater force when we consider Eamonn Callan's argument that RLE is bound significantly to drive the characters and values of students towards more liberal positions.[50]

Here it is important to see why the ideal of free reason cannot similarly be turned against directed education. The reason is that liberal legitimacy is fundamentally a political principle targeting the exercise of state power, not that of private citizens. Just as private citizens are permitted, in ways states are not, to encourage others to adopt a particular faith or pursue particular goals, so too are they allowed to shape their child's education in ways the state may not. Since we are imagining authentic education, and not the straw man of indoctrination, such children will develop knowledge and skills such that their own political views reflect the exercise of their reason, not merely the thoughtless parroting of another's will. Should it then turn out that many citizens so educated nonetheless reject liberal values, that would suggest either that liberalism is not unerringly vindicated by reason or that citizens will endorse it only if educated in a manner designed from the outset to achieve that outcome. The truth of either would cast serious doubt on the liberal project as a whole.

The second problem with defending RLE through the alignment strategy is that since the *raison d'être* of the liberal state is protecting citizens' freedom, it should compel RLE only when alternative measures of achieving the relevant good are not available. But such measures often exist. Consider a religion which teaches that sex is a sacred act properly occurring between a man and woman. The liberal state cannot respect

---

[50] Harry Brighouse, "Civic Education and Liberal Legitimacy," *Ethics* 108 (July 1998), 726–7; Eamonn Callan, "Political Liberalism and Political Education," *Review of Politics* 58 (Winter 1996), 5–33.

a citizen's holding such a view and at the same time demand that she be equally happy renting an apartment to a homosexual couple as to a husband and wife. But this is not an obvious concern for the MVL state, because its scope extends not to a landlord's happiness in renting, but to her willingness to do so. Since the latter can be advanced by a range of measures (oversight agencies, informing citizens of legal remedies, etc.) that do not involve reshaping citizens' religious commitments, the MVL state should concentrate chiefly on the former.

This approach, I realize, may generate citizens who honor liberal ideals of justice with less than maximal enthusiasm. But that is unavoidable for a liberalism that seeks not to erase diversity but to manage it while securing equal freedom for all. The alternative is a totalizing civic liberalism that brings under public scrutiny too many commitments that are properly private. Consider, for example, Stephen Macedo's observation that "only where the Catholic Church itself adopts the sort of leveling of authority that is associated with Protestantism does it appear to promote a social order supportive of active citizenship and healthy liberal democracy."[51] If so, expanding the state's role in promoting civic virtues might in principle condone its imposing measures that disadvantage Catholic schools relative to Protestant ones. (How Muslim or Jewish schools fare is anyone's bet.) This gets the order of justification exactly backwards. The MVL state exists to secure its citizens' freedom; it cannot constrain those freedoms to ensure its own survival. That is the political equivalent of destroying the village to save it. We should not, then, resolve the debate over RLE by considering how parental objections satisfy some criterion of liberal citizenship specified without reference to the strength of parents' interests in transmitting norms to their young.[52] Rather, the nature and scope of those requirements must be worked out partly by considering the commitments liberal citizens believe they must honor. This is not unprincipled capitulation, but the proper task of a liberal theory that takes seriously its citizens' claims to freedom.

---

[51] Macedo, *Diversity and Distrust*, 133, drawing on Robert Putnam's work in Northern Italy. Along the same lines, if one follows Tracy Higgins's suggestion that religions with gendered structures of authority "convey more effectively than gender-stereotyped parochial school curriculum the fundamental inferiority of women," does it not follow that liberal regimes ought to constrain the practice of Catholicism? ("Why Feminists Can't (or Shouldn't) be Liberals," 1637). Okin squarely faces the logic here: "Why not argue," she writes, "that unless and until they reform themselves, as many variants of religion have already done, so as to accommodate sex equality, sexist religions too are to be discouraged or even excluded altogether from the just society?" ("Justice and Gender," 1558).

[52] The approach I'm rejecting is implicit in Amy Gutmann's assertion that "parents do not have a right to pass on their own religious beliefs if that's inconsistent with requirements of liberal democratic citizenship" ("Civic Education and Social Diversity," 576).

PRINCIPLES OF APPLICATION: A SKETCH

Thus far I have focused on broad conceptual questions about the sort of education MVL states may require. I conclude by suggesting how the approach I've defended can help us think through two prominent controversies over compulsory education in liberal states: the teaching of evolution, and sex education. To be sure, specific recommendations in such debates will have to be sensitive to changeable pragmatic considerations (e.g.: Is it possible to teach the content in question only to some students and not to others? Will lack of exposure to disputed material undermine the students' preparation for subsequent material?). Nonetheless, the argument I have advanced suggests various *prima facie* criteria for determining what should and should not be required in a curriculum. Strengthening the case for mandatory inclusion, four factors are especially important.

1. Teaching the material enhances minimal autonomy.
2. Teaching the material promotes and corroborates moral equality.
3. Teaching the material significantly bolsters requisite civic virtues otherwise at risk.
4. Teaching the material has intrinsic educational importance, either because it concerns a matter of great human significance or because of its value as preparation for later study in some significant area.

Against mandatory inclusion two considerations are paramount. The first sets forth a necessary condition any objection must meet to gain a hearing. Only when it is satisfied does the second consideration come into play.

A. The objection to the proposed material is consistent with the fundamental commitments of MVL and minimal universalism (e.g. political equality, moral equality, equal freedom).
B. The proposed material significantly challenges normative frameworks allegiance to which is permitted in the MVL state.

Teaching evolution

At first glance the case for requiring the teaching of evolution seems largely independent of considerations 1–3 above (though in a moment I shall mention a possible connection to the civic virtues). The strongest reason in its favor, of course, is that evolution is far and away the best theory we have about a matter of great importance. The origin of our species, and the course of life on our planet generally, possess an obvious significance that, say, the history of rock and roll does not. Such claims for significance would be strengthened, it's worth noting, by showing the relative centrality of understanding evolution to science generally – for example, by showing that an understanding of other important issues (e.g. the genome, cell structure) requires a grasp of evolutionary theory.

What of the case against it? Let me say straight away that the most frequent objection pressed by opponents of evolution – that evolution has no greater *bona fides* as a scientific account than creationism – is fundamentally misguided. The overwhelming consensus of scientists with no obvious metaphysical axes to grind establishes evolution just as securely as it does atomic theory or the structure of DNA, and with respect to the relative merits of competing accounts of the natural world, this group must surely have the final word. But there exists a quite different objection, one both more interesting and more powerful, which states that the case for mandatory teaching of evolution does not hinge on its superiority as a scientific account. This second objection stresses the distinction between, on the one hand, judging a view like creationism as largely without warrant, and on the other, permitting mandatory teaching designed to replace that view with a sounder one: it suggests that even if the judgment be granted, the permissibility does not directly follow, for there may be independent considerations against requiring the material in question.

This objection presents a more difficult challenge to the mandatory teaching of evolution for the simple reason that schools cannot teach everything known to be true and must make choices about what to require in a curriculum. Usually such choices involve comparing the relative merits of different materials along criteria (1) to (4) above. If we think only in those terms, the case for requiring evolution, given its intrinsic importance, will be quite strong. But unlike knowledge of mathematics or literacy, for example, many citizens believe that the teaching of evolution carries a distinct cost. We cannot, then, resolve the matter without considering how such objections fare against the two criteria sketched above.

Few objections to requiring the teaching of evolution will, I think, be disqualified by (A). There is no reason to think such opposition corresponds to a diminished commitment to basic liberal norms of moral decency, political equality, and so on. To the contrary, some citizens may endorse those norms precisely because of religious views they see evolution as threatening. (It is not wholly irrelevant here that a little learning about evolution can breed opposition to liberal norms: social Darwinism recommends indifference to the poor, just as evolutionary psychology can be employed to defend bogus claims of racial or sexual differences.)

This compatibility between opposing evolution and endorsing basic liberal commitments is important, for a common move among those who would require the teaching of evolution is to argue that just as we dismiss parents who object to certain material for reasons that are racist or sexist in nature, so too should we pay no heed to parents who reject evolution. That point would be relevant if I were arguing that any parental opposition is a reason to exclude material, but (A) distinguishes my view from that position.

Turning to (B), it is undeniable that evolution challenges the permissible normative frameworks (largely religious ones) of many liberal citizens. Though some faiths have achieved a reconciliation with evolutionary biology, many have not, and in a liberal state such questions are properly decided by adherents of the faith in question. Mandating the teaching of evolution thus either drives citizens to find some such reconciliation or undermines parents' ability to pass on religious ideals the liberal state has otherwise deemed permissible. Doing either might be justified if lacking an understanding of evolution significantly disadvantaged one in life or meant that one had simply not received the good of education, but the first claim is implausible, the second arbitrary. In the previous chapter I noted that the liberal commitment to freedom gives citizens the right to do the wrong thing; my argument here is that, within limits, they also have the right to believe the wrong thing, and to try to get their children to do the same.

This right is not absolute, however, and may be overridden by especially powerful considerations. Consider the possibility that global climate change presents an urgent threat that states must actively address. It may be that arguments for this view involve claims about the Earth's history that depend on or are strongly corroborated by the theory of evolution, and are thus at odds with permissible religious doctrines.[53] If so, the need for citizens to make informed decisions about such a grave matter might override the *prima facie* objection against requiring the teaching of evolution. But if this concession brings my argument in the end closer to the position of robust liberals, it differs in seeing that outcome as an unfortunate departure, forced by contingent challenges, from basic liberal ideals.

Sex education: two models

Working out what MVL implies for mandatory sex education is complicated by the fact that the nature of such education is ambiguous. At

---

[53] Thanks to Beth Parks for drawing my attention to this point.

a minimum, sex education informs students about human beings' basic sexual functionings as they relate to biological reproduction, in a manner that promotes responsible choices and personal health. More maximal accounts seek also to instill particular attitudes towards our sexual natures, sexual identities, and appropriate modes of expressing both, as in Debra Haffner's suggestion that "sexuality education encompasses sexual knowledge, beliefs, attitudes, values, and behaviors."[54] To ask how MVL stands with respect to mandatory sex education is thus to ask two questions. May the MVL state mandate any form of sex education for all its citizens? If so, what form should it take?

Mandating some such class is recommended, in varying degrees, by all four criteria mentioned above. (1) Becoming a parent is an event of great consequence that significantly restructures one's obligations and range of acceptable choices. Additionally, sexual activity has potentially serious consequences for personal health. Learning about responsible and healthy sexual practices thus protects one's range of effective freedom. (2) Given that the physical effects of sexual activity fall disproportionately on women, improving citizens' understanding of reproduction can help promote equality in the conditions of men and women. It is also possible, though this point is more speculative, that learning that contraceptive options exist for both men and women can promote a more equal assumption of responsibility towards pregnancy prevention, further enhancing equality between the sexes. (3) Responsible citizenship involves limiting the demands one places on others. Since all citizens within the liberal state are guaranteed access to the basic goods needed for a decent life, responsible family planning may be one aspect of responsible citizenship. Given limits to the Earth's carrying capacity, this point applies as well to people whose children do not draw direct resources from the state. (4) Finally, the facts of biological reproduction are intrinsically significant, the sort of thing any person should know.

Critics of sex education might grant these considerations but insist that such lessons should be taught at home. But this point holds for many other subjects already taught in schools, and in any case, any duplication of lessons at home and school is offset by the great importance such knowledge has. (Various studies reveal an astonishing lack of knowledge about sex among US citizens.)[55] Still, it cannot be denied that sexual

[54] Debra Haffner, "Foreword: Sexuality Education in Policy and Practice," in *Sexuality and the Curriculum*, ed. James T. Sears (New York: Teachers College Press, 1992), vii.

[55] For some sense of the level of misinformation, see Michael Carrera *et al.*, "Knowledge about Reproduction, Contraception, and Sexually Transmitted Infections among Young Adolescents in American Cities," *Social Policy* 30, no. 3 (Spring 2000), 41–50.

matters are both more intimate and more likely to connect to questions of value about which citizens care deeply, than, say, planar geometry or the Plantagenet lineage. What really concerns parents who reject sex education, of course, is the fear that it will be taught in a way that undermines values taught in the home. Do such objections have the same weight they did in the context of teaching evolution?

They do not, at least when sex education conforms to minimal accounts, because sex education differs from teaching evolution in two important ways. First, the facts that sex education treats have direct implications for citizens' freedom and well-being in a way that knowledge of evolution simply does not. Second, in contrast to teaching evolution, teaching about human sexuality and reproduction does not challenge the basic normative frameworks endorsed by citizens. Teaching that condoms exist and that some people use them to prevent pregnancy, for example, does not endorse such efforts in a manner at odds with certain beliefs about sex, any more than teaching students that persons sometimes blow themselves up to protest against government policy endorses similar action.

This defense of sex education assumes that a real distinction exists between transmitting facts and endorsing norms, such that efforts to do the first do not inevitably do the second. That assumption can be problematic: Was your colleague rude, or just being efficient? Did the riot police restore order, or murder the protesters? Notwithstanding such difficulties, the distinction, at least with respect to sex education, remains broadly relevant. There is surely a difference between acknowledging the fact of nocturnal emissions and encouraging boys to see masturbation as a harmless option they should pursue, between acknowledging that some persons are attracted to others of the same sex and seeking to convince students that all forms of sexual relations are morally equivalent, between teaching the biology of sexual reproduction and "helping people achieve as much sexual satisfaction and pleasure as possible."[56] And lest this point seem ideologically one-sided, I hasten to add that minimal approaches similarly prohibit attempts to communicate the evils of masturbation, the superiority of heterosexism, or the view that pleasure is not a legitimate aim of human sexual activity.

Advocates of more maximal approaches may still maintain that minimal approaches implicitly privilege heterosexism as the proper mode of

[56] R. Jones, "Sex Education in Personal and Social Education," in *Personal and Social Education: Philosophical Perspectives*, ed. P. White (London: Kogan Page, 1989), 57, quoted in Michael J. Reiss, "Conflicting Philosophies of School Sex Education," in *Philosophy of Education: An Anthology*, ed. Randall Curren (Malden, MA: Blackwell, 2007), 553.

sexual relationship. I doubt this is inevitable, but even if it were, this would be an unintended (and from the standpoint of MVL, unfortunate) consequence of a program justified by the fact that heterosexual sex potentially has the momentous consequence of producing a new life (with all its attendant obligations) whereas homosexual sex does not. It is thus not a judgment about the intrinsic superiority of heterosexual sex that warrants emphasizing it in the classroom, but its connection with other matters over which the state properly has some say. To assert this is not to deny the merits of the sort of goal Peter McLaren has endorsed: "to shed a new critical understanding on the construction of male and female sexual identity as it has been mapped by sovereign regimes of patriarchal scientific discourses and colonized by phallic desire, and to challenge regressive and insidiously harmful myths about gay and lesbian sexuality."[57] It is only to say that such goals should not be the aim of a mandated program of sex education.

I suspect that many who advocate more maximal approaches endorse a view of sexuality as a domain from which normative constraints have largely disappeared (assuming the consent of all parties), one where personal pleasure reigns as the sole criterion. While that view is not without merit, neither are its competitors. Many citizens who object to more maximal approaches worry that they will lead children to adopt a casual attitude to sexuality at odds with a view of our sexual natures as potential sites of the sacred, whose exploration merits cautious deliberation bound by norms that sharply constrain bodily desires, and see combating such permissiveness as a central parental duty. Though the MVL state should not aid such efforts, neither should it undermine them through a program of compulsory education that takes sides on such debates. Liberal citizens are just deeply divided on important questions of sexual morality – not just which norms ought to govern our sexual lives, but whether there are any such norms at all – and, given the central place sexual morality occupies within many normative frameworks (a testament to the importance both of reproduction and of sexuality generally), it is hardly surprising that such divisions occasion fierce disagreement. The minimal approach to sex education offers the best way to meet important goals while remaining consistent with the idea of the MVL state.

---

[57] Peter McLaren, "Foreword: Border Anxiety and Sexuality Politics," in *Sexuality and the Curriculum*, ed. James T. Sears (New York: Teachers College Press, 1992), xii. To be clear, McLaren offers this as the goal of a book on sexuality education, not as a goal of sex education itself.

The approach to sex education outlined here, along with that concerning the teaching of evolution, remains quite broad and schematic. But there is only so much specificity that moral principles, already relatively imprecise, can achieve. In the face of practical debates under conditions of deep diversity, there is often no alternative to leaving what William Galston calls "the plane of moral abstractions" and trying instead to resolve this particular conflict, with these particular values at stake, in the most appropriate way.[58] I have tried to identify those factors that are especially important in working towards such a resolution. Given the legitimacy of the interests on all sides, it's not clear that an account of compulsory education in the MVL state can or should do more.

[58] Galston, *Liberal Pluralism,* 106.

CHAPTER 10

The limits of modus vivendi liberalism

It must be acknowledged that the modus vivendi liberalism I have outlined is not entirely satisfying. In two main areas it seems especially inadequate. The first concerns the worry that MVL fails to provide precisely what we want from a political theory – viz., a rationally vindicated solution to the problem of moral conflict that all parties within a political community would wholeheartedly accept. MVL does not resolve the moral dissensus that is the context for liberal theory through a more complete and reflective account, it might be said, but instead acquiesces to such conflict and shows us only how to manage it. In thus failing to articulate a rational harmony among the competing parties of liberal society, it fails to reconcile us to our social world in the manner of philosophical reflection at its best.

In *The Law of Peoples*, John Rawls gives elegant expression to this general worry. The book begins and ends with Rawls's discussion of a realistic utopia, by which he means a vision of the sort of collective moral improvement genuinely possible given the realities of the human condition. In the context of that discussion, Rawls says this:

Eventually we want to ask whether reasonable pluralism within or between peoples is a historical condition to which we should be reconciled. Though we can imagine what we sometimes think would be a happier world – one in which everyone, or all peoples, have the same faith that we do – that is not the question, excluded as it is by the nature and culture of free institutions. To show that reasonable pluralism is not to be regretted, we must show that, given the socially feasible alternatives, the existence of reasonable pluralism allows a society of greater political justice and liberty. To argue this cogently would be to reconcile us to our contemporary political and social condition.[1]

Such reconciliation would not only be theoretically satisfying, given the goals of moral inquiry, but would as well, Rawls suggests, have important

---

[1] Rawls, *The Law of Peoples*, 12.

practical consequences concerning our need to relate to the social world in a certain way. Confidence in such a reconciliation, he says, "gives meaning to what we do today" and bolsters motivation for constructive political engagement. Without it, we risk "the dangers of resignation and cynicism." Indeed, if human beings under conditions of freedom can live alongside one another only on modus vivendi terms, Rawls darkly concludes, "we might ask, with Kant, whether it is worthwhile for human beings to live on the earth."[2]

Though Rawls makes these comments in discussing the challenge of diversity between societies, not within them, his concern with reconciliation there continues a theme broached in *Political Liberalism*. This is not surprising, given that Rawls's approach to the international realm mirrors in various ways his approach to diversity within liberal states as well. (Note that the long passage above refers to both kinds of disagreement.) In *Political Liberalism*, for example, the possibility that there exists a substantive account of public reason that can be endorsed by citizens committed to diverse comprehensive views is what allows Rawls to answer affirmatively what he calls "a torturing question in the contemporary world, namely: Can democracy and comprehensive doctrines, religious or nonreligious, be compatible?"[3] This last question, I suggest, anticipates the Kantian question with which *The Law of Peoples* concludes and explains Rawls's reference in *Political Liberalism* to the goal of "reconciliation by public reason."

It is difficult not to admire Rawls's ambitious claims for political philosophy here. What is less clear is the importance of the sort of reconciliation he stresses in assessing options in political philosophy generally, and MVL in particular. That importance can be defended, I just suggested, either as a vital motivating force in our practical lives or as a requirement of theoretical unity or completeness. Regarding the former, I see little reason to think that if one abandons Rawls's hopes of a realistic utopia, one's own actions will then seem to lack meaning, ushering in resignation and cynicism. Such consequences might follow if the only alternative to living under norms one wholeheartedly embraces is a state of affairs where one could in no way pursue a flourishing life, but such a dichotomy omits the range of second-best options (or third-, fourth-, etc.) in which human beings the world over fashion satisfying lives and which they often go to great lengths to defend. Though political philosophers may be dismayed that some citizens will not wholeheartedly endorse the political terms

---

[2] Ibid., 128.   [3] Rawls, *Political Liberalism*, 177, 175.

governing the liberal state, such misgivings are likely to have far less effect on everyday citizens who do not share the former's idiosyncratic concerns. It's hard to see why the disabling doubts and cynicism Rawls imagines must arise for them.

As for the ideal of theoretical completeness, where that refers to reason vindicating a single set of principles as ideal to govern fundamental political questions, that hope is already rendered dubious by the conjunction of the justificatory requirement, deep diversity, and value pluralism. If reconciliation involves seeing the liberal state as protecting what Rawls calls "a society of greater political justice and liberty," that goal MVL does not deliver. But this limitation is just an unavoidable consequence of taking seriously the liberal commitment to citizens' ultimate sovereignty. So long as discerning authoritative political principles was a privileged task for the philosopher, seeking the theoretical closure that reconciliation gestures to was not a bootless pursuit. But the liberal ideal of justification means that the content of such principles cannot be worked out in the philosopher's mind alone, and must also accommodate the thinking of citizens who in various degrees depart from the conception of rationality to which philosophical understanding aspires. If we accept, as I have argued, (1) that acceptable political principles will secure the rational endorsement of those they govern, (2) that the criterion of rationality cannot be set so high as to exclude large numbers of citizens, and (3) that such a level of rationality is met by people committed to a range of ways of life and attendant frameworks of value, the project of reconciliation in liberal states is unlikely to succeed. I am not denying that it would be a welcome achievement, and might even give us confidence that the world was made to human purposes. My point is just that, given liberal commitments, it cannot be a necessary condition for an adequate approach to politics, and MVL cannot be faulted for failing to deliver it.

The second lingering source of dissatisfaction with my overall argument is that the MVL state, because of its relatively modest normative commitments, cannot function as a collective agent for moral progress, and cannot combat objectionable norms and practices, in ways that might seem desirable. For though I have argued that liberal states often have no good grounds to oppose the values illiberal groups endorse, many of those values, I acknowledge, seem both mistaken and troubling. For example, some believe that men and women are designed to occupy fixed roles within the social order, or that sexual relations between persons of the same sex are intrinsically corrupting, or that profound and illuminating works of art and literature are an offense against God. Since MVL sharply limits what the state may do to move citizens away from such beliefs and towards what many will see as much sounder views, this must occasion some dismay.

Such frustration is mitigated, however, by two considerations. The first returns on more interventionist liberals a reply that liberals standardly offer against conservatives: believing that the liberal state should tolerate a practice implies neither that one endorses it nor even that one sees it as non-objectionable. When weighing state action to combat objectionable norms and practices, two issues are crucial: (1) To what degree do those norms and practices result from the exercise of the expressive liberty that liberal states value? (2) How far does tolerating those norms and practices harm the interests of other non-consenting citizens? When important expressive liberties are involved, the degree of harm will have to be relatively serious to justify state involvement. Kukathas captures this point neatly: "If people are given freedom, they may use their freedom badly; if they are granted rights, they may use them to do wrong."[4] For liberals, state involvement is warranted only when those wrongs rise above a certain threshold. This means that citizens who regard themselves as especially enlightened in moral matters will often have to tolerate a world in which, in their eyes, others are acting immorally. One hopes the sting of this should be alleviated somewhat by the knowledge that, in liberal regimes, this is an affliction to which many other citizens are similarly subject.

The other consideration mitigating frustration that the MVL state cannot be a more active agent of moral progress is that state power is only one mechanism that might lead people to revise their values, and is as well the one most likely to generate opposition in those it seeks to work upon. In liberal states such change should chiefly come from two other sources. One is the presence of arguments against dubious or unsound frameworks advanced by persons both within and outside such groups. It's important to see that an argument against state intervention is not an argument that citizens should not lobby to transform or overturn norms and practices they find objectionable. There is much that those who oppose what they see as objectionable norms of various groups can and should do – exhortation, moral critique, consciousness-raising, political activism, and so on. Through its firm commitment to freedoms of speech, association, movement, and so on, the MVL state creates an environment maximally open

---

[4] Kukathas, *The Liberal Archipelago*, 142. See also Jeremy Waldron, "A Right to do Wrong?," 21–39.

to such exchanges. Requiring an education that promotes rational reflection, informs citizens of their rights, and ensures awareness of alternatives further enhances conditions for such exchanges and positions citizens to both criticize and respond as they see fit.

The second source for change in a cultural group's norms has to do with the tacitly liberalizing effect of living in a liberal society that tolerates robust diversity and enforces the requirements of moral equality in all interactions subject to public scrutiny. Several factors contribute to this liberalizing dynamic – economic transactions, mass media, shared use of common public space, compulsory education – and these can place enormous pressure on a group's traditional norms and practices. One common result of this dynamic is that groups face the option of either changing in the direction of liberal norms or appearing increasingly obsolete in the eyes of younger members.[5]

My point here is that advocates of MVL can perfectly well both welcome revisions in the norms of various groups and believe that these are likely to come about as a result of living in the liberal state. What chiefly distinguishes them from more interventionist liberals is their belief that the state should not itself be the agent of such change, but should instead create conditions in which citizens might bring such change about (or not, as they decide).[6] This insistence on free citizens as the necessary agents of such change is, I have said, the only position compatible with the liberal view that the nature of public institutions should reflect citizens' ultimate sovereignty. Indeed, it is hard not to conclude that strong support for the state as the agent of moral progress, in the manner favored by more robust liberals, reflects one of two fears about what will happen without it: the first is that many citizens will continue to pass on deeply mistaken moral frameworks, ideals, values, and so on; the second is that many will remain either unaware of what justice requires or unmoved to do it. While neither fear is wholly groundless, each is hard to square with the strong confidence in citizens' rationality and capacity for moral self-governance that underpins the liberal project. While a liberalism structured by such fears is not self-refuting, it is nonetheless one that lacks the confidence of its convictions.

---

[5] In her study of young women caught between their family's traditional norms and the culture of their public high school, Laurie Olsen notes that many express their intention to raise their own children in ways that depart from those traditional norms and show the influence of liberal ideals (Olsen, *Made in America: Immigrant Students in Our Public Schools* [New York: New Press, 1997], quoted in Spinner-Halev, *The Boundaries of Citizenship*, 90).

[6] In *The Law of Peoples* Rawls speaks of "a division of labor" between political and social institutions on the one hand and civil society on the other (127).

I do not pretend, however, that MVL offers a conclusive rebuttal to the two worries I have been discussing; its imperfections must be granted. In the end, advocates of the modus vivendi approach must take their stand here, acknowledging that while their defense of liberalism does not give us everything we want in a political theory, this is no reason to reject it; no theory does. It is not surprising that political theorists might find this fact especially frustrating, but we should not let such vexation lead us to conclude that there must exist a liberal solution to the problem of moral diversity, just over the horizon, which all citizens might wholeheartedly endorse if only we could find it. Nor, finally, should we forget that it is a singular accomplishment to arrive at lasting terms of peaceful coexistence among people who value very different ideals, worship very different gods, and pursue very different ends, many of which are bound to appear deeply misguided to fellow citizens. Achieving more than this may be a task appropriate for beings quite different from us. Living humanely alongside those with whom we deeply disagree is challenge enough.

Bibliography

Ackerman, Bruce, *Social Justice in the Liberal State*, New Haven: Yale University Press, 1980.

Ahmed, Leila, *Women and Gender in Islam: Historical Roots of a Modern Debate*, New Haven: Yale University Press, 1992.

Al-Hibri, Azizah, "Is Western Patriarchal Feminism Good for Third World/ Minority Women?," in *Is Multiculturalism Bad for Women?*, ed. Joshua Cohen, Matthew Howard, and Martha Nussbaum, Princeton: Princeton University Press, 1999, 41–6.

Arneson, Richard, "Human Flourishing versus Desire Satisfaction," *Social Philosophy and Policy* 16 (Winter 1999), 113–42.

Arneson, Richard, and Ian Shapiro, "Democratic Autonomy and Religious Freedom," in *Political Order: NOMOS 38*, ed. Ian Shapiro and Russell Hardin, New York: New York University Press, 1996.

Audi, Robert, *Religious Commitment and Secular Reason*, Cambridge: Cambridge University Press, 2000.

Audi, Robert, and Nicholas Wolterstorff, *Religion in the Public Square: The Place of Religious Convictions in Political Debate*, Lanham, MD: Rowman & Littlefield, 1997.

Baber, Harriet, "Adaptive Preference," paper presented March 28, 2004, at the APA Mini-conference on Global Justice, Pasadena, CA.

Barry, Brian, *Culture and Equality: An Egalitarian Critique of Multiculturalism*, Cambridge, MA: Harvard University Press, 2001.

Justice as Impartiality, New York: Oxford University Press, 1995.

The Liberal Theory of Justice, Oxford: Oxford University Press, 1973.

Benditt, Theodore, "Compromising Interests and Principles," in *Compromise in Ethics, Law and Politics: NOMOS 29*, ed. J. R. Pennock and J. W. Chapman, New York: New York University Press, 1979, 26–37.

Benedict, Ruth, "Anthropology and the Abnormal," *Journal of General Psychology* 10 (1934), 59–82.

Benhabib, Seyla, *The Claims of Culture*, Princeton: Princeton University Press, 2003.

Benjamin, Martin, *Splitting the Difference: Compromise and Integrity in Ethics and Politics*, Lawrence, KS: University of Kansas Press, 1990.

Benn, Stanley, "Freedom, Autonomy, and the Concept of a Person," *Proceedings of the Aristotelian Society* 66 (1975–6), 109–30.

A Theory of Freedom, Cambridge: Cambridge University Press, 1988.

Berkowitz, Peter, *Virtue and the Making of Modern Liberalism*, Princeton: Princeton University Press, 1999.

Berlin, Isaiah, "Two Concepts of Liberty," in *Four Essays on Liberty*, New York: Oxford University Press, 1969, 118–72.

Billig, Michael, *Arguing and Thinking: A Rhetorical Approach to Social Psychology*, Cambridge: Cambridge University Press, 1996.

Bird, Colin, "Mutual Respect and Neutral Justification," *Ethics* 107 (October 1996), 62–96.

Brighouse, Harry, "Channel One, the Anti-Commercial Principle, and the Discontinuous Ethos," in *Philosophy of Education: An Anthology*, ed. Randall Curren, Malden, MA: Blackwell, 2007, 208–20.

"Civic Education and Liberal Legitimacy," *Ethics* 108 (1998), 719–45.

School Choice and Social Justice, New York: Oxford University Press, 2000.

Brower, Bruce, "The Limits of Public Reason," *Journal of Philosophy* 91 (January 1994), 5–26.

Burkett, Elinor, "God Created Me to Be a Slave," *New York Times Magazine*, October 12, 1997, 56–60.

Burtt, Shelley, "Comprehensive Educations and the Liberal Understanding of Autonomy," in *Citizenship and Education in Liberal-Democratic Societies*, ed. Walter Feinberg and Kevin McDonough, New York: Oxford University Press, 2003, 179–207.

Caldwell, John C., "Routes to Low Mortality in poor Countries," *Population and Development Review* 12 (1986), 171–220.

Callan, Eamonn, "Autonomy, Child-Rearing, and Good Lives," in *The Moral and Political Status of Children*, ed. David Archard and Colin Macleod, New York: Oxford University Press, 2002, 118–41.

Creating Citizens, New York: Clarendon Press, 1997.

"Liberal Legitimacy, Justice, and Civic Education," *Ethics* 111 (October 2000), 141–55.

"Political Liberalism and Political Education," *Review of Politics* 58 (Winter 1996), 5–33.

Caney, Simon, "Liberal Legitimacy, Reasonable Disagreement and Justice," in *Pluralism and Liberal Neutrality*, ed. Richard Bellamy and Martin Hollis, Ilford: Frank Cass, 1999, 19–36.

Card, Claudia, "Rape as a Terrorist Institution," in *Violence, Terrorism and Justice*, ed. R. G. Frey and Christopher Morris, New York: Cambridge University Press, 1991, 296–319.

Carens, Joseph, and Melissa Williams, "Muslim Minorities in Liberal Democracies: The Politics of Misrecognition," in *Secularism and its Critics*, ed. Rajeev Bhargava, Delhi: Oxford University Press, 1998, 137–73.

Carrera, Michael, *et al.*, "Knowledge about Reproduction, Contraception, and Sexually Transmitted Infections among Young Adolescents in American cities," *Social Policy* 30, no. 3 (Spring 2000), 41–50.

Case, Anne, "Health, Income and Economic Development," in *Annual World Bank Conference on Development Economics 2001/2002*, ed. B. Pleskovic and N. Stern, Washington DC: World Bank, 2002, 221–41.

Christiano, Thomas, "The Incoherence of Hobbesian Justifications of the State," *American Philosophical Quarterly* 31 (January 1994), 23–38.

Cladis, Mark, *A Communication Defense of Liberalism: Emile Durkheim and Contemporary Social Theory*, Stanford: Stanford University Press, 1992.

Cohen, Joshua, "Moral Pluralism and Political Consensus," in *The Idea of Democracy*, ed. David Copp *et al.*, Cambridge: Cambridge University Press, 1993, 270–91.

Cookson, Catharine, *Regulating Religion: The Courts and the Free Exercise Clause*, New York: Oxford University Press, 2001.

Crowder, George, *Liberalism and Value Pluralism*, New York: Continuum, 2002.

"Pluralism and Liberalism," *Political Studies* 42 (1994), 293–305.

Dagger, Richard, *Civic Virtues: Rights, Citizenship, and Republican Liberalism*, New York: Oxford University Press, 1997.

D'Agostino, Fred, *Free Public Reason: Making it Up As We Go*, New York: Oxford University Press, 1996.

Diamond, Jared, "Vengeance is Ours," *New Yorker*, April 21, 2008, 74ff.

Donner, Wendy, *The Liberal Self: John Stuart Mill's Moral and Political Philosophy*, Ithaca: Cornell University Press, 1991.

Double, Richard, "Two Types of Autonomy Accounts," *Canadian Journal of Philosophy* 22, no. 1 (March 1992), 65–80.

Dworkin, Gerald, "Autonomy and Behavior Control," *Hastings Center Report* 6 (February 1976), 23–8.

"Non-Neutral Principles," in *Reading Rawls: Critical Studies on Rawls' A Theory of Justice*, Stanford, CA: Stanford University Press, 1989, 124–40.

The Theory and Practice of Autonomy, New York: Cambridge University Press, 1988.

Dworkin, Ronald, "Justice and Rights," in *Taking Rights Seriously*, Cambridge, MA: Harvard University Press, 1977, 150–83.

Sovereign Virtue: The Theory and Practice of Equality, Cambridge, MA: Harvard University Press, 2000.

Elster, Jon, *Sour Grapes: Studies in the Subversion of Rationality*, New York: Cambridge University Press, 1983.

Feinberg, Joel, *The Moral Limits of the Criminal Law,* vol. iii: *Harm to Self,* New York: Oxford University Press, 1984.

Finnis, John, *Natural Law and Natural Rights*, Oxford: Oxford University Press, 1990.

Fishkin, James, "Liberty vs. Equal Opportunity," *Social Philosophy and Policy* 5 (1978), 32–48.

Foot, Philippa, "Utilitarianism and the Virtues," in *Consequentialism and its Critics*, ed. Samuel Scheffler, New York: Oxford University Press, 1988, 224–42.

Frankfurt, Harry, "Equality as a Moral Ideal," *Ethics* 98 (October 1987), 21–43.

"Freedom of the Will and the Concept of a Person," in *Free Will*, ed. Gary Watson, New York: Oxford University Press, 1982, 81–95.

Fried, Charles, *Right and Wrong*, Cambridge, MA: Harvard University Press, 1978.

Galston, William, "Civil Education in the Liberal State," in *Liberalism and the Moral Life*, ed. Nancy Rosenblum, Cambridge, MA: Harvard University Press, 1989.

Liberal Pluralism, Cambridge: Cambridge University Press, 2002.

Liberal Purposes, New York: Cambridge University Press, 1991.

The Practice of Liberal Pluralism, New York: Cambridge University Press, 2005.

"Two Concepts of Liberalism," *Ethics* 105 (April 1995), 516–34.

Gaut, Berys, "Moral Pluralism," *Philosophical Papers* 22, no. 1 (1993), 17–40.

"Rawls and the Claims of Liberal Legitimacy," *Philosophical Papers* 24 (1995), 1–22.

George, Robert P., *Making Men Moral*, Oxford: Clarendon Press, 1993.

"Natural Law and International Order," in *International Society*, ed. David Mapel and Terry Nardin, Princeton: Princeton University Press, 1998, 54–69.

Gilles, Stephen, review of Stephen Macedo, *Diversity and Distrust*, *Education Next* 1, no. 1 (Spring 2001), www.hoover.org/publications/ednext.

Gilman, Sander, "'Barbaric' Rituals?," in *Is Multiculturalism Bad for Women?*, ed. Joshua Cohen, Matthew Howard, and Martha Nussbaum, Princeton: Princeton University Press, 1999, 53–8.

Goldsmith, M. M., "Hobbes' 'Mortall God': Is There a Fallacy in Hobbes' Theory of Sovereignty?," *History of Political Thought* 1 (1980), 33–50.

Gray, John, *Enlightenment's Wake: Politics and Culture at the Close of the Modern Age*, New York: Routledge, 1995.

Isaiah Berlin, Princeton: Princeton University Press, 1996.

Two Faces of Liberalism, New York: New Press, 2000.

"Two Liberalisms of Fear," *Hedgehog Review* 2 (Spring 2000), 9–23.

Green, Leslie, "Internal Minorities and Their Rights," in *The Rights of Minority Cultures*, ed. Will Kymlicka, New York: Oxford University Press, 1995, 256–72.

Greenawalt, Kent, *Private Consciences and Public Reasons*, New York: Oxford University Press, 1995.

Greenberg, Blu, *On Women and Judaism: A View from Tradition*, Philadelphia, PA: Jewish Publication Society of America, 1981.

Greene, Jay P., "The Surprising Consensus on School Choice," *The Public Interest* 144 (Summer 2001), www.thepublicinterest.com.

Griffin, James, "Are There Incommensurable Values?," *Philosophy and Public Affairs* 7 (1977), 39–59.

Gutmann, Amy, "Children, Paternalism, and Education: A Liberal Argument," *Philosophy and Public Affairs* 9 (1980), 338–58.

"Civic Education and Social Diversity," *Ethics* 105 (April 1995), 557–79.

Democratic Education, rev. edn., Princeton: Princeton University Press, 1999.

"How Limited is Liberal Government?," in *Liberalism Without Illusions: Essays on Liberal Theory and the Political Vision of Judith Shklar*, ed. Bernard Yack, Chicago: Chicago University Press, 1996, 64–81.

Haffner, Debra, "Foreword: Sexuality Education in Policy and Practice," in *Sexuality and the Curriculum*, ed. James T. Sears, New York: Teachers College Press, 1992, vii–viii.

Hampshire, Stuart, *Innocence and Experience*, Cambridge, MA: Harvard University Press, 1989.

Justice is Conflict, Princeton: Princeton University Press, 2000.

Haworth, Lawrence, *Autonomy: An Essay in Philosophical Psychology and Ethics*, New Haven: Yale University Press, 1986.

"Autonomy and Utility," in *The Inner Citadel: Essays on Individual Autonomy*, ed. John Christman, New York: Oxford University Press, 1989, 155–69.

Higgins, Tracy, "Why Feminists Can't (or Shouldn't) Be Liberals," *Fordham Law Review* 72 (April 2004), 1629–41.

Hill, Thomas, "The Problem of Stability in *Political Liberalism*," in *Respect, Pluralism, and Justice: Kantian Perspectives*, Oxford: Oxford University Press, 2000, 237–59.

Honig, Bonnie, "'My Culture Made Me Do It'," in *Is Multiculturalism Bad for Women?*, ed. Joshua Cohen, Matthew Howard, and Martha Nussbaum, Princeton: Princeton University Press, 1999, 35–40.

Hurka, Thomas, *Perfectionism*, Oxford: Oxford University Press, 1993.

"Why Value Autonomy?," *Social Theory and Practice* 13, no. 3 (Fall 1987), 361–82.

Ignatieff, Michael, *Isaiah Berlin: A Life*, London: Chatto & Windus, 1998.

Jones, R., "Sex Education in Personal and Social Education," in *Personal and Social Education: Philosophical Perspectives*, ed. P. White, London: Kogan Page, 1989, 54–7.

Kekes, John, "Cruelty and Liberalism," *Ethics* 106 (July 1996), 834–44.

The Morality of Pluralism, Princeton: Princeton University Press, 1993.

Kraybill, Donald, *The Riddle of Amish Culture*, Baltimore: Johns Hopkins University Press, 1989.

Kuflik, Arthur, "Morality and Compromise," in *Compromise in Ethics, Law and Politics: NOMOS 29*, ed. J. R. Pennock and J. W. Chapman, New York: New York University Press, 1979, 38–65.

Kukathas, Chandran, "Are There Any Cultural Rights?," *Political Theory* 20, no. 1 (February 1992), 105–39.

"Is Feminism Bad for Multiculturalism?," *Public Affairs Quarterly* 15 (April 2001), 83–98.

The Liberal Archipelago, New York: Oxford University Press, 2003.

Kymlicka, Will, "Liberal Individualism and Liberal Neutrality," *Ethics* 99 (July 1989), 883–905.

Liberalism, Community and Culture, New York: Oxford University Press, 1989.

Multicultural Citizenship, New York: Oxford University Press, 1995.

"The Rights of Minority Cultures: Reply to Kukathas," *Political Theory* 20, no. 1 (February 1992), 140–6.

Larmore, Charles, *The Morals of Modernity*, Cambridge: Cambridge University Press, 1996.

Patterns of Moral Complexity, Cambridge: Cambridge University Press, 1987.

Levinson, Meira, *The Demands of Liberal Education*, New York: Oxford University Press, 1999.

Levinson, Sanford, "The Confrontation of Religious Faith and Civil Religion: Catholics Becoming Justices," *DePaul Law Review* 39 (1990), 1047–82.

Lleras-Muney, Adriana, "The Relationship between Education and Adult Mortality in the US," *Review of Economic Studies* 72, no. 1 (January 2005), 189–221.

Lomasky, Loren, "But is it Liberalism?," *Critical Review* 4 (Winter 1990), 86–105.

Lukes, Steven, *Liberals and Cannibals: The Implications of Diversity*, New York: Verso, 2003.

McCabe, David, "Knowing About the Good: A Problem with Anti-Perfectionism," *Ethics* 110 (January 2000), 311–38.

Macedo, Stephen, *Diversity and Distrust: Civic Education in a Multicultural Society*, Cambridge, MA: Harvard University Press, 2000.

"Liberal Civic Education and Religious Fundamentalism: The Case of God v. John Rawls," *Ethics* 105 (April 1995), 468–96.

Liberal Virtues: Citizenship, Virtue, and Community in Liberal Constitutionalism, New York: Oxford University Press, 1990.

"The Politics of Justification," *Political Theory* 18 (May 1990), 280–304.

Macedo, Stephen, and Leif Wenar, "The Diversity of Rights in Contemporary Ethical and Political Thought," in *The Nature of Rights at the American Founding and Beyond*, ed. Barry Shain, Charlottesville, VA: University of Virginia Press, 2007, 280–302.

MacIntyre, Alasdair, *After Virtue*, 2nd edn., Notre Dame, IN: University of Notre Dame Press, 1984.

McLaren, Peter, "Foreword: Border Anxiety and Sexuality Politics," in *Sexuality and the Curriculum*, ed. James T. Sears, New York: Teachers College Press, 1992, ix–xiv.

Maddock, Kenneth, *The Australian Aborigines: A Portrait of Their Society*, Ringwood: Penguin, 1972.

Madison, James, *The Federalist* no. 10, in *The Federalist Papers*, ed. Clinton Rossiter, New York: Penguin, 1961.

Mason, Andrew, *Community, Solidarity, and Belonging*, Cambridge: Cambridge University Press, 2000.

May, Simon Cabulea, "Principled Compromise and the Abortion Controversy," *Philosophy and Public Affairs* 33 (Fall 2005), 317–48.

Mill, John Stuart, *On Liberty* (1859), various editions.

Utilitarianism (1863), various editions.

Mills, Claudia, "'Not a Mere Modus Vivendi': The Bases for Allegiance to the Just State," in *The Idea of a Political Liberalism*, ed. Victoria Davion and Clark Wolf, Lanham, MD: Rowman & Littlefield, 2000, 190–203.

Mirhosseini, Akram, "After the Revolution: Violations of Women's Human Rights in Iran," in *Women's Rights, Human Rights*, ed. Julie Peters and Andrea Wolper (New York: Routledge, 1995), 72–7.

Mitchell, Basil, "Introduction," in *The Philosophy of Religion*, Oxford: Oxford University Press, 1971.

Moon, J. Donald, *Constructing Community: Moral Pluralism and Tragic Conflicts*, Princeton: Princeton University Press, 1993.

Moore, Margaret, "On Reasonableness," *Journal of Applied Philosophy* 13 (1996), 167–77.

Nagel, Thomas, "Moral Conflict and Political Legitimacy," in *Authority*, ed. Joseph Raz, New York: New York University Press, 1990, 300–24.

Narayan, Uma, *Dislocating Cultures: Identities, Traditions, and Third-World Feminism*, New York: Routledge, 1997.

Neal, Patrick, *Liberalism and its Discontents*, New York: New York University Press, 1997.

"Perfectionism with a Liberal Face? Nervous Liberals and Raz's Political Theory," *Social Theory and Practice* 20, no. 1 (Spring 1994), 25–58.

Nehamas, Alexander, *Nietzsche: Life as Literature*, Cambridge, MA: Harvard University Press, 1985.

Nietzsche, Friedrich, *The Gay Science*, trans. Walter Kaufmann, New York: Vintage, 1974.

Noggle, Robert, "The Public Conception of Autonomy and Critical Self-Reflection," *Southern Journal of Philosophy* 35 (1997), 495–515.

Nussbaum, Martha, "A Plea for Difficulty," in *Is Multiculturalism Bad for Women?*, ed. Joshua Cohen, Matthew Howard, and Martha Nussbaum, Princeton: Princeton University Press, 1999, 105–14.

Sex and Social Justice, New York: Oxford University Press, 1999.

Women and Human Development: The Capabilities Approach, New York: Cambridge University Press, 2000.

Oakeshott, Michael, *Morality and Politics in Modern Europe,* ed. Shirley Letwin, New Haven: Yale University Press, 1993.

On Human Conduct, Oxford: Clarendon Press, 1975.

Okin, Susan Moller, "Feminism and Multiculturalism: Some Tensions," *Ethics* 108, no. 4 (July 1998), 661–84.

"Is Multiculturalism Bad for Women?," in *Is Multiculturalism Bad for Women?*, ed. Joshua Cohen, Matthew Howard, and Martha Nussbaum, Princeton: Princeton University Press, 1999, 9–24.

"Justice and Gender: An Unfinished Debate," *Fordham Law Review* 72 (April 2004), 1537–67.

Justice, Gender, and the Family, New York: Basic Books, 1989.

"Mistresses of Their Own Destiny: Group Rights, Gender, and Realistic Rights of Exit," *Ethics* 112 (January 2002), 205–30.

Olsen, Laurie, *Made in America: Immigrant Students in Our Public Schools*, New York: New Press, 1997.

Owen, J. Judd, *Religion and the Demise of Liberal Rationalism*, Chicago: University of Chicago Press, 2001.

Parekh, Bikhu, *Rethinking Multiculturalism: Cultural Diversity and Political Theory*, Cambridge, MA: Harvard University Press, 2000.

"A Varied Moral World," in *Is Multiculturalism Bad for Women?*, ed. Joshua Cohen, Matthew Howard, and Martha Nussbaum, Princeton: Princeton University Press, 1999, 69–75.

Paris, David, "The 'Theoretical Mystique': Neutrality, Plurality, and the Defense of Pluralism," *American Journal of Political Science* 31 (November 1987), 909–39.

Patten, Alan, "Democratic Secession from a Multinational State," *Ethics* 112 (April 2002), 558–86.

Post, Robert, "Between Norms and Choices," in *Is Multiculturalism Bad for Women?*, ed. Joshua Cohen, Matthew Howard, and Martha Nussbaum, Princeton: Princeton University Press, 1999, 65–8.

Quinn, Warren, "Putting Rationality in its Place," in *Virtues and Reasons: Philippa Foot and Moral Theory*, ed. Rosalind Hursthouse *et al.*, Oxford: Clarendon, 1995, 181–208.

Rachels, James, and William Ruddick, "Lives and Liberty," in *The Inner Citadel: Essays on Individual Autonomy*, ed. John Christman, New York: Oxford University Press, 1989, 221–33.

Rawls, John, "Fairness to Goodness," *Philosophical Review* 84, no. 4 (October 1975), 536–54.

"The Idea of an Overlapping Consensus," *Oxford Journal of Legal Studies* 7 (1987), 1–125.

The Law of Peoples: with "The Idea of Public Reason Revisited," Cambridge, MA: Harvard University Press, 1999.

Political Liberalism, New York: Columbia University Press, 1993.

A Theory of Justice, Cambridge, MA: Harvard University Press, 1971; rev. edn. 1999.

Raz, Joseph, *Engaging Reason: On the Theory of Value and Action*, Oxford: Oxford University Press, 1999.

Ethics in the Public Domain, New York: Oxford University Press, 1994.

"Facing Up: A Reply," *Southern California Law Review* 62 (1989), 1153–235.

The Morality of Freedom, Oxford: Clarendon Press, 1986.

Regan, Donald, "Authority and Value: Reflections on Raz's *Morality of Freedom*," *Southern California Law Review* 62 (1989), 995–1095.

"The Value of Rational Nature," *Ethics* 112 (January 2002), 267–91.

Reich, Rob, "Testing the Boundaries of Parental Authority over Education," in *Moral and Political Education: NOMOS 43*, ed. Stephen Macedo and Yael Tamir, New York: New York University Press, 2002, 275–313.

Reiss, Michael J., "Conflicting Philosophies of School Sex Education," in *Philosophy of Education: An Anthology*, ed. Randall Curren, Malden, MA: Blackwell, 2007, 553–60.

Rose, Carole, "Women and Property: Gaining and Losing Ground," *Virginia Law Review* 78 (1992), 521–59.

Safi, Omid, ed., *Progressive Muslims: On Justice, Gender, and Pluralism*, Oxford: Oneworld, 2003.

Sangari, Kumkum, and Sudesh Vaid, eds., *Recasting Women: Essays in Indian Colonial History*, New Brunswick, NJ: Rutgers University Press, 1990.

Sartre, Jean-Paul, *Existentialism and Human Emotions*, trans. Bernard Frechtman, New York: Philosophical Library, 1957.

Schoeman, Ferdinand, "Rights of Children, Rights of Parents, and the Moral Basis of the Family," *Ethics* 91 (October 1980), 6–19.

Sen, Amartya, "More than One Hundred Million Women are Missing," *New York Review of Books* 37, no. 20 (1990), 61–6.

Shachar, Ayelet, *Multicultural Jurisdictions: Cultural Differences and Women's Rights*, Cambridge: Cambridge University Press, 2001.

Sher, George, *Beyond Neutrality: Perfectionism and Politics*, New York: Cambridge University Press, 1997.

Sher, George, and William Bennett, "Moral Education and Indoctrination," *Journal of Philosophy* 79 (November 1982), 665–77.

Shklar, Judith, *Legalism*, Cambridge, MA: Harvard University Press, 1964.

"The Liberalism of Fear," in *Liberalism and the Moral Life*, ed. Nancy Rosenblum, Cambridge, MA: Harvard University Press, 1989, 21–38.

Ordinary Vices, Cambridge, MA: Harvard University Press, 1984.

Shweder, Richard A., " 'What About Female Genital Mutilation?' and 'Why Cultural Understanding Matters'," in *Why do Men Barbecue? Recipes for Cultural Psychology*, Cambridge, MA: Harvard University Press, 2003, 168–216.

Simmons, A. John, *Justification and Legitimacy: Essays on Rights and Obligations*, New York: Cambridge University Press, 2001.

Smart, J. J. C., "An Outline of a System of Utilitarian Ethics," in J. J. C. Smart and Bernard Williams, *Utilitarianism: For and Against*, New York: Cambridge University Press, 1963, 3–74.

Spinner-Halev, Jeffrey, *The Boundaries of Citizenship*, Baltimore: Johns Hopkins University Press, 1994.

"Feminism, Multiculturalism, Oppression, and the State," *Ethics* 112 (October 2001), 84–113.

Surviving Diversity: Religion and Democratic Citizenship, Baltimore: Johns Hopkins University Press, 2000.

Stocker, Michael, *Plural and Conflicting Values*, Oxford: Clarendon Press, 1990.

"The Schizophrenia of Modern Ethical Theories," *Journal of Philosophy* 73 (August 1976), 453–66.

Sunstein, Cass, *Free Markets and Social Justice*, New York: Oxford University Press, 1997.

Talisse, Robert, "Liberalism, Pluralism, and Political Justification," *Harvard Review of Philosophy* 13 (2005), 57–72.

Tamir, Yael, "The Land of the Fearful and the Free," *Constellations* 3 (1997), 296–314.

Taylor, Charles, "Cross-Purposes: The Liberal-Communitarian Debate," in *Liberalism and the Moral Life*, ed. Nancy Rosenblum, Cambridge, MA: Harvard University Press, 1989, 159–82.

Sources of the Self, Cambridge, MA: Harvard University Press, 1989.

"What is Human Agency?," in *Human Agency and Language: Philosophical Papers*, vol. 1, New York: Cambridge University Press, 1985, 15–45.

Teson, Fernando, "Kantian International Liberalism," in *International Society: Diverse Ethical Perspectives*, ed. D. Mapel and T. Nardin, Princeton: Princeton University Press, 1998, 103–13.

Tuck, Richard, "Rights and Pluralism," in *Philosophy in an Age of Pluralism: The Philosophy of Charles Taylor in Question*, ed. James Tully, Cambridge: Cambridge University Press, 1994, 159–70.

Wadud, Amina, *Inside the Gender Jihad: Women's Reform in Islam*, Oxford: Oneworld, 2006.

Qu'ran and Woman: Reading the Sacred Text from a Woman's Perspective, 2nd edn., New York: Oxford University Press, 1999.

Waldron, Jeremy, "Autonomy and Perfectionism in Raz's Morality of Freedom," *Southern California Law Review* 62 (1989), 1097–152.

"A Right to do Wrong?," *Ethics* 92 (October 1981), 21–39.

"Theoretical Foundations of Liberalism," *Philosophical Quarterly* 37 (April 1987), 127–50.

"Toleration and the Rationality of Persecution," in *John Locke: A Letter Concerning Toleration in Focus*, ed. John Horton and Susan Mendus, London: Routledge, 1991, 98–124.

Wall, Stephen, *Liberalism, Perfectionism, and Restraint*, Cambridge: Cambridge University Press, 1998.

Walzer, Michael, "On Involuntary Association," in *Freedom of Association*, ed. Amy Gutmann, Princeton: Princeton University Press, 1998, 64–74.

Thick and Thin: Moral Argument at Home and Abroad, Notre Dame, IN: Notre Dame University Press, 1994.

Weinstock, Daniel, "Beyond Exit Rights: Reframing the Debate," in *Minorities within Minorities: Equality, Rights and Diversity*, ed. Avigail Eisenberg and Jeffrey Spinner-Halev, Cambridge: Cambridge University Press, 2005, 227–46.

"The Graying of Berlin," *Critical Review* 11, no. 4 (Fall 1997), 481–501.

Williams, Bernard, "Introduction" to Isaiah Berlin, *Concepts and Categories*, New York: Viking, 1979, xi–xviii.

Wolf, Susan, "Sanity and the Metaphysics of Responsibility," in *Responsibility, Character, and the Emotions*, ed. F. Schoeman, New York: Cambridge University Press, 1988, 46–62.

"Two Levels of Pluralism," *Ethics* 102 (July 1992), 785–98.

Wolfe, Alan, *One Nation, After All*, New York: Viking, 1998.

Young, Robert, *Personal Autonomy*, London: Croom Helm, 1986.

Index

robust liberal education (RLE) 196–7
civic virtues 217–27
conception of critical reasoning 223–4
concern over liberal legitimacy 229
equal opportunity 212–17
self-rule and 205
Rousseau, Jean-Jacques 11
Ruddick, William 49

Sartre, Jean-Paul 20
Scanlon, Thomas 7
Schumpeter, Joseph 114
sex education 233–7
maximal v. minimal accounts 234–6
Shachar, Ayelet 144, 167, 168–71, 180
joint governance 168–9
Shapiro, Ian 198
Sher, George 41
Shklar, Judith 126–32
Simmons, A. John 148, 164
Smart, J. J. C. 50
Spinner-Halev, Jeffrey 192
Stocker, Michael 16, 17–18
subsidiarity 143–8

Tamir, Yael 130–2
Taylor, Charles 20, 179
Tuck, Richard 139

value pluralism 15–25
agent-relative constraints and 21–2
argument from truth 105–9
importance of choice and 100–1
incommensurability 17–19
noncomparability thesis 17–18
objectivity and 22–4
reasons for choice and 20–1
uncombinability thesis 16–17
underdeterminacy thesis 20

Waldron, Jeremy 5, 7, 75
Wall, Stephen 30, 35, 57, 109–11
Walzer, Michael 138, 189
Weinstock, Daniel 180–1
Weir, Peter, *see Witness*
well-being, in political argument 11–13
structure and content 14–15
tracking value and 112–15
Williams, Bernard 103, 105
Witness (film) 22, 113
Wolf, Susan 22